Pregnant with Meaning

Teen Mothers
and the Politics
of Inclusive
Schooling

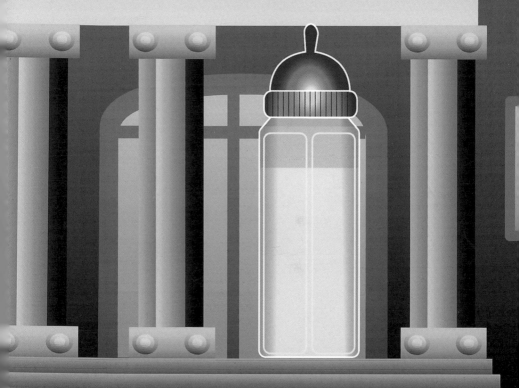

H I G H   S C H O O L

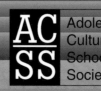

AC
SS

Adolescent
Cultures,
School &
Society

Deirdre M. Kelly

Pregnant with Meaning

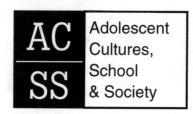

Joseph L. DeVitis & Linda Irwin-DeVitis
General Editors

Vol. 13

PETER LANG
New York • Washington, D.C./Baltimore • Boston • Bern
Frankfurt am Main • Berlin • Brussels • Vienna • Oxford

Deirdre M. Kelly

Pregnant with Meaning

Teen Mothers and the Politics of Inclusive Schooling

PETER LANG
New York • Washington, D.C./Baltimore • Boston • Bern
Frankfurt am Main • Berlin • Brussels • Vienna • Oxford

Library of Congress Cataloging-in-Publication Data

Kelly, Deirdre M.
Pregnant with meaning: teen mothers
and the politics of inclusive schooling / Deirdre M. Kelly.
p. cm. — (Adolescent cultures, school, and society; vol. 13)
Includes bibliographical references and index.
1. Teenage mothers—Education—Social aspects—British Columbia
Case studies. 2. Pregnant schoolgirls—Education—Social aspects—
British Columbia Case studies. 3. Feminism and education. I. Title.
II. Series: Adolescent cultures, school & society; vol. 13.
LC4094.2.B8K45 306.43—dc21 99-37975
ISBN 0-8204-4536-3
ISSN 1091-1464

Die Deutsche Bibliothek-CIP-Einheitsaufnahme

Kelly, Deirdre M.:
Pregnant with meaning: teen mothers
and the politics of inclusive schooling / Deirdre M. Kelly.
—New York; Washington, D.C./Baltimore; Boston; Bern;
Frankfurt am Main; Berlin; Brussels; Vienna; Oxford: Lang.
(Adolescent cultures, school, and society; Vol. 13)
ISBN 0-8204-4536-3

Cover Illustration: Dan Hubig
Cover design: Patrick Dunne

The paper in this book meets the guidelines for permanence and durability
of the Committee on Production Guidelines for Book Longevity
of the Council of Library Resources.

Printed in the United States of America

In memory of KJ,
whose activism and accepting spirit
provided support for many teen mothers

Acknowledgments

I thank David Beers, Pamela Courtenay-Hall, Jane Gaskell, Sheila Martineau, Paul Orlowski, John Taylor, and Allison Tom for reading and commenting on one or more draft chapters of the book. Dan Hubig magnanimously agreed to supply the cover illustration on short notice.

The Social Sciences and Humanities Research Council of Canada provided a generous grant to support the research on which this book is based. Thanks also to the folks at Peter Lang Publishing (especially Chris Myers) and series co-editor Joseph DeVitis for their interest.

Anita Bonson, Sheila Martineau, Diane Purvey, Kelly Tuffo, and Athena Wang provided excellent research and clerical assistance on the research project. Sheila deserves special recognition. Not only did she serve as my apprentice ethnographer at City School, but she conducted interviews with one third of the teachers at Town School. During the period of intensive fieldwork at City School, Sheila and I exchanged field notes regularly to keep each other informed, share stories, and test interpretations; we met formally at least once a week to compare observations and discuss emerging themes. After the fieldwork, Sheila continued to assist me with data coding and analysis as well as library research. Her contribution to the study has thus been considerable, and I value the friendship that has emerged from our shared experiences, particularly as we navigated the micropolitics of school-based research together.

For helping me to maintain my sanity and sense of humor, especially through the rough patches of writing, my special thanks go to Antoine Altasserre, Maggie Beers, Jane Gaskell, Ricki Goldman-Segall, Nora Kelly, Brenda and Del Lowery, Gaby Minnes Brandes, Bill Richardson, Wallace Robinson, Peter Seixas, and Allison Tom, and to members of my extended Kelly-Beers-Wade family.

I would also like to express my gratitude to the many young people, teachers, administrators, and community workers who generously gave of their time to participate in the study. Ms. Long, the coordinator of Town School's Young Parents Program, stands out in my mind for her unflagging interest in the project, her insight, compassion, good sense, and razor-sharp wit. Although I am compelled to use pseudonyms in order to protect the privacy of all the research participants, you know who you are, and thank you!

And, finally, I would like to thank my partner and soul mate, Dave Beers, for his willingness over the years to discuss ideas, his invaluable editorial suggestions, his art direction of the book's cover, and his companionship.

Table of Contents

Tables

Chapter 1

Introduction:
Locating the Study in Historical
and Political Context

On April 28, 1998, the topic for an internationally televised debate was the character of Amanda Lemon, age 18, of Xenia, Ohio. Lemon's 3.8 grade point average and community volunteer work caused her to be invited to join the local chapter of the National Honor Society, but that decision was reversed on the grounds that the graduating senior was also a mother. The existence of her child was proof that Amanda Lemon had engaged in sex, which was reason enough for the teachers who made up the honor society selection committee to rule her inadequate in the character department. The ensuing controversy landed Lemon on CNN's *Talk Back Live* program, an orchestrated management of public discourses meant to appear as a kind of electronic town hall meeting beamed throughout the United States, Canada, and beyond.[1]

Invited to consider just how much stigma should be applied to Amanda Lemon for conceiving, bearing, and then raising a 9-month-old child, the millions of viewers heard Dr. James Smith, Superintendent of Xenia Schools, explain why he wasn't budging: "[T]here's [sic] four components of a National Honor Society student and again it can not only be just academics, but also character and service and leadership. When that was reviewed, again she did not meet the character component of those four." Viewers heard a radio talk show host named Steve Malzberg say, "Pregnancy and sexual conduct is taken into consideration so . . . she has to suffer the consequences of that. . . . She should be applauded because she didn't dump her baby in a dumpster. She didn't throw her baby out the window when it was born or strangle it and throw it in the toilet. But not rewarded for that." Viewers heard an audience member named Gail say,

"I was a school teacher and when you set these standards, you've got to live by them. . . . I think in today's society we keep giving and giving and giving and we don't stick by those standards." Viewers heard a Pentecostal minister, Barbara Reynolds, note that teen motherhood "is often a ticket to poverty."

Viewers also heard from some who supported Lemon's appeal to have the decision reversed. Ann Stone of the group Republicans for Choice declared that "to say this isn't a punishment is not to look at reality. You ask her if she feels like she's being punished. Ask her schoolmates. Ask the people in her town. They're all going to tell you she's being punished when she should in fact be rewarded for doing such a great job of keeping her grade point average up. She, in fact, is a role model in that sense."

Tammy Williams, who also bore a child in high school, said, "It's hard to be a teen mother, go to school, do extra-curricular activities, and volunteer your time as well. It's like you're juggling. You have to be a mother/daughter—a daughter to your parents, a mother to your child as well as a student to your school. And that's a lot of roles that she has to play. And by her just playing these roles and being a member of the National Honor Society is just an accomplishment in itself."

Back and forth, interweaving, various discourses about teen mothers filled the airwaves. Teen mother as character flawed or otherwise damaged; teen mother as enemy of the chaste; teen mother as eroder of standards that form the national backbone; teen mother as welfare drain; teen mother as role model to those who might otherwise choose abortion; teen mother as a juggler of many roles—and so not only needing but deserving the wider support of family and society if she is to succeed in the world.

It fell to Amanda Lemon herself to point out the contradictions implicit in the Xenia National Honor Society chapter's litmus test. "When I had a meeting with the principal and one of the advisors, I asked, 'If you're going to judge character, then what about the people that do have sex and what about the people that have had abortions, if you want to get like that?' And I was told by one of the people that they do know people on the National Honor Society that have had abortions, but that I [represent] *visual* evidence [that premarital sex occurred]."[2]

Nothing was resolved, of course, in the hour spent with Amanda Lemon in CNN's approximation of the electronic global village, but the episode dramatized three major themes of this book: (a) how teen mothers, in a climate that is perceived to be liberalizing, continue to be made scapegoats blamed for a variety of negative social trends; (b) how teen mothers, in trying to describe and assign meaning to their own lives, struggle against and internalize the many competing discourses about the "teen mother" identity; and (c) what challenges face schools that are striving to be more inclusive of teen mothers and other groups stigmatized for their difference. If the CNN program demonstrated anything certain, it is this: Teen mothers remain highly politicized icons at a time of great social anxiety and gradual shift toward a more conservative, individualistic model of what is owed to, and expected of, the North American citizen.[3]

Like a reed poking up against the current, British Columbia school policy presents an experiment that counters the North America–wide resistance to fully including teen mothers in society. In British Columbia increasing numbers of teen mothers have been encouraged to attend mainstream high schools with day care and other support on site.[4]

As the following chapters show, this reed of an initiative is small and often twisted by surrounding forces, making it an experiment that is highly constrained and problematic, yet significant. Public debate swirls around it, while inside the schools, administrators, teachers, fellow students, and the teen mothers themselves engage in the politics of interpreting the needs of teen mothers (Fraser, 1989). All of this presented a rich opportunity to study teen mothers and the politics of inclusive schooling, and so I conducted two ethnographic studies of British Columbia schools that are seeking to integrate teen mothers.

Sheila Martineau, a research assistant, and I did the bulk of the fieldwork at City School[5] and its well-established Teen-Age Parents Program during school year 1993–1994, preceded by my pilot set of observations and interviews in 1992–1993. In the case of Town School, I followed the Young Parents Program from the time the first funding proposal was submitted in 1992 through twists and turns over 2 years until the day care opened and through its first year of implementation, 1994–1995.[6]

While their teen parent programs differ in some key respects, both Town and City Schools are large public secondary schools, with mostly working-class and poor students in grades 8 to 12. For more detailed comparative descriptions, see Tables 1.1 and 1.2. At both sites I spent several days per week over the course of a year, observing hundreds of regular classes, special classes for teen parents, and extracurricular activities and interviewing hundreds of students, teachers, school administrators, school trustees, community representatives, and school-based child care staff members. Sheila and I "shadowed" dozens of teen mothers through their school day. I visited teen parents in their homes, both those in school and those who were planning to return. I commissioned essays

Table 1.1   City and Town Schools at a Glance

	City School	Town School
location	Pacifica (a metropolis)	Midland (population 40,000)
school type	public secondary, grades 8–12	public secondary, grades 8–12
school reputation and academic ranking based on grade 12 provincial exam and graduation rate data	prides itself in being respectful of differences; ranked near the bottom among Pacifica's high schools	considered a "second chance" school; ranked lowest among Midland's high schools
neighborhood	multiethnic, working class, gentrifying	majority White, low income and working class
teen pregnancy, abortion, and live birth rates, based on an average over the past decade	below the provincial averages; of the women aged 15–19 who do get pregnant, an above-average proportion obtain abortions	above the provincial average in rates of pregnancy and birth, below in rate of abortion; may reflect strong "pro-life" presence in Midland
student population	1,300	1,100
English as a second language (ESL)	one third of students enrolled in ESL classes	no ESL classes
languages spoken at home	over 30 different ones; 25% of students have Chinese as their first language	12% of students in the Midland School District speak a language other than English at home
immigrant or ethnic and racial status	half of students born outside of Canada, in 46 different countries	75% of the students are of European descent (White), 11% Asian (most with ties to India), 11% Aboriginal,[1] and 3% other ethnicities

[1] In Canada the term "Aboriginal" includes both First Nations peoples as well as the Métis. The term "Métis" was originally applied to people of French and North American "Indian" ancestry who formed a distinct cultural group but is now used more generally to indicate a person of both Native and European ancestry. Among many participants in my study, including most First Nations teen mothers, the most common designation for Aboriginal people was "Native" or, less often, "Native Canadian." This term was not considered pejorative in the British Columbian context (by contrast, the term "Indian" is considered pejorative). In this book, I use Aboriginal, First Nations, and Native somewhat interchangeably.

from non-parenting students and asked teen mothers to keep journals. I collected and analyzed pertinent district, community, school, and program documents.

Table 1.2   School-Age Mothers Programs at a Glance

	City School	Town School
history of special program	district-wide Teen-Age Parents Program (TAPP), founded in 1982	district-wide Young Parents Program (YPP), founded in 1994
educational component of special program	choice of self-paced instruction in self-contained classroom or various degrees of integration into regular classes	mostly full integration into regular classes; other options available at nearby Midland Alternative Education Center
child care component of special program	nonprofit Community-Based Organization (CBO) operates on-site day care for 20 infants/toddlers	nonprofit Youth Society (YS) operates on-site day care for 12 infants/toddlers
other components of special program	CBO offers weekly support group and coordinates overall program, including the Advisory Committee, charged with advocacy, setting policy, ensuring ongoing program evaluation	YS offers informal one-on-one parenting and other support, consults community advisory committee; early school leavers may enter YS's GED prep/parenting program
cumulative student enrollment, with age range	In 1993–1994, 31 women, aged 16 to 19 years	In 1994–1995, 19 women, aged 17 to 20 years
race/ethnicity of teen mothers	17 White (European) 5 Aboriginal 5 Aboriginal & White 3 Latino 1 South Asian	11 White (European) 5 Aboriginal 3 Aboriginal & White
living arrangement of teen mothers formally interviewed	10 alone w/kid(s) 9 with partner 4 with parent(s) 1 with girlfriend	5 alone w/kid(s) 4 with parent(s) 1 with partner 1 with girlfriend

Dilemmas of Difference and the
Ideal of Inclusive Schooling

Within these settings, as I attended closely to the politics of how the needs of teen mothers were being interpreted and addressed, there was a rich opportunity to see at work the *dilemma of difference*. To ignore the differences of subordinate groups, argues legal scholar Martha Minow, "leaves in place a faulty neutrality, constructed so as to advance the dominant group and hinder those who are different." But attending to the differences of subordinate groups can highlight their deviance from the norm. "The dilemma of difference is the risk of reiterating the stigma associated with assigned difference either by focusing on it or by ignoring it" (Minow, 1984, pp. 159, 202).

Besides their parental status, school-age mothers are often different in ways that mark them as "abnormal" and in need of "special" treatment. Many of the young women in my study, for example, were considered different from the unstated norm of mainstream schooling by virtue of being poor or working class and academically underprepared. Not a few were immigrants or people of color who lacked proficiency in English. Thus, the lessons I draw from the attempts to include them in regular classes and activities will interest those concerned about enhancing the prospects of students in inner-city schools as well as others on the margins (such as dropouts, pushouts, and those labeled as having learning or emotional disabilities).

At City and Town Schools, the negative representations and restrictive interpretations of the needs and identities of teen mothers sometimes led—contrary to stated policy aims—to exclusionary practices. Yet I also found teen mothers and some of their peers and community and school officials challenging stigmatizing attitudes and making innovations and applauding efforts to build more inclusive schools.

By *inclusive schooling,* I mean the ideal of including a wide variety of students, particularly those who have been traditionally excluded, either formally or informally. This meaning encompasses the narrower, technical meaning given to inclusive schooling in the field of special education, which equates inclusion with the provision of services to students with disabilities in the general education classes of their neighborhood schools (see, e.g., Lipsky & Gartner, 1996). It also includes efforts to challenge institutionalized practices of racism, sexism, class discrimination, and heterosexism.

Across Western industrialized societies, schools face a crisis of consensus over inclusiveness. Those who want schools to sort and reward students who are most "productive" within a competitive economy that offers limited numbers of "knowledge-based jobs" are pitted against those who see the classroom as a key public arena for challenging social injustices, for countering the very sorting process their opponents encourage. The schools I studied in depth are fully representative of this struggle. As a result, this book seeks to contribute to the literature on the politics of detracking (or destreaming) the curriculum.

Both City and Town Schools were attempting to move away from pregnancy and parenthood as a basis for grouping students for differentiated instruction. Although in certain contexts, tracking may not be "inherently detrimental to lower-track students" (Page & Valli, 1990, p. 13), evidence is mounting to suggest that tracking as it is currently practiced is often neither equitable nor effective (e.g., Oakes, Gamoran, & Page, 1991; Curtis, Livingstone, & Smaller, 1992).

To help the increasing numbers of school practitioners involved with alternatives to tracking, Oakes has called for studies "of schools in the process of detracking that focus simultaneously on the technical, normative, and political dimensions of their efforts" (1992, p. 20). This book represents one such study. More generally, this study helps to flesh out what progressive educators and scholars mean by *inclusive schooling* (e.g., Brantlinger, 1997; Skrtic, 1995) and *multicultural education* (e.g., Carlson, 1994; Sleeter, 1996).

In this book I also seek to make a methodological contribution. I am committed to research that bridges public discourses, educational policies, and the views of teen mothers. Taken as a whole, the various chapters of *Pregnant with Meaning* show how the politics of inclusive schooling shape, and are shaped by, the politics of representation (in this case, of teen pregnancy and motherhood). In making this case, I draw on feminist appropriations of Foucault's discourse theory (for further discussion, see Chapter 4).

I spotlight the complex of meanings associated with teen mothers and the rival, ideologically driven interpretations of their needs—in short, how they are represented in both authoritative and marginalized discourses (see especially Chapters 2–4). By focusing on competing discourses, however, I do not mean to suggest that I believe "discursive empowerment" should replace struggles for "social and economic enablement" (Ebert, 1996, p. 291). Both are necessary and in fact linked, just as cultural injustice and economic injustice are usually intertwined and mutually reinforcing. "Cultural norms that are unfairly biased against some are institutionalized in the state and the economy; meanwhile, economic disadvantage impedes equal participation in the making of culture, in public spheres, and in everyday life. The result is often a vicious circle of cultural and economic subordination" (Fraser, 1997, p. 15).

After documenting how teen mothers are culturally devalued and unequal participants in the making of culture, I turn (in Chapters 5–8) to an analysis of the politics of integrating teen mothers and the local struggles to make the institution of schooling more inclusive. By highlighting the "stigma stories" that persist and calling attention to the silences that result, I aim to inform debate about the politics of inclusion.

A Critical Feminist Stance

How does a critical feminist ethnographer approach such a study if she believes, as does Fraser (1997), that creating truly inclusive schools will involve both cultural recognition and socioeconomic redistribution? This proved to be no small question; in fact, my striving toward an answer has become a central theme in my work and therefore in this book. Methodology, in the pages that follow, was not merely a means to investigation, but became its own subject for intense scrutiny, a scrutiny that leads, ultimately, to self-searching.

I concluded that I must place my local analyses of cultural dynamics and the politics of particular research sites in historical context, mindful of the political economy and broader sociocultural patterns or ideologies. I was required to reflect upon, and locate myself within, the complex workings of power that I witnessed as I studied up, down, and across the contested arena of schools and sought to balance advocacy against self-censorship. I felt a responsibility to speak about, for, and with marginalized groups directly affected by educational reforms; in this case, teen mothers.

To be sure, I am mindful enough of poststructuralist theorizing not to want to create a "totalizing" narrative for the diverse, and in some ways arbitrary, grouping that is teen mothers. I reflect (in Chapter 9) on the risk of misrepresenting teen mothers even as I attempt to rewrite the prevailing cautionary tales about them. I struggle with how the researcher/writer might acknowledge that victims are created within the current social and economic order without burdening those who are victimized with the simplistic and stigmatized identities that various observers—left, right, and center—would impose upon them. I challenge the prevalent and all-too-easy dichotomous political construct: If teen mothers are not victims, then they are the architects of their own fates who deserve public wrath. Conversely, if teen mothers are not free agents, they are helpless victims who deserve public sympathy and protection judged by experts to be in their own best interest.

This methodological approach combines well with a critical feminist stance. It attends simultaneously to the agency and lived experiences of the participants in research (especially the most vulnerable); the extra-local context of research sites, including various asymmetrical power relations; and the documentation of oppressive ideologies and practices with an eye toward envisioning more emancipatory alternatives.

There are a number of feminist lenses through which to view the subordination of women; there is no unified feminist perspective. But a feminist stance typically indicates, at a minimum, a focus on gender—an oppressive, ideological structure that is socially produced through unequal relations of power—and a political commitment to "changing unequal power relations between men and women in society" (Weedon, 1988, p. 1). Such structures as the sexual division of labor; power relations between men and women; institutions such as the family, school, and childrearing; and associated political struggles (e.g., over reproductive rights) help to organize gender and sexuality (Connell, 1987).

In synthesizing and extending feminist thinking on the issue of teen pregnancy and motherhood, I have found the work of multicultural and critical (poststructuralist, socialist, and materialist) feminists most useful. This work highlights the intersection of multiple axes of subordination and domination. It recognizes that people can simultaneously be oppressor and oppressed and that no one form of oppression is primary. Patricia Hill Collins (1990), for example, has made this case persuasively: These ideas are embedded in her concept of the "matrix of domination," formed by interlocking systems of oppression. Such analyses have sensitized me to the age, race, class, and gender subtexts of the dominant discourse about teen mothers.

The feminist theorists whose work, in my view, speaks most directly to the situations of teen mothers, have combined the insights of radical political economists with postmodern insights about language and subjectivity (e.g., Fraser, 1989, 1997; Mohanty, 1991). As a shorthand way to signal the importance of a deep restructuring of the existing political economy and dominant cultural valuations to the creation of a more just society, I refer to the stance I take in this book (and develop in Chapters 9 and 10) as "critical feminism."

In sum, I hope this book will be taken as an argument that critical feminist ethnography is, in fact, worth doing—this at a time when "a growing chorus of [academic] colleagues . . . presume that if you are interested in policy and/or social practice, your data are thereby less trustworthy" (Fine & Weis, 1996, p. 265). My goals are to help us understand how largely subordinated groups, such as teen mothers, perceive and respond to their positioning and also to help envision and work toward opportunities for positive social change.

Placing City and Town Schools in the Historical
Context of School Inclusiveness

Throughout the first half of the twentieth century, it was common policy to exclude pregnant and mothering students from public schools on the grounds that they posed a threat (see, e.g., Solinger, 1992, pp. 109–110). Administrators feared, for example, that school-age mothers, married or not, would, by their very presence, prompt discussions about sexuality that were "considered undesirable for unmarried girls to hear" (McGowan, 1959, p. 487). There is evidence to suggest that some young mothers, particularly those who were married, were quietly accommodated *individually* in continuation and adult schools (Kelly, 1993a, pp. 62–63). But "the idea of providing classes on a group basis for unwed mothers," even in public alternative schools, was resisted (Solinger, 1992, pp. 140–141).

By the 1960s attitudes toward teen pregnancy had begun to shift. In the United States, federal policies and financial assistance quietly encouraged the establishment of about 40 school-centered "rehabilitation" projects offering a range of educational, health, and welfare services to poor, predominantly African American, "pregnant school-aged girls" (Solinger, 1992, pp. 213–217). These projects, located in most major cities across the United States, were often affiliated with public school systems but did not enroll pregnant teens or "unwed mothers" in regular classes (Sedlak, 1983; for a case study of one such project see Rains, 1971).

By decade's end, exclusion from the regular school system was still prevalent.[7] The civil rights movement for racial equality, however, and the second wave of the women's liberation movement were helping to set the stage for legal inclusion. Young women and their parents, supported by community action groups, began filing lawsuits to protest their exclusion based on pregnancy and marital status (National Education Association, 1970, p. 89).

In 1971, the U.S. Supreme Court ruled in *Ordway v. Hargraves* that it was illegal for schools to expel from regular classes students who were known to be pregnant (Luker, 1996). Congress added force to this decision by passing Title IX of the Education Amendments of 1972, which took effect in 1975. Title IX expressly prohibits the exclusion of students from their "education program" or "any extracurricular activity" on the basis of pregnancy, parental status, or marital status; schools that do not comply face the loss of federal funds. "Due process and equal protection concerns also convinced lower courts to begin striking down public school policies that excluded unwed mothers but not unwed fathers" (Rhode, 1993, p. 308).

Historically, Canadians have made less use of the courts to fight discriminatory school policies than have their U.S. neighbors. Nevertheless, important U.S. judicial rulings and legislation have influenced educational policy in Canada (Little, 1990). Also reflecting a shift in public attitudes, schools in British Columbia and elsewhere moved from a policy of formal exclusion to formal inclusion of pregnant and mothering students in the early 1970s (e.g., Morgan, 1973). Special programs for pregnant and parenting teens began to spring up in the late 1970s across North America.

There is no doubt that over the past two or three decades educational opportunities have improved for young North American women who find themselves pregnant and decide against abortion. Their high school graduation rates have increased accordingly (Upchurch & McCarthy, 1989), although they still lag behind women who did not give birth in their teens (U.S. General Accounting Office, 1998). Yet school officials do not always want to accommodate pregnant and mothering teens in regular high school settings, classes, or activities.

A 1989 survey of 12 geographically and demographically diverse schools in the United States found that nine were in violation of Title IX. Common violations included "channeling pregnant and parenting students into specific courses of study, not allowing excused absences for prenatal or postnatal care or problems associated with pregnancy, and not reinstating students to the status they held at the beginning of a leave for pregnancy." Some schools discouraged pregnant students from holding leadership positions (Snider, 1989, p. 5; cf. Dunkle, 1990; Earle, 1990). Zellman and Feifer (1992) were part of a research team that found in visits to school-based teen parent programs throughout the United States "that, despite widespread endorsement of mainstreaming, strong sentiment for isolation—particularly for younger teen mothers—remains. At the same time, most isolated programs lack the teaching staff and resources to serve the youngest mothers and provide limited curricular choices to all enrollees" (p. 1392). As I discovered in California, districts commonly establish special programs and day cares at alternative sites, forcing pregnant and mothering teens to choose between needed services and access to a university preparatory curriculum (Kelly, 1993a).

It seems that many school administrators today favor "mainstreaming" pregnant and parenting teens but do not necessarily believe in providing them with special services (Buie, 1987; Weiner, 1987). In some communities, district attempts to establish day care programs in regular high schools have created controversy (Stern, 1993). In Medicine Hat, Alberta, for example, a conservative city alderman used his radio talk show to denounce plans to build a high school day care and declared "that the mothers should be made to look after the [babies] in the proper manner." When a reporter asked him about those who would be unable to complete their education without child care assistance, the alderman replied, "A lot of them are probably too dumb to educate anyway, if they've got in this position" (Ormiston, 1993).

Local school districts in both the United States and Canada wield the most control over what services, if any, will be provided to pregnant and parenting teens and how—in a way that encourages integration into the mainstream or separation from it. Because the provision of education is so decentralized in both countries, it is difficult to know what is typically provided and how the programs are usually organized.

Given the ingrained resistance to mainstreaming, it is not surprising that pregnant and mothering teens appear to have remained largely "ghettoized" in alternative programs, often off-campus or otherwise self-contained. The programs that get showcased in government reports and popular media accounts are often comprehensive and self-contained, located on a separate campus from regular high schools. They feature education, health, counseling, and child care components. Two that recur in the popular, academic, and policy literatures on teen pregnancy and parenthood are the Lawrence Paquin School in Baltimore, Maryland, and the New Futures School in Albuquerque, New Mexico (e.g., U.S. Department of Education, 1987). Both are alternative schools that no doubt bring together more resources than most: on-site day care, career counseling, health services, and classes in prenatal and postnatal care. A number of qualitative academic studies, focused either directly or indirectly on the schooling experiences of teen mothers, have been done in the context of alternative programs in the United States (Holm, 1995; Horowitz, 1995; Jacobs, 1994; Kelly, 1993a; Lesko, 1990; McDade, 1987). Thompson (1995), in a more popular account, interviewed pregnant and mothering young women across the country and reported that most attended demonstration or high school equivalency programs in alternative settings.

Several policy surveys have also found that many pregnant and mothering students are schooled in alternative settings. In a study of eight school-based comprehensive programs in three states, Weatherley, Perlman, Levine, and Klerman found that most "served pregnant students in self-contained facilities, either off campus or in alternative schools," and "enrollees returned to their regular schools the semester after delivery" (1985, p. 74). School districts in California commonly locate programs for "pregnant minors" and teen parents in continuation schools (Cagampang, Gerritz, & Hayward, 1987). In a survey of 220 child care programs for teen parents in all 50 states and the District of Columbia, Marx, Bailey, and Francis (1988) found that only 22% were located in regular comprehensive high schools, and even these were often self-contained.

A few other studies on the school experiences of teen mothers have found them being served in largely self-contained programs composed of special classes within a regular high school (Lustig, 1997; Pillow, 1997). A study of a program within a large, urban high school in the Midwest found that teen mothers were formally included in "regular" classes with non-parenting peers but were found to be treated like "pariahs" and effectively excluded from the "larger life of the school" (Herr, 1991, p. 24). A case study of a high school in Regina, Saskatchewan, had its special program for teen mothers "separated from the rest of the school, providing a safe haven but unable to challenge the stereotypes that abound" (Gaskell, 1995, p. 165).

Lesko (1995) reviewed the literature and concluded that many "U.S. school districts cling to the model of temporary alternative schools followed by return to the regular school" after the young women have delivered their babies (p. 193). Upon return to regular school, support services, especially on-site child care, is lacking. In the only estimate that I have run across, the Wall Street Journal reported: "Child care is available in approximately 11% of school districts, according to a 1986 reader survey by Capitol Publications Inc., in Alexandria, Va., which publishes newsletters for educators. Educators believe there has been a small increase since the survey was published" (Stern, 1993, p. 1). My review suggests that districts that provide services for teen mothers usually locate them in alternative settings or in self-contained classrooms within regular schools.

At this moment, then, school districts throughout North America are in the process of moving beyond formal integration of pregnant and mothering students, are inquiring into the meaning and practice of inclusion, and are at a crossroads. Some policy researchers and pundits recommend separate schools (Buie, 1987; Whitehead, 1994), while others urge supported integration (Earle, 1990).

Hence the significance of British Columbia, and Town and City Schools in particular, which have formally pursued supported integration over the last decade. Dale-Johnson (1995) collected detailed information about 32 education-based programs with day care centers for young parents in British Columbia. Of those, 7 were run as alternative schools or located within alternative education centers, although in 4 cases some students elected to use the day care while attending classes in a regular high school nearby; 13 programs, including the Town School program, had day cares located on the campus of a regular high school and all teen parents were integrated; and 12 programs, including the City School program, had day cares located on the campus of a regular high school and teen parents had the option of attending regular classes or pursuing all or part of their academic program within a special classroom. In sum, 91% of the B.C. programs enabled young parents to attend regular classes while providing them with child care and other support services.

What accounts for this development in British Columbia? Three factors have come together to support a full integration policy. First, a B.C. school act passed in 1989 mandated the integration of special education students (those with learning, behavioral, and physical disabilities) into neighborhood schools, and this legislation provided ideological support for integrating pregnant and parenting students more fully into regular classes.[8]

A second factor was the commitment to developing school-based day care—during the schoolday for school-age parents as well as after-school care for parents of all ages—by the B.C. Ministry of Women's Equality. (This ministry had lead responsibility for issues relating to child care in the province.) The provision of day care, although usually couched in gender-neutral terms, effectively allocates resources to help young women with children remain in school, given that they are usually the sole or primary caregiver.

Dovetailing with this "equal opportunities" feminist perspective was a third factor, namely a shift in government policy regarding single mothers, from treating women as mothers and wage workers to treating women as primarily wage workers (Evans, 1996; cf. Naples, 1997). This shift has been particularly evident in the debates about welfare reform across North America, in the rise of welfare-to-work ideology, and in the targeting of single mothers, particularly teen mothers, as a welfare "problem." Keeping teen mothers in school by providing day care services for their children has come increasingly to be seen as serving a dual purpose: enabling teen mothers to get jobs and off welfare and breaking the cycle of "welfare dependency" for the next generation. The idea that the caregiving activities of single mothers are paramount, especially until their children reach school age, has come under attack.

In Ontario, for example, policymakers have recently sent a message that teen mothers should think of themselves first and foremost as future paid workers. A new policy will deny welfare benefits to teen mothers who do not promptly return to school; older single parents do not have to join the "workfare" program—which requires all able-bodied welfare recipients to complete 17 hours a week of school, training, or work in order to get paid—until their children are of school age. The unstated assumption of this policy is that teen mothers are bad parents who do not deserve time to bond with their infants (Southam Newspapers, 1999).

Placing British Columbia within the Current North American Political Mood

As the Ontario example indicates, it is Canada's societal similarity to the United States, rather than any utopian difference, that makes British Columbia's approach to integrating teen mothers worth the attention of American policymakers and educators. In both nations, a new consensus about "family values" and neoliberal economic policies thwarts progressive reform not just in schools but in virtually every other public institution.

As I drafted the grant for this study in 1992, educators across North America were facing right-wing campaigns against school-based condom machines and child care centers for teen parents, abortion, and sexuality education in general. A group of prominent communitarians[9] (among them U.S. President Bill Clinton) began what sociologist Judith Stacey describes as a "centrist campaign for family values" (1996, p. 63). Like social conservatives, the communitarians blamed sex education, among other things, for the rise in single motherhood and stressed above all the importance for children of being raised by two parents, a mother and father joined in marriage. Allied to this, in both the United States and Canada, politicians across the spectrum targeted single mothers as a "welfare problem," undeserving of state aid, and unfit unless working for pay outside the home (Brodie, 1996; Fraser & Gordon, 1994; Naples, 1997).

This new consensus lay behind the 1996 passage in the United States of the Personal Responsibility Act (P.R.A.), predicated on the wrong-headed assumption that teen childbearing and the sexual and reproductive decisions of poor, single women in general cause poverty and other social problems (see Chapter 4; Geronimus, 1997). The P.R.A. allocated $250 million for abstinence-until-marriage programs but nothing for sexuality education, contraception, or abortion.

Most relevant to my study, conservatives and communitarians alike wrung their hands over allowing teen mothers and their children to be integrated into regular high school classes. Writing in *Forbes Magazine,* Peggy Noonan, former speech writer for U.S. Presidents Reagan and Bush, urged "'official' disapproval and 'unofficial' succor" to "unwed" teen mothers (1992, p. 69). Using the same logic, communitarian Barbara Dafoe Whitehead, co-director of the Institute for American Values, called in the *Atlantic* for

> some imaginative measures to "uglify" unwed teenage motherhood or even to re-establish some of the disincentives that worked in the past, including separation of the girl from her peer group. Perhaps teenage mothers should attend special high schools, as they do in some cities, rather than mixing with the general high school population. This contemporary version of being "sent away"—though it would not interrupt education—would segregate teenage mothers from nonpregnant teenagers and perhaps change a peer culture that views schoolgirl pregnancy as an unobjectionable, even enviable, event. (1994, p. 77)

Perhaps the most influential battle cry to re-stigmatize teen mothers came when Bill Clinton, in his 1995 State of the Union address, "vowed to enlist parents, religions and community groups in a national campaign against 'our most serious social problems, the epidemic of teen pregnancies and births where there is no marriage'." Clinton was joined by moderate Democrats, who "called for a media campaign that includes stigmatizing single-motherhood as 'a selfish act'" (Gallman, 1995, p. 8A).

Why are many public policymakers in both the United States and Canada still approaching the issue of teen pregnancy and parenthood from a puritanical vantage point? When we know that a strong social safety net, non-moralistic and accessible contraception and abortion services, and open and responsible sexuality education supported by government and mass media lead to lower teen pregnancy and birth rates (see Chapter 3), why instead do we tolerate growing inequality, measures that cut and further stigmatize welfare, barriers to contraception and abortion, and a patchwork sex education curriculum based largely on scare tactics?

The human cost of the new consensus is sobering. Secondary students are being denied a respectful sexuality education curriculum. Young women's desires go unacknowledged. It has been hard to ignore the highly publicized cases of high school-aged women hiding their pregnancies, giving birth in secrecy; one young woman literally closeting her baby at home while she continued to attend school (see Lambert, 1997). As the social safety net frays, the life chances of a significant portion of the next generation worsen.

Although the attacks on anti-poverty programs, reproductive rights, and inclusive schooling are more virulent in the United States, the same consensus that fuels these attacks is on the rise in Canada, where my study was located. A symbol of this growing cross-border consensus can be discerned in a comparison of two politicians, each a prominent conservative in his respective country. In March of 1995, Canadian national Reform Party leader (now official Opposition leader in the House of Commons) Preston Manning traveled to Washington, D.C., to meet with the speaker of the U.S. House of Representatives, Republican Newt Gingrich. The two men spoke of their common political agendas. Both oppose "big government," support market economics, and espouse "traditional values" (both were raised Baptists). In what Canada's newsweekly *Maclean's* described as a "political love-in on Gingrich's weekly cable-TV show," the Republican leader credited Manning and the Reform Party's 1993 campaign as a model and inspiration for the GOP's successful electoral program (Newt's axis, 1995).

For his part, Manning basked in Gingrich's endorsement but, for the benefit of Canadians watching at home, he also attempted to portray himself as more moderate than his American ally. When introduced as "a real revolutionary in our midst," Manning replied: "A revolutionary should neither look like one nor act like one to get ahead in our country" (Newt's axis, 1995). At a press conference, Manning took pains to state that he did not agree with some of the harshest measures proposed in the Republican agenda, specifically the denial of welfare to teenage mothers (Canadian Press, 1995a).

The meeting between Manning and Gingrich points to some of the similarities as well as some of the differences in the political cultures of the two men and their countries. In addition, it shows how the political debates cross the border—in both directions. First to the differences. In an effort to gain wider credibility, Manning did not want to be perceived by his fellow Canadians as "revolutionary," whereas this label harks back to a proud beginning for many Americans. Nor does Manning want to be seen as intent on destroying social programs—an important way that many Canadians distinguish their national identity from that of Americans. And it is evident that Canada's social safety net produced markedly lower poverty rates than did the social programs of the United States in the mid-1980s (Blank & Hanratty, 1993). In addition, Canada has a more equitable way of funding its public schools and a universal health insurance system.

Indeed, the difference between the health systems of the two countries provides one explanation for the fact that the teen pregnancy rate in the United States is more than twice as high as that of Canada.[10] Canada's system provides coverage for virtually all of its citizens, often including reproductive and contraceptive services.[11] In the United States, "government-sponsored health programs cover primarily individuals aged 65 and older and people with disabilities (Medicare) and those with very low incomes (Medicaid). Most health care coverage in the United States is provided through private, employment-based health plans with varying levels of coverage. But about 15% of the U.S. population is uninsured" (Delbanco, Lundy, Hoff, Parker, & Smith, 1997, p. 70). U.S. plans provide limited, if any, coverage of reproductive and contraceptive services. Such services, furthermore, are provided by relatively inaccessible specialists, whereas in Canada these services are provided through primary care providers, such as general practitioners (p. 70).

By comparison, Canada's universal health system represents a nod toward a social democratic welfare state model, and, historically, Canada has had more generous and universal social programs than in the United States. But over the past 25 years, there has been a "dramatic reversal" (Cohen, 1993, p. 266). Taken overall, Canada is enough like the United States that both can be termed an archetypal liberal welfare state. Both countries, for example, have stigmatizing, means-tested welfare programs that provide only modest benefits.[12] In both countries, the middle classes are "institutionally wedded to the market" rather than to the welfare state (Esping-Andersen, 1990, p. 32); they rely, for example, on private pensions and child care arrangements. Without having forged "middle-class loyalties" to the welfare state, both countries thus are vulnerable to periodic welfare-state backlash movements and tax revolts (p. 33). Although Gingrich is no doubt the most famous political leader to have appealed to middle-class anger at the welfare state by invoking negative images of teen mothers, politicians throughout both countries have done likewise.

In addition, both Canada and the United States have similar anti-modern, "pro-life," "pro-family" movements to which politicians like Manning and Gingrich appeal for support. In fact, the two movements have made alliances across national boundaries (e.g., the influential Christian Coalition, led by Pat Robertson in the United States). Leaders have spearheaded attacks on reproductive rights, creating barriers to access to abortion and contraception. "Pro-life" supporters in British Columbia, for example, have, in the recent past, gained control of regional hospital boards and brought abortions to a halt. More recently, they have formed the majority on school boards and insisted on an abstinence-only approach to sexuality education (cf. Donovan, 1998b).

Many Canadians, like many Americans, continue to take a moralistic stance toward teen sexuality and contraception. Neither government has played an active role in providing public information about reproductive health. Sex education programs vary by province or state and by school district. It is not surprising that Canada's teen pregnancy, birth, and abortion rates are higher than in countries such as the Netherlands, which combine a major sexuality education program with a very liberal, nonmoralistic contraception policy (see Chapter 3).

But unlike the case with issues such as sex education and abortion, conservative politicians seem to have hit upon an issue in teen motherhood (and single-parent families generally) that resonates beyond social conservatives in North America. Direct or veiled attacks on teen mothers seem to promise savings to taxpayers in two ways: They reduce the amount spent on teen mothers directly, and they supposedly discourage others from becoming teen mothers who feel entitled to make a claim on the state's resources. In this political climate, centrist leaders such as Canadian Prime Minister Jean Chretien and U.S. President Bill Clinton have presided over decentralization and reduced funding of social programs to the provinces and states, where punitive measures have been taken against teen mothers as supposed examples of the "undeserving" poor.

In sum, Canada's teen pregnancy and birth rates are lower than those in the United States. However, for reasons shared with the United States—the class character of its liberal welfare state, its strict Protestant roots, and the ascendancy of conservative populism in its present political culture—an increasing number of Canada's citizens seem predisposed to see teen mothers as icons of welfare dependency. Indeed, Canada's newspaper of record, the *Globe and Mail,* reported recently that for "many" Canadians, teen pregnancy "is a proxy for the state of the nation's moral health" (Mitchell, 1998, p. A6). As Gingrich's admiration for Reform Party strategy suggests, it is not just that conservative attitudes are drifting across the border into Canada; the animus toward the welfare state is also homegrown.

Pregnant Students: No Uniform Meaning

Given the similarities between Canadian and American political climates today, it is hardly surprising that in both places teen mothers, by virtue of their life experiences, age, gender, class, and sometimes race, face routine disparagement in their everyday lives, as well as disrespectful stereotypes in public policy, academic, mass media, and other cultural representations. Spurned National Honor Society candidate Amanda Lemon and her fellow teen mothers have become lightning rods for stigma from many quarters of society and across opposing ideological stances. Their very presence in a public high school is read by liberals, conservatives, and radicals alike as a potent signal of societal shift.

The symbol is so potent, and yet the discourses interpreting that symbol clash so, that many mainstream news reports on the subject of teen mothers in regular school settings often invite contradictory, confused conclusions. Where discourses collide, policy and the life options of teen mothers are shaped (the reason I have woven discourse analysis throughout this book).

Consider one recent wire story without byline, which began: "Gone are the days when teens automatically dropped out of school and gave up babies for adoption. Now some private schools even have special uniforms for pregnant students." The article's author thus offered the special uniforms as evidence that the social stigma attached to teen motherhood has all but vanished.

Yet at the same time, the article sounded an alarm through a series of unsubstantiated claims: that teen pregnancy rates are rising and possibly outpacing schools' ability to "cope," that teens are becoming mothers at younger and younger ages, that their pregnancies are often "intentional" and "a ticket to a welfare cheque," and that "virtually everyone agrees something should be done" (Canadian Press, 1995b). Framed in this way, the image of the special uniform, rather than signaling a welcome step toward more inclusive schooling, can be read as profoundly unsettling.

Why might this be? Perhaps because the uniform, particularly a private school uniform, symbolizes elite social status—an elite status that presumes moral and academic superiority. Adapting it to fit the body of a presumably unmarried, pregnant schoolgirl suggests a lowering of moral and, by extension, academic standards—even contamination by the undisciplined masses. As well, the school uniform is designed to deny natural body contours. It is meant to be desexualizing and has become associated with keeping school-age young women "looking more child-like and innocent" (Meadmore & Symes, 1996, p. 185). The obviously pregnant and sexualized wearer of the school uniform thus violates a number of binary oppositions that implicitly help to organize schooling as it is widely experienced, namely: rational mind-emotional body, masculinity-femininity, and adult-child.

Here, then, is an extremely visible example of the dilemma of difference that pregnant (and, by extension, mothering) girls imply within schools. No doubt the reporter is correct in noting that a school uniform tailored for pregnant students represents a move away from outright exclusion from a private school as well as the common practice of segregating pregnant and mothering teens in public alternative schools or classes. But as that reporter also implies (perhaps unwittingly), it remains to be seen whether uniform clothing can help cause the teen mother to be seen, and treated, uniformly with other students. Whether it does will depend on the nature and degree of integration into the mainstream the teen mothers enjoy and whether some of the organizing principles of "regular" schooling are challenged and transformed in the process.

Notes

1. All quotes are taken from Cable News Network (1998, pp. 2–3, 5–6, 10, 19).

2. Responding to a similar 1998 instance, the American Civil Liberties Union's (ACLU) Women's Rights Project filed a federal lawsuit on behalf of two other young mothers in Grant County, Kentucky, whose school denied them membership in the National Honor Society. The ACLU charged that the decision violates Title IX of the U.S. Education Amendments of 1972 (American Civil Liberties Union, 1998).

3. I recognize that this usage is continentally incorrect because it excludes Mexico, but here and throughout the book, I use the term "North America" as a shorthand reference to Canada and the United States only.

4. In 1993–1994 alone, British Columbia's Ministry of Education (in conjunction with the Ministry of Women's Equality) made available to school boards $19.5 million in capital funding to support school-based child care programs, with priority given to young parent programs (British Columbia Ministry of Education, 1993, p. 2). A number of young parent programs joined existing ones, and by 1995, over 30 were in operation around the province, most of them with day care centers located in or near regular school settings (Dale-Johnson, 1995; Rivers and Associates, 1995). Provincial funding to operate these programs comes mainly in the form of child care subsidies, block grants, and staff salaries and amounts to about $9.5 million annually (Rivers and Associates, 1995).

5. City School and all other names of organizations and people associated with the two ethnographic case studies are pseudonyms.

6. The British Columbia Alliance concerned with Early Pregnancy and Parenthood (BCACEPP), sponsored by the YWCA in Vancouver, maintains a comprehensive, up-to-date, and province-wide list of school-based young parent programs, including information about whether each program is offered in a regular or alternative school setting. As part of the pilot study, I became a member of BCACEPP and contacted a number of programs, ultimately selecting two that met the following criteria: (a) one located in a city and one in a town, (b) had either a well established or a brand new regular school-based day care facility, (c) encouraged teen parents to integrate into the mainstream, including regular classes, to the greatest extent possible, (d) had program administrators committed to the goal of lessening the stigma attached to teen parenthood, and (e) had staff and students willing to participate in a year-long research project.

7. "A survey conducted by the Children's Bureau in 1968 found that more than two-thirds of the nation's school systems had a policy of expelling pregnant students immediately, whether they were married or not. The remaining one-third let them stay on only until their families had made 'appropriate arrangements' for alternative instruction (usually tutoring at home). Only one school permitted such students to continue their education on the premises. Young men were rarely if ever

expelled from school after getting married or after impregnating a young woman" (Luker, 1996, p. 62).

8.   For some time now, advocates for teen mothers in the United States have been using the "least restrictive environment" concept from the field of special education to argue against policies that segregate pregnant and parenting adolescents in special classes and schools (see, e.g., C. P. Smith, 1982, p. 256).

9.   The term "communitarian" refers to those who critique liberal individualism and seek to strengthen interdependence, neighborhood and civic institutions, and "community" in general; communitarians, however, define community in disparate ways, reflecting a wide range in ideological perspectives.

10.   In Canada in 1994, among women aged 15 to 19, the total teen pregnancy rate per 1,000 was 48.8; the abortion rate was 22.0, the stillbirth/miscarriage rate was 2.1, and the live birth rate was 24.7 (Wadhera & Millar, 1997, pp. 11–12, 14).
      In the United States in 1992, 112 pregnancies occurred per 1,000 women aged 15 to 19; of these 61 ended in births, 36 in abortions, and 15 in miscarriages (Henshaw, 1997, p. 115). The live birth rate among teens has been declining since 1991; in 1996 (the last year for which data are available), the U.S. National Center for Health Statistics (1997) reported the birth rate for women aged 15 to 19 was 54.7 per 1,000 (Donovan, 1998a, p. 151).
      In 1988, the most recent year for which comparable international figures are available, Canada's teen pregnancy rate was 40 per 1,000 women aged 15 to 19, while the analogous U.S. rate was 97 per 1,000 (Alan Guttmacher Institute, 1994, p. 76).

11.   Access to contraception and abortion services in Canada is far from barrier-free. For example, only two provinces pay the full costs of abortion, four pay partial costs, and four pay no costs. "Access to abortion still varies considerably across Canada, and there is significant financial hardship involved for women in many settings, particularly in remote Northern areas and in PEI [Prince Edward Island], Newfoundland, and Saskatchewan (the three most rural provinces)" (Barrett, King, Levy, Maticka-Tyndale, & McKay, 1997, p. 308).

12.   In Canada, the primary means-tested assistance program is Social Assistance (SA). Low-income individuals are not excluded from this program based on their family composition as they are in the United States. However, "most nonworking households with an employable family member will receive UI [Unemployment Insurance] rather than SA," which means that so-called welfare (i.e., SA) recipients tend to be single women with young children or families with long-term employment problems (Blank & Hanratty, 1993, p. 197). Thus, despite a difference in program rules, in reality Canada's social welfare system, like the American system, "is currently divided into two gender-linked [and unequal] subsystems: an implicitly 'masculine' social insurance subsystem tied to 'primary' labor force participation and geared to (white male) 'breadwinners'; and an implicitly 'feminine' relief subsystem tied to household income and geared to homemaker-mothers and their 'defective' (i.e., female-headed) families" (Fraser, 1989, p. 9).

Chapter 2

Pregnant with Meaning:
Teen Mothers as Catch-all Enemies

The targets of displaced resentments or guilt are often "catch-all" enemies: people who become magnets for the suspicions and anger of many different groups and therefore serve to condense and transform a range of discontents and also to build political coalitions.

—Murray Edelman

In many communities across North America, teen mothers have become a "symbol of suspect status," thus making them likely "'catch-all' enemies" (Edelman, 1988). The image of the teen mother is pregnant with meaning; as a "condensation symbol," the image "draws its intensity from the associations it represses" (Edelman, 1988, p. 73). For people concerned about changing family structures and gender relations and sexual "permissiveness," teen mothers represent adolescent female sexuality out of control. For those worried about the breakdown of traditional lines of authority, teen mothers represent rebellion against parents and other adults. For those anxious about global economic restructuring, teen mothers represent dropouts who refuse to compete yet expect the welfare system to support their "poor choices." For those distressed about poverty and child abuse, teen mothers represent both the cause and consequence. Unstated assumptions about "the good mother," "the good student," and "the good citizen"—shaped by inequalities based on age, gender, sexuality, class, and race—often form the backdrop to the ongoing morality play about teen mothers.

Why is it important to detail the various negative stereotypes attached to the category "teen mother"? To the extent that these repressed associations can be identified, explicated, and viewed in a fuller social context, it will be that much easier for those who feel teen mothers are being unfairly scapegoated to challenge the political uses to which they are being put and to present alternative views. This is my general aim in this chapter and the two that follow.

Teasing out the many meanings of teen mothers helps us understand when, why, and how schools have responded to teen pregnancy and parenthood, including the politics of integration and the evolving shape of the programs designed to serve students who are pregnant or parents. In addition, an analysis of the negative stereotypes that circulate in public discourse begins to reveal how teen mothers interpret their experiences and represent themselves to others. The largely negative social identities available to teen mothers also constrain their capacity to make claims on the state.

Before analyzing the various stereotypes attached to teen mothers, a few preliminary observations are in order. First, how a particular teen mother is positioned in the "matrix of domination"—formed by interlocking systems of oppression based on race, class, gender, age, sexuality, ethnicity, and religion (Collins, 1990, p. 225)—will determine which stereotypes stick most and to whom. By virtue of their age, all teen mothers are disadvantaged vis-à-vis adults who hold greater economic, political, and social power, and they are therefore vulnerable to discrediting labels (e.g., "children having children"). But a Native teen mother, unmarried and living in poverty, is liable to be stereotyped much more readily than a married, White teen mother who presents herself as middle class.

Second, in keeping with the dominant discourse, I will use the term "teen mother," although it is far from a neatly bounded, coherent category. Who counts as a teen mother? A married 19-year-old? A 12-year-old made pregnant by an abusive father? A 20-year-old still attending high school? A teenager who places her baby for adoption?

Third, by scrutinizing the various stereotypes associated with teen mothers, I am not saying that there is never any truth to them. But I am critical of the practice of reducing any person to a stereotype or set of stereotypes. Failing to see a woman who happened to give birth to a child while in her teens in all her complexity risks turning her into the Other, a degraded category.

Fourth, this is not an exercise in laying out the bad images of teen mothers for its own sake; I am interested in exploring "the politics underlying certain representations" (hooks, 1990, p. 5). I am not under the illusion that if a particular stereotype can simply be revealed as partial or erroneous, it can be replaced or erased. "Stereotypes are tied to historical social relations, and . . . the chances of success in challenging a stereotype will depend upon the social location of the group in question" (Barrett,

1985, p. 70). Rather than occupying a privileged social location, teen mothers make up one of the most marginalized groups in society. Indeed, it is their marginal status and relative lack of power that make them such good "catch-all enemies." In the remainder of this chapter, I focus on the images of teen mothers that are most often evoked and that mark them as either unworthy of public support or as pitiable yet incompetent to lead autonomous lives.

"Stupid Sluts"

Some [students] are hard on teen mothers and think they're stupid for getting pregnant . . . mostly because they didn't use protection and they got themselves into that situation.

—Lois, age 15, Town School

I hear that all the time, [that when a girl is pregnant, she's a slut, and when a guy has gotten a girl pregnant, he's a stud]. That's just the way it is in society. That's the way it always has been. That's the way society thinks.

—Rose, mother, age 19, Town School

Nearly every teen mother I talked to mentioned being tarred by the "stupid slut" label; they felt this most acutely when it came from their peers, friends, or family members. Paradoxically, this stigma persists, despite the fact that premarital heterosexual activity is more widespread than ever before, if not necessarily endorsed for teenagers by adults (Bozinoff & MacIntosh, 1992; Laumann, Gagnon, Michael, & Michaels, 1994, p. 322). To understand this paradox, it is important to look at the changes accompanying the advent of the birth control pill as well as the continued dominance of the romantic love discourse, which glosses over a persistent sexual double standard.

In 1960 the U.S. Food and Drug Administration approved the oral contraceptive pill, which marked an important turning point in how people viewed extramarital pregnancy. Throughout the 1950s, many people considered premarital sex to be morally wrong, and young women who became pregnant felt shamed or blamed (Solinger, 1992, pp. 24–25). Over the next two decades, however, as birth control advocates worked to redefine teen pregnancy as a medical problem, the moral issue shifted from premarital sex to the use of contraception (Nathanson, 1991, p. 71).

Although sexual meanings are still contested within and between subcultures, "the dominant system of sexual meanings" (Irvine, 1994, p. 20) in Canada and the United States today suggests that a young woman is not so much condemned for having sex outside of marriage as she is for "irresponsible" contraceptive practices. Yet the prevalent double standard, which morally evaluates women's sexual practices but not men's, still places the onus on women to manage sexual and reproductive choices. This means that young women who find themselves pregnant risk being seen as not only "stupid," but as "sluts" as well. (An estimated 24% of American female adolescents become pregnant at least once before age 18 [Furstenberg, Brooks-Gunn, & Chase-Lansdale, 1989].)

"It takes two to tango," I often heard people in my study say, as they wondered aloud why so many young men showed a lack of contraceptive responsibility. But that phrase implies that men and women interact as equal partners. The reality is much more complicated; decisions about whether and when to have heterosexual intercourse and to use contraception are made within contexts of unequal power relations.

Inequalities based on gender, for example, permeate such major institutions as the labor market, the family, and organized religion. Men across differences of class, race, and ethnicity are still seen as the proper initiators of sexual activity. The potential for violence continues to cloud sexual decisions in young women's lives. A major, national study of U.S. sexual practices found that:

> 37 percent of younger females who participated in the survey said the reason they had sex for the first time was peer pressure, and only 35 percent said it was out of affection for their partner. In addition, nearly 29 percent of young females said that first intercourse was not wanted or was forced. This is in stark contrast to the response of young males who said that peer pressure accounted for only 4 percent of their reason for first intercourse, and 92 percent reported wanting it. (Trubisky, 1995, p. 1, citing Laumann et al., 1994)

Further, even with "assertiveness training," a significant number of young women find it difficult to insist that male partners use a condom (Lever, 1995, p. 174).

Even though they often do not have access to a feminist analysis, many young people, both boys and girls, recognize the existence of the double standard, but they consider it "the way the world works" and therefore accept it. As a tenth-grade girl, who interviewed her peers about the meaning of the prevalent label "slut," reported in an article she wrote for a big city newspaper:

> Some boys say that guys who sleep around are "players," and admit that they applaud them. (Although the term "himbo" is being used to describe a male bimbo, like Fabio for example, it hasn't yet entered into the mainstream language, so people aren't familiar with the term.) (Sayo, 1996, p. A2)

Similarly, at Town School, a counselor told me that he had heard a student using the term "male slut" to criticize boys for "sleeping around." Yet this term had not made it into common parlance.

The double standard is partially masked by the fact that girls, but not necessarily boys, continue to think about sex within the framework of romantic love. A national survey of Canadian teens found that 88% of boys and 85% of girls approve of premarital sex if two people "love" each other; 77% of boys but only 51% of girls approve if two people "like" each other; and 75% of boys but only 40% of girls approve if two people have dated a few times (Bibby & Posterski, 1992, pp. 28, 39). In the context of "love" or emotional intimacy, girls—who continue to be held responsible for their own as well as male behavior—may feel better able to negotiate the timing of sexual intercourse, the use of contraception, and what to do about a pregnancy should it occur. But girls face a dilemma: If they wait too long to have sex, they risk losing their boyfriend; if they do not wait long enough, they risk being labeled a slut. The discourse of romantic love "provides no clues about *how* to draw this line [between good girl and slut] or what to do if one is uncertain whether one is in love" (Canaan, 1986, p. 205).

For many teenage boys, having heterosexual intercourse is a culturally sanctioned way of proving their masculinity; whether the expression of their physical desire occurs within the context of emotional intimacy is less important. What remains largely hidden and unchallenged is the extent to which young men structure the sexual decisions of young women by asking for sex while remaining silent about their emotions (Canaan, 1986). In conversations I had with young women who were not mothers, I found that they were much more confident about what they would do in the abstract than in the context of a real relationship:

> If you're going to sleep with someone, you should like him and even love them. So if guys say they love you, they should have enough respect to do it [use a condom]. I would never, ever do it [have sex] unless I knew that the guy had something. That's stupid. (Lisa, age 15, Town School)

I chanced to interview Michelle, a popular 14-year-old at Town School, just days after her boyfriend, Mike, broke up with her because she refused to have sex with him. Mike humiliated Michelle by calling her a "fat, stingy pig" in the presence of mutual friends and then began dating one of her "close friends." Her feelings in the aftermath were complex: Michelle was clear that Mike was a "jerk," but she mourned the loss of her relationship and struggled with emerging sexual desire:

Me and a friend talk all the time in science class and math class, "I'm never going to do that," but yet sometimes you want to. There's something there that's telling you that now's the right time, but then something's [telling you] maybe you shouldn't. What if you get pregnant? Even if you are using protection and stuff like that, anything is possible.

In the context of real rather than hypothetical relationships—ones featuring conflicting emotions, unequal power relations, coercion, and unnamed sexual desire—it is much easier to see how some young women find themselves pregnant.

There is some evidence to suggest that a woman's pregnant body in and of itself is stigmatized. "Pregnancy remains the most 'visible' sign of sexual difference" (Françoise Verges quoted in Jones, 1993, p. 218). Men, especially, tend to avoid and stare at pregnant women, which women often interpret as a social stigma (Taylor & Langer, 1977). A number of studies suggest that compared to non-pregnant women, pregnant women, teenagers in particular, face a higher risk of battering from male partners (for a review, see Parker & McFarlane, 1991; see also, Kelly, 1993a, esp. pp. 154–155).

In the school context, a pregnant girl "violates the ideological opposition of mind and body that has been incorporated into the ritual organization of the school, as well as into its curriculum and instruction" (McDade, 1987, p. 60). Or as one City School teacher put it, "There are a few comments on the part of the students, and I think raised eyebrows on the part of the teachers, when you see somebody who is in their seventh or eighth month [of pregnancy] parading through the halls. It still doesn't seem to quite fit with what a school is basically for."

Although students and teachers alike in both Town and City Schools agreed that pregnant and parenting students were widely accepted, the students tended to report that being pregnant as a teenager was potentially more discrediting than being a mother. Upon further analysis, however, the stigma evoked by pregnancy usually seemed at root to be about the "stupid slut" label. In short, girls did not want to risk "ruining their reputations" (to quote Susan, age 15) by being seen with their pregnant peer, while boys wanted to avoid being perceived as the father-to-be.

A girl's visibly pregnant body advertises that she has had sex; her difference makes it difficult to impossible to control who knows her "business." She is the subject of rumors and interrogation and may be assumed to be a "stupid slut" unless and until she can convince her peers otherwise. Students were most understanding of girls who (a) became pregnant in the context of a love relationship, (b) were still with the father-to-be, and (c) had been using some form of contraception. These young women could be forgiven, because "everyone makes mistakes." Yet even these girls remained vulnerable to rumors started by peers who, for whatever reason, never liked them to begin with. Further, regardless of whether pregnant girls are accepted at school or not, they continue to provoke anxiety among other girls who are uncertain about whether willingness to have sex is required in order to attract and keep a boyfriend:

> I saw one girl in the hallway, and she was pregnant, and basically when you walk by you're like, "Oh, they're pregnant"—like you can tell. It's really weird for you, because you're thinking, "Oh, they don't seem like the type" [to have sex], like, "Why can they get a guy, and you can't?" (Sylvia, age 13, Town School)

In sum, a young woman who does not protect herself by ensuring that both she and her male sexual partner use contraception is "stupid"; but a young woman who looks too prepared too early in a relationship is a "slut." The young woman who finds herself pregnant and chooses not to have an abortion risks being labeled a "stupid slut."

"Children Having Children"

> Getting pregnant gives teenagers power over their parents. They use their body as a weapon.
>
> —Sex education consultant

> Most of these youth are dealing with issues around physical, sexual, emotional and verbal abuse. They suffer from low self-esteem, anger, fear of trusting others, a need for unconditional love and a lack of positive role models in their lives.
>
> —Young parent program counselors

The phrase "children having children" came into general use in the late 1970s and early 1980s, concurrent with teen pregnancy's official emergence as a social problem (Luker, 1996, esp. pp. 71–80). Yet this "discourse of infantilization" (B. Clark, 1994, p. 33) had been used previously to degrade single mothers of all ages, especially low-income, racial and ethnic minority women, as incapable of making their own independent decisions. Because immaturity and dependence are theoretically temporary states—something people can grow out of—these labels may be considered more "'polite' way[s] of rendering other distinctions" (B. Clark, 1994, p. 35). (I will be analyzing some of these "impolite" distinctions bound up in the phrase "children having children" later in this chapter.)

The spectacle of 14-year-olds announcing their intentions to become teen mothers on TV talk shows surely feeds public concern about "babies having babies." But in reality women aged 18 or 19 years account for two thirds of births to teenagers in Canada as well as the United States (Wadhera & Millar, 1997, p. 13; Rhode & Lawson, 1993, p. 3). We do not commonly categorize this 18- to 19-year-old age group as "children."

Indeed, as Anna, a 17-year-old honor roll student at Town School, reminded me, it was common historically for women her age to become mothers:

> A lot of times they say, "Kids having kids." But really people used to have kids when they were that young in the olden days, and that was perfectly acceptable. It's just now it's different 'cause that was supposed to be your whole life, was having and raising children—that was your career. Whereas now you have college and [a career outside the home].

In the not-so-distant past, a "family economy" was prevalent in North America, and children worked on the family farm or at the family business from about the age of 6 or 7 years, while older female children cared for siblings too young to work (Hays, 1996, pp. 27–28). In most societies around the world today, and in pockets of North America, it is common for women to share the rearing of small children with older, usually female, children (Hays, 1996, p. 20, citing Weisner & Gallimore 1977).

Given that the vast majority of teen mothers are, by some definitions, considered legal adults, and that in other times and contexts young women have successfully participated in childrearing, why does the phrase "children having children" continue to resonate? This stereotype has come to embody two related but contradictory sets of anxieties about teen mothers. To a large extent, these are elaborations of how adults have alternately portrayed children in general: as either threats or victims (Thorne, 1987).

"Teen Rebel, Teen Mom"

One important subcategory of the "children having children" label, then, is the teen mother as threat. Numerous mass media articles on the subject of teen pregnancy have expressed the concern that teenagers use pregnancy and parenthood as a ticket to instant adulthood and as a way of rebelling against parental authority. To the extent that young women take mothering seriously and show they can handle adult responsibilities, adults wonder about their incentive to conform to the authority of other institutions, such as the school, where teen mothers are still defined as children.

A related fear is that teenagers in general are more likely to take their cue from each other than from adults. As the visibility and acceptability of pregnant and parenting students in mainstream schools has increased, so have anxieties that they have become "celebrities" among their peers. Describing teen pregnancy as "fashionable" and teen motherhood as "baby chic" plays on the stereotype of teenagers as superficial and gullible trend-followers. In this scenario, pregnant and mothering teens are cast as misguidedly trying to achieve status in the eyes of their peers.

I witnessed a flash point for such worries at Town School, where a significant minority of teachers and administrators portrayed the teen mothers' bringing their children into the main part of the school as "show and tell." Whereas other teachers saw the same behavior as ordinary parental pride, these teachers used language that cast it as "selfish," "immature," and potentially "abusive." Their accounts implied that the babies were treated as objects and less than human ("toys," "pets," "dolls"). By "prancing their babies around" the school, as one administrator put it, the teen mothers were perceived to be "flaunting" their non-conformity.

A variant of the "teen rebel" stereotype is the teen mother as "street kid." The very term suggests a young woman outside of parental and other social controls. Life on the streets implies alcohol and drug addictions, violence, participation in petty crime and gang activity, prostitution, craftiness ("street smarts"), and a general toughness.

"The Girl Nobody Loved" Revisited

The flip side of the teen mother as an in-your-face threat to adult authority, and the other important subcategory of the "children having children" label, is the teen mother as victim of adult dysfunction and abuse. Feminist historian Rickie Solinger has surveyed the psychological explanations for white single pregnancy in the post-World War II era, characterizing them with the catchphrase "the girl nobody loved" (1992, ch. 3). In the 1950s, for example, psychiatrists argued that "unwed mothers" got pregnant on purpose, albeit unconsciously, as evidenced by their lack of contraceptive use and unwillingness to get an abortion. The experts often identified the underlying causes of pregnancy as family and gender "dysfunctions." Both parents, but especially mothers, were blamed for not offering their daughters "appropriate models of sex roles or gender characteristics" (Solinger, 1992, p. 91). In one formulation, the unwed mother was described as "creating the lost love object [her mother] by herself, within herself, through pregnancy" (p. 94).

Although today psychologists no longer define all young single mothers as mentally ill, echoes of "the girl nobody loved" are still heard. A number of professionals to whom I spoke at both Town and City Schools asserted that a particular type of student was vulnerable to pregnancy. Collectively, they painted the following portrait: Those "at risk" are "lonely hearts," "people in crisis," "kids on the verge," "a little bit on the outside," who "don't have a big circle of friends." They have "low self-esteem," "are basically unloved," and come from "dysfunctional families" and "unstable homes." As a result, they "seek attention from boys" and "want somebody to love." This discourse, still prevalent in media and academic accounts of teen pregnancy and parenthood, stigmatizes both the teen mother (as psychologically disturbed) as well as her family (as abusive) (see Chapter 4).

The 1990s version of "the girl nobody loved" departs somewhat from the 1950s version by shifting the locus of blame. In the earlier construct, the teen mother was mainly a victim of herself and, at a remove, her family, particularly her mother. The teen mother today is more likely to be described as the victim of child abuse. This argument takes two forms, which are sometimes linked. First, researchers have recently taken note of the fact that perhaps "half of all babies born to minor women are fathered by adult men," thus prompting policymakers in the United States to explore statutory rape laws as a means of preventing teen pregnancy (Donovan, 1997, p. 30). Yet, according to a national survey in the United States, "[o]nly 8% of all births to 14–19-year-olds are to unmarried minors with a partner five or more years older" (Lindberg, Sonenstein, & Martinez, 1997, p. 61). There is a cultural norm that heterosexual women date men who are older than they are. Still, in cases where the age difference between teen mothers and their adult male partners is substantial, many psychologists see an unconscious desire for a father substitute (Thompson, 1995, pp. 235–236).

To the extent that teen mothers are said to exhibit an "Oedipal complex" because of abusive parenting, this first argument connects to a second: that young women get pregnant and have babies because they have been sexually and physically abused. Researchers have posited five possible links between child sexual abuse and early pregnancy (but see Roosa, Tein, Reinholtz, & Angelini, 1997): (a) the pregnancy results directly from sexual abuse; (b) there are "similarities in the family dynamics of incest victims and adolescent mothers," namely "a powerful father figure, a mother who is devalued, and a daughter who is assigned maternal responsibilities"; (c) "a sexually abused girl may learn that her purpose is to fulfill the sexual desires of others," which may lead to "promiscuity" at an age when people do not tend to use contraception consistently; (d) low self-esteem resulting from sexual abuse may create "needs for immediate gratification," and unprotected sex may be one way to "distance a victim in some way from her anxious emotions"; and (e) the pregnancy may be planned consciously as a way to escape from a bad environment (Butler & Burton, 1990, pp. 73–74).

This latter hypothesis, that young women deliberately set out to become mothers, seems to be the one that has most captured the public imagination. While liberals seem inclined to blame "the abusers" and, less often, "the pressure cooker of poverty [that] creates the conditions in which most abuse occurs" (Durning, 1997, p. E3), conservatives read into this further evidence that teen mothers are "calculating" and looking for the "easy way out" (traits also associated with "welfare moms"; see below).

The 1990s version of "the girl nobody loved" more often scrutinizes and affixes blame to the sexual partners of teen mothers, although this is usually done by highlighting their power advantage by virtue of age rather than gender. It also excavates sexual abuse from among the vaguely named family and gender dysfunctions identified in the 1950s version. But there are important continuities between the two, as well. In both the 1990s and the 1950s version of this construct, the issue of young women's sexuality, their own desires and agency, is played down (recall that most women become teen mothers at age 18 or 19).

Whether teen mothers are cast as unloved victims or as rebellious threats, by virtue of their age, they are seen as children who must be "helped" by adults. Defining teen mothers as by that very fact "immature" inevitably shapes the programs and policies established to address their needs; thus, supervision, monitoring, and surveillance become the resulting watchwords of such programs. People often assume teen mothers were themselves born to teen mothers who had dropped out of school, lived hard lives, and perhaps abused drugs; they grew up on welfare and suffered child abuse. Teen mothers are destined to recreate their multiple disadvantages, it is argued, unless professionals can intervene to help them "break the cycle."

"Welfare Moms"

It's no wonder that a quarter of a million joined the ranks of the poor when our benevolent government encourages young women to live on welfare and reproduce like rabbits.

—Warland, 1993, letter to the editor, Vancouver Sun

Having a baby and receiving welfare is a way to get away from your family—a legitimate way out. I wonder, does this explain the trend for girls to keep their babies? Other girls, who are under 19 and living independently on welfare, think, "If I get pregnant, I'll get more money."

—Pregnancy counselor, Midland

Once people know that I'm on assistance, I've heard the term "welfare bum." . . . Girls in my computer class will laugh, "It's Welfare Wednesday—the bars are going to be packed tonight."

—Anastasia, mother, age 19, Town School

Despite research to the contrary (see Chapter 4), it is widely believed that teen motherhood causes poverty and welfare dependency and that teens get pregnant in order to obtain welfare benefits. Allied to these beliefs, whether voiced in school corridors or over the airwaves of North American media, are negative stereotypes about welfare recipients in general as the undeserving poor. They are considered undeserving for several reasons. First, they are said to be "lazy bums" who "sit around waiting for their welfare checks to arrive" rather than working or trying to find work. Second, they are accused of spending their money "irresponsibly" on such things as holidays or drugs and alcohol. Third, they are thought to be "promiscuous" and "recklessly" fertile, procreating without being able to support their children financially. In short, they cannot, as some social scientists might put it, "delay gratification."

Being a "welfare mother," in the eyes of some people, is also in and of itself evidence of being a "neglectful mother." This is particularly true of teenagers, because they cannot claim to have become single mothers through more legitimate paths such as widowhood or divorce or even the breakup of a long-term relationship. They cannot claim to have temporarily fallen on economic hard times while already mothers. To bring a child into the world without the ability to provide for it materially, so the reasoning goes, models irresponsible decision making and "dependency" and selfishly consigns the child to poverty and all of its accompanying ills.

Once a young woman finds herself a mother on welfare, she faces at least two double binds. First, although many families today require two incomes to lift them above poverty level, government rules such as "no man in the house" make it difficult for women on welfare to reunite with former partners or forge stable, new relationships. Yet to remain single on welfare can help stigmatize young women as "sluts"; they are vulnerable to the ability of people with power over them, such as landlords, to pressure them for sexual favors. Second, although teen mothers are told to make something of themselves and break the "cycle of welfare dependency," they face public pressure to get off welfare right away. Yet most of them know that they need not only a high school diploma but a post-secondary education in order to obtain work that pays a living wage and covers the cost of child care.

Advocates for teen mothers are well aware of these double binds:

> The fact that welfare pays more than a lot of minimum wage, entry-level jobs—that's a real problem when you've got a child. . . . I really think a mother at home is the best thing *for* the baby, especially for the first few years. But, it's a stigma to be on welfare. (former staff member, Teen-Age Parents Program, City School)

A youth consultant in British Columbia told me about being asked by a service group to help write a proposal for an entry-level employment program for young mothers aged 19 and over. She advised against an entry-level jobs approach, explaining, "If they're going to be at entry level, how are they going to be able to support their child? What you have to be doing is gearing towards jobs that are more attractive than being on welfare." To this, the consultant got a response she said she "will never forget": "Well," people in the group told her, "that would mean a job of X-thousand a year; that's as much as I make. They're not going to take jobs away from me. Why would I be training these young people in a way that would make them just as good as I am?"

"Dropouts"

> Usually the teachers, they don't think less of girls who get pregnant, but you can tell there's a little bit of a difference from before. . . . Just kind of thinking maybe they're a misfit type.
>
> —Lisa, age 15, Town School

> After that much of a problem with attendance, commitment becomes an issue, and any time that starts to sneak its ugly head into a school system, it's like wearing a sign on the front of your head that [reads] "I've got an attitude" or "I'm marginal."
>
> —Teacher, City School

The term "dropout" implies that a student makes an independent, final decision to leave school without graduating; it attaches blame squarely on the individual. It glosses over the number of people who are expelled for tardiness and absenteeism or other disciplinary infractions. It includes those who read institutional practices—such as academic failure, standardized testing, ability grouping and tracking, and in-grade retention—as covert messages of rejection. It also counts among its ranks those who eventually return or obtain their diploma or equivalent through alternate means. "Dropouts" are negatively stereotyped as psychologically disturbed, below average in intelligence, irrational, unreliable, lacking in persistence, and otherwise deviant (Fine, 1991; Kelly & Gaskell, 1996).

The dropout label haunts most teen mothers, regardless of whether they have ever actually left school or not. Those who were out of school prior to getting pregnant can be said to have shown a lack of commitment, which then gets read as a character flaw that may manifest itself again when "the going gets too tough." They have looked for "the easy way out" in the past, so the argument goes, and will probably do so in the future. Those who have never left school are still made to feel like "slackers" if they rely on welfare in order to combine new motherhood with full-time schooling. Fran, who was struggling to remain on the honor roll, explained the contradictions she was facing:

> People are [saying], "It's our tax dollars, and what are you using it for? Why aren't you working?" I find it hard. I understand that there are mothers out there going to school and working [for pay], but I don't know how they do it. And I also feel my grades would just drop. (age 18, Town School)

From a different direction, some teen mothers reported criticism from family, friends, and others that they had "abandoned" their children by putting them into day care while they attended classes. Yet to resolve this dilemma by leaving school to provide full-time care for their children—even in cases where their children were chronically ill—would have relegated them to "dropout" status, no matter how well they did as stay-at-home mothers.

"Neglectful Mothers"

> Most of these girls come from dysfunctional families; they haven't learned proper behavior, they don't know how to behave, how to care for children. They haven't been cared for themselves; how are they going to look after a child? When that child starts to say "no," when that child doesn't love them, how are they going to manage? They have nothing to fall back on. They'll just dump the kid somewhere.
>
> —Teacher, Town School

> There are "bad" teen moms and "good" teen moms, and when you meet one "bad" teen mom, that sets the picture for everybody. You're like, "Oh, I saw this girl, she was smacking her kid around on the bus." And anytime you meet anybody who says, "Yeah, I'm a teen mom," then that's the thing that comes into your mind. Not, "Oh, she had a child at a young age." So I think if more people

meet the "good" teen moms, then the image of this girl who's been abused and is therefore abusing her child who will then abuse is destroyed.
—Mina, mother, age 18, City School

Many of the negative stereotypes already discussed reinforce the stereotype of the teen mother as neglectful and abusive. If she is promiscuous, she is immoral. If she is having a child to spite her parents or gain status in the eyes of her peers, she is immature and selfish. If she planned her pregnancy as an escape from an abusive home life, she is confused in her thought process. If she brought a child into the world without being able to support it financially, she has doomed her child to poverty and possibly a lifetime of misery. If she has left school, she has irrationally given up a chance for a credential and ticket to a good job. In all these ways, she can be said to have proven herself to be a poor role model for her child and thus a bad mother. Related stereotypes arise from preconceptions about teenagers. Young women are assumed, for example, to be self-absorbed and obsessed with their body image and therefore liable to starve themselves during pregnancy, thus abusing their child in the womb.

Contrary to such widespread beliefs, several authoritative reviews of the literature and some carefully done studies suggest that a mother's age is far less important than other factors in determining the potential abuse and neglect of her children (Buchholz & Korn-Bursztyn, 1993; Geronimus, Korenman, & Hillemeier, 1994; Miller & Moore, 1990; Phoenix, 1991b). One U.S. study using demographic data on over 30,000 parents—who had either maltreated their children or whose children were in out-of-home care—found that adolescent parents were not overrepresented in either category (Massat, 1995).

Studies of child abuse have focused on easily accessible groups, such as single mothers on welfare, and often do not use control groups (Martineau, 1992). Yet child abuse typically occurs under conditions of isolation, stress, or both—conditions that cut across differences based on socioeconomic and marital status (Martineau, 1993).

Although maternal age does not appear to be a prime determinant in child abuse and neglect, teen mothers face discrimination based partly on their age, which can add to their stress and isolation. Many of the teen mothers in my study were having to cope with negative judgments and tremendous scrutiny. Programs for parents of all ages that provide social, emotional, and financial support can alleviate the stress and isolation that factor into child abuse and neglect.

Women of various ages in North America today face what Sharon Hays has called the "cultural contradictions of motherhood":

In a society where over half of all mothers with young children are now working outside of the home, one might well wonder why our culture pressures women to dedicate so much of themselves to child rearing. And in a society where the logic of self-interested gain seems to guide behavior in so many spheres of life, one might further wonder why a logic of unselfish nurturing guides the behavior of mothers. (1996, p. x)

The ideology of "intensive mothering" (Hays, 1996) fuels feelings of isolation, boredom, depression, and exhaustion yet, at the same time, makes such feelings difficult to acknowledge publicly.

It may well be that public anxiety over the ability of young women to mother reflects harder-to-express worries about the major transformations in economic, gender, and family relations that affect us all. A study of 15-year-old girls revealed that when asked to describe what life was like for mothers, many focused on negative aspects, yet most went on to agree with the formal proposition that "It's a good life for mothers at home with a young child." Without alternative models of motherhood available to them, several of the ways that the girls came to terms with the negative aspects of motherhood involved "locat[ing] the problems and contradictions of motherhood in young mothers" (Prendergast & Prout, 1980, p. 526).

In short, many of the problems facing teen mothers are problems for all women with children, and teenagers appear to cope as well or as poorly as others with similar levels of support. Yet the stresses generated in large part by structural mismatches—more and more women, for example, need to work outside the home for pay, but many do not have access to a living wage or affordable, quality child care services—get displaced onto teen mothers.

Flash Point: The Case of Teen Mothers Who Smoke

The negative stereotypes and accompanying narratives about teen mothers often remained latent in the school settings that I studied. But the anger underneath the surface occasionally broke out. Cigarette smoking became the flash point at City School. One of the designated smoking areas, and the one the teen mothers who smoked favored because of its proximity to their homeroom, happened to be in front of the school, where it was visible from the administrative offices.

Official school policy is, of course, opposed to smoking because of the overwhelming evidence that cigarette smoking is unhealthy, even lethal. Yet the anger that some school staff members directed at teen mothers who smoked went beyond a concern for their health. Their anger was fueled by other worries and was shaped by most of the negative stereotypes about teen mothers that I have just analyzed. Foremost among these was the latent image of the cunning welfare claimant.

Most teachers were aware that the Teen-Age Parents Program participants had a special lunch program that became a proxy for welfare benefits. A recurring theme in informal conversations with staff was anger that teen mothers bought cigarettes but got their noontime meal for free. One teacher referred to the teen mothers as "little princesses," while another implied that some of "her little guys" (eighth graders) were going hungry and that they were more deserving than the teen mothers who wasted their money on cigarettes. Not all teachers agreed with this, and some felt compelled to defend the teen mothers:

> I just turn to them [in the staff room] and say, "Well, you have to prioritize in your life, and that's a priority for them." I said, "I teach *not* to smoke," but I said, "Certainly, if it's a priority for them and that helps them get through their day, then I'm not going to say they can't have a program."

Another teacher publicly questioned the ability of teen mothers who smoke to serve as "role models" for their children, thus invoking the "neglectful mother" stereotype. Later, in a formal interview, he returned to this theme:

> The only behavior that I find really disturbing . . . is that damn smoking that they all engage in—you know, the stress reliever. . . . Not only because it's so expensive and it's so stupid and they've got this young person and it's not a good—there's just so many things that are wrong with it.

He readily acknowledged that other City School students (and, I might add, teachers) smoked, but "the only ones I see are the silly moms." The smokers could be considered neglectful mothers because (a) they spent money on cigarettes that could have gone toward their children, (b) they admitted to being under "stress," (c) they might be exposing their children to the dangers of secondhand smoke, and (d) their children might see them smoking and take up the habit.

A third set of worries about smoking tapped into the stereotypes of teen mothers as "street kids" or "rebels." Smoking, several staff members said, underscored these young women's "toughness." One teacher saw smoking as a marker of changing gender relations:

> When I first started teaching, the girls were very quiet and subdued, and if there was any noise and racket, it was the boys that did it. But over the years, . . . the girls have changed; they're certainly more outgoing, more rebellious. One thing

I've noticed being a non-smoker: They smoke a lot more. Less boys smoke and more girls smoke.

One of the classmates of the teen mothers cited cigarette smoking as one reason she felt "they look low class."

Smoking became, for at least some of the middle-class teachers, a metaphor for the purported inability of teen mothers to repress their desires. One teacher, talking about why young women become pregnant and become mothers, told me, "It's like smoking. They have needs they don't seem to have control over." This language evokes the stereotypes of the "stupid slut" and the welfare claimant unable or unwilling to suppress her sexuality and fertility. Brodkey has called attention to how the middle-class campaign against smoking has focused on the "character of *smokers* rather than, say, the cost and quality of health care or the political influence of the tobacco industry" (1996, p. 133). In the case of the focus of school adults on the morality of individual teen mothers, deeper questions about why young women start smoking in the first place—such as a desire to be thin or to fit in—went unasked.

Images Refracted through Lenses of Gender, Sexuality, Class, and Race

An understanding of the many meanings currently attached to teen pregnancy and motherhood would be incomplete without examining how these negative images are refracted through the lenses of gender, sexuality, class, and race. Together, these four lenses represent the major intersecting axes of subordination that position teen mothers. The relations of unequal power based on gender, sexuality, class, and race shape who is likely to become a teen parent, how this event will be interpreted by those in positions of power, and with what consequences.

Relations of unequal power intersect in ways such that teen mothers are disproportionately found among the poor and working class and among certain racial and ethnic minority groups. In the comparatively infrequent cases in which middle-class White girls become teen mothers, they are less likely to experience the stigma, surveillance, and attendant risk of losing their children that face those who must rely on welfare for survival. Those who share particular traits beyond teen motherhood—such as being Native, poor, and unmarried—become ensnared by mutually reinforcing, negative stereotypes.

Gender and Sexuality

Teen pregnancy and motherhood—and more broadly, youth sexuality—serve, as I have tried to show, as a "condensation symbol" (Edelman, 1988) for multiple social anxieties, including unsettling changes in gender roles and relations. In a culture where many still consider it "normal" for young men to "sow their wild oats" and initiate sexual relationships and for women to be the guardians of morality, we can see that this particular condensation symbol is highly gendered.

With the latest backlash against the welfare state, we have witnessed some attempts to stigmatize the men who father children born to teen mothers as "deadbeat dads" and statutory rapists. This stigma, however, has two perverse effects. First, it reinforces the traditional equation of fatherhood with breadwinner, which may discourage young men without access to the primary labor market from taking responsibility for actual childrearing. Second, it shifts attention from unequal gender relations to age differences, though age differences may be less significant, given the difficulty that women of *all* ages have in negotiating sexual relationships with men. Furthermore, it is still quite easy for men, who do not bear the visible mark of pregnancy and who are less likely than women to take responsibility for childrearing, to evade scrutiny and avoid stigma, making the talk about deadbeat dads and child abusers more rhetorical than real in its consequences.

By contrast, women's sexuality—spotlighted during pregnancy—has, historically, been used as a means to devalue and exclude them from public places such as the workplace and school. Even today, there is little room in supposedly gender-neutral organizations for reproductive concerns (Acker, 1990); students are often treated as asexual (Wolpe, 1988). Although it is no longer legal to deny pregnant and mothering girls access to an education, it is still common to segregate them, sometimes coercively (Snider, 1989) and in ways that are not always in their best interest (Kelly, 1993a).

Although pregnancy may devalue young single women in some ways, in other contexts it also offers the valued role of motherhood and seems to confirm one's heterosexuality. A teen mother at Town School, for example, told me that as stigmatized as she felt, nobody suspected her of being a lesbian, apparently the most despised category at her high school. An Ontario study found that young lesbians faced such pressure and hostility that some resorted to having sex with a variety of men in order to conceal their sexual orientation; this behavior sometimes resulted in pregnancy (cited in Lees, 1994, p. 288). A federal politician from Nova Scotia, whose daughter had become a mother at age 15, explained the social hierarchy between teen mothers and lesbians this way: Her daughter's situation was "immoral" but "natural." In contrast, "for a child to come home and say 'I am a lesbian'—it is immoral. Not only is it immoral, it is also unnatural and it does defy nature" (Canadian Press, 1994, p. A6).

Social Class

Poor people, by virtue of being at the bottom of the social class hierarchy, have historically been stigmatized as sexually promiscuous. A teacher at City School, for example, told me, "In certain socioeconomic groups, [changing sexual partners often] is common, but these are basically one step up from street kids." Lower-class and ethnic minority women

> carry a stigma that overrides their sexual unorthodoxy; they are already outside
> the social pale. Providing adolescent women who are poor and black with hu-
> manitarian assistance not only does not establish or legitimize new sexual norms;
> it calls attention to and reinforces the traditional sexual values of the dominant
> community. (Nathanson, 1991, p. 163)

The middle class can hide the "problem" of teen pregnancy partly through abortion and lobbying to provide services for teen mothers away from the most affluent neighborhoods. Among "middle-class families," explained a City School teacher, the "prevailing attitude is, 'It's a mistake; we'll get rid of the mistake . . . because there's a whole life ahead of you'." "Among well-to-do teens who get pregnant accidentally, about three-fourths seek an abortion; among poor teens, the proportion is less than one-half," according to U.S. data (Luker, 1996, p. 154).

In both Midland and Pacifica where my research took place, I heard reports that predominantly middle-class schools subtly and not so subtly tried to push visibly pregnant students out and into alternative programs located in working-class neighborhoods. Bonnie, an upper-middle-class teen mother at City School, said students would have "shunned" her if she had turned up pregnant at her affluent neighborhood school, where "having a kid early" would "be considered a failure."

Sociologists have argued that in advantaged communities, people are likely to view teen parenthood as a serious obstacle to economic and marital success (Furstenberg, 1991, p. 134). Brewster, Billy, and Grady (1993), using data from a U.S. national survey of White females, showed that young women postponed sexual intercourse, used more effective birth control methods, or both if they lived in areas with more local labor market opportunities for women and if adults in their neighborhood had higher levels of educational attainment. Conversely, women who lived in poor neighborhoods, who attended inferior schools, and who had fewer good job opportunities faced a greater likelihood of teenage childbearing (McCrate, 1990, 1992).

Race

Unequal class relations are intricately intertwined with unequal race relations in both the United States and Canada. "As John D'Emilio and Estelle Freedman note, the white middle class has routinely justified oppression by casting people of color as sexually deviant, for 'images of sexual depravity served to strengthen class and race hierarchies'" (Irvine, 1994, p. 11). In a story that reveals racism, class bias, and sexism, a former teacher in a young parents program, a woman of color, told me how she had entered the staff room one day in time to overhear herself referred to as "the madam and her girls." Her colleague's comment invoked the negative stereotype of the Black woman as prostitute and cast the teen mothers—low-income White and Native women—as sexually irresponsible.

Like teen mothers of African descent, Native teen mothers belong to subordinate, racialized "castes." Native people must cope with the legacy of colonialism, racial oppression, and poverty. A Native parent at Town School who had been a teen mother told me: "For generations every aspect of our lives was controlled by the government and the church as well. . . . Because many of the children were put in residential school, the need to practice traditional parenting was almost lost." She also attributed teen pregnancy among Natives to "poverty, isolation from mainstream society, alcoholism, and the lack of self-image."

Contradictory and Overlapping Negative Images

When the various stereotypes of teen mothers are teased apart and examined side by side, one begins to see how they contradict as well as imply each other. If a young woman doesn't use contraception effectively, then she's "stupid" and "irresponsible," but if she plans ahead and insists on using contraception, then she's a "slut." The stereotype of the teen mother pregnant by accident due to non-use or improper use of contraception is at odds with another stereotype, the teen mother who plans her pregnancy in order to escape parental control and obtain welfare benefits. She is "tough" and can no longer be considered a child by virtue of hard living out on the streets, but she is also a "victim," a "baby having a baby." She is at once too independent and too dependent.

The stereotypes also overlap; any one of several traits may evoke the same negative image. Receiving welfare, having black skin, having been homeless, and being pregnant out of wedlock can all imply promiscuity. Similarly, living in poverty, being young, leaving school early, and being Native can all suggest that one is a neglectful mother.

These contradictory and overlapping images can create a confusing hall of mirrors for teen mothers, particularly those who come from low-income backgrounds and have fewer options. They may detest living on welfare but know that if they try to combine motherhood, school, and paid work, they will not get enough education to enter the primary labor market. If they enroll their children in day care while working hard in school, they may be criticized for neglecting their maternal duties. If they leave school to care for their children full time, they may be branded a dropout and welfare scrounger.

As "catch-all enemies" teen mothers are vulnerable to potentially repressive public policies. People who resent using tax money for welfare as well as those who see "the poor as a cultural, moral, or genetic threat to the respectable classes" (Edelman, 1988, p. 68) both have incentives to want to limit the reproductive rights of young women, especially those who are poor, Black, or Native (see Roberts, 1997). In the course of my study, I have had more than one well-intentioned, White, middle-class person wonder aloud, as one teacher did, "if we shouldn't give something to people so they can't have children until a certain age." As I will explore in the next chapter, impulses to suppress the sexual and reproductive choices of young people often exist just below the surface of a seemingly neutral and benign discourse about informed decision making.

Chapter 3

The Good Choices Discourse: A Fashionable, Flawed Attempt to Avoid Stigma

Perhaps the most recent and increasingly marshaled negative stereotype of single teen mothers is that they are "people who make bad choices." This stereotype is evoked, for example, when people refer disapprovingly to the "teen mom lifestyle"—the term "lifestyle" implying something freely chosen. The unstated assumption is that most teen mothers are personally responsible for their choice and therefore blameworthy; people thus attribute to them a "conduct stigma" (Page, 1984, p. 6).

By focusing on the choices of teen mothers, some people hope to avoid stigmatizing the teen mothers or their children as *persons;* instead, they want to stigmatize their *practices,* such as the choice to raise their babies themselves. This is analogous to the attempt to keep the practice of "homosexuality" stigmatized, while "the homosexual" "increasingly is awarded civil rights and civil liberties" (see Epstein, 1987, p. 47). Whether this distinction between people and their behavior can be maintained is dubious. A policy analyst in the area of teen pregnancy put it this way: "A lot of us are uncomfortable about moralizing. How do you stigmatize the behavior without stigmatizing the children? Do we want to make the kids feel lousy and like outsiders? I don't think we have a very good answer to that" (quoted in Gallman, 1995, p. 8A).

"Sociologists from Max Weber to Pierre Bourdieu have noted how groups of individuals use behavior patterns as 'markers' to distinguish themselves from others" (Luker, 1996, p. 92). A clear example of this process was provided in an interview with a teacher at Town School, by her own description a member of the "upper middle class" and a vocal opponent of school-based day care programs for teen parents. Halfway through the interview, Ms. Wick revealed that her own daughter (a recent graduate of Town School) had become a mother at age 18. She was careful to show how her daughter did not fit the usual stereotypes by contrasting her behavior with that of the type of pregnant girl who would have been stigmatized at Town School:

> She was into other kinds of activities and behaviors that would certainly put her into a group of people that my daughter wouldn't want to be associated with, [behaviors like] parties, drugs, alcohol, promiscuity. . . . [If] they were into those kinds of activities anyway and then they got pregnant, it was sort of, "Well, it figures."

In addition, Ms. Wick explained that her daughter never went on welfare, eventually married the father of her child, "they both have jobs, and they have bought a house, so everything has worked out." The low-income teen mothers, whose more constrained choices helped shape a different behavior pattern, thus served as a negative referent against which Ms. Wick could favorably compare her middle-class daughter's achievements.

The Good Choices Discourse:
Spanning the Ideological Divide

Talk about choices, good and bad, not only allows White, middle-class people such as Ms. Wick to distinguish themselves from the people most likely to become single teen mothers. What I will call the "good choices discourse" also allows those who espouse it the illusion of rising above moral debates and conflicting beliefs and values to the realm of "facts" and the weighing of costs and benefits. This discourse provides a seemingly non-moralistic language to professionals and front-line employees of the welfare state as they give information to patients, teach clients communication skills, and train students to make rational, informed decisions.

But this language simply reframes many of the same stigmas explored in the previous chapter. A young woman who finds herself pregnant, for example, is no longer labeled a "slut"; rather, her failure to use contraception wisely and well, if at all, constitutes a bad choice. Women under the age of 20 years who give birth and decide to raise their own babies are still grouped together; how and why they arrived at the same destination is deemed largely irrelevant. The choices embedded in their status as teen mothers are labeled "bad" on the basis of an often unstated cost-benefit assessment. Inevitably, there is slippage; the discourse that casts the choices of teen mothers in a negative light affects the way people with real influence over their lives—doctors, caseworkers, principals, judges—treat them. In short, young women with children find themselves discredited, stigmatized as people who make bad choices.

Talk about good and bad choices easily spans the conservative-liberal ideological divide because such talk can be vague about what constitutes (a) goodness or badness or (b) a choice. Also left undefined might be who, ultimately, makes the choices. Thus, the discourse has potent practical implications for building a coalition in support of programs. When Town School undertook a supported integration initiative for pregnant and parenting teens, the main discourse of the teachers revolved around the school's role in encouraging "good choices" regarding pregnancy and parenthood. My many interviews showed that the good choices discourse proved to be remarkably supple in its ability to allow conversation and agreement among conservative and liberal teachers, although what they meant by "choice" was filtered by their respective ideological lenses. Nevertheless, they agreed that teen parenthood was a bad choice, a consensus at least partially rooted in the common identity of the teachers as "middle-class taxpayers" concerned about "welfare dependency." Both conservatives and liberals framed the problems facing teen parents as individual rather than structural ones (for a fuller discussion of these dynamics, see Kelly, 1998).

Encouraging teenagers to make good choices is hardly a controversial stance, and conservatives and liberals alike consider single teen motherhood to be a decidedly bad choice. They differ, however, in their analysis of human nature and how people make decisions and therefore they also differ over matters of policy that affect the sexual and reproductive lives of young people.

Cognitive linguist George Lakoff (1996) traces such differences in worldview to underlying metaphors of the ideal family: at the center of conservative ideology is the "strict father" model, while liberal ideology centers on the "nurturant parent" model. The strict father "teaches children right from wrong by setting strict rules for their behavior and enforcing them through punishment" (p. 66). A key metaphor in this model is moral strength. Children are viewed as "naturally tending toward evil unless some strong corrective action is taken" (p. 76).

Teenagers engage in sexual activity, for example, because they are morally weak and lacking in self-control. A morally strong person, according to conservatives, should be able to "just say no" to sexual desire; "chastity" constitutes a "good" choice. In having made the "wrong" choice, the pregnant teenager deserves punishment. "Tough love" means teaching children "to accept the consequences of their own irresponsibility"; in the process, they develop moral strength (p. 97). Punishment is also important in maintaining "moral boundaries" (p. 85); the young woman who has sex outside of marriage and chooses to keep her baby rather than place the baby for adoption, for instance, must be marked as deviant so that others in the community are not led astray.

Rejecting this reward-and-punishment model, the nurturant parent model espoused by liberals posits:

> Children develop best through their positive relationships to others, through their contribution to their community, and through the ways in which they realize their potential and find joy in life. Children become responsible, self-disciplined, and self-reliant through being cared for and respected, and through caring for others. (p. 108)

Key metaphors include nurturance and empathy. For example, liberals would support young parent programs because society should help those who need help.

Many liberals are silent, however, about whether becoming a mother as a teenager is, or ever could be, a good choice. Lakoff, for example, himself a liberal, presents reasons that liberals support the right of a pregnant teenage woman to choose to have an abortion: she is "in trouble" and deserves to be helped and to pursue her self-development (pp. 269–270). One explanation for the silence of liberals on this matter stems from the Enlightenment notion that the role of society is not to prescribe and enforce certain choices but rather to ensure that individuals have access to the proper information and to the intellectual maturity to make the best choices on their own. This, I would contend, leads liberals to idealize an individualistic, rational decision-making model that does not match the way people reason and act in matters of sexuality any more than the reward-and-punishment model espoused by conservatives.

Both models fail to acknowledge the complexity of the human decision-making process. The liberal model, in particular, assumes that if we provide people with information on the consequences of various actions, they will act independently and with enlightened self-interest. It ignores the fact that decisions are made in the context of particular cultures, relationships, and conversations with others. In real life people often make decisions in response to particular *situations* that are more or less risky (Nathanson, 1991, p. 183).

Although the conservative and liberal models of how and why people make decisions are distinct—and hence their explanations for, and responses to, teen pregnancy and motherhood differ—both ideological perspectives frame the "problems" of teen pregnancy and motherhood in individual terms. They share the individualistic (or humanist) model of the person as autonomous, full of potential, operating within an open structure of opportunity, exercising freedom of choice (Davies, 1991, p. 43). From this set of assumptions, one takes away the notion that teen pregnancy and birth rates would decline if young people had better training in how to make "responsible" decisions. The individualistic good choices discourse leaves unexamined the material and cultural conditions that constrict the choices available; for example, the barriers to access to contraception and abortion services, mixed messages about sexuality, and the pervasiveness of poverty, child abuse, and unequal power relations based on age, race, class, and gender (cf. Males, 1994).

Not surprisingly, then, both conservatives and liberals accept as common sense that becoming a teen mother is a clear-cut bad choice. In interviews with middle-class professionals, I was repeatedly struck by their inability to see any benefits at all (personal or otherwise) to teen motherhood and their propensity to portray this choice in the bleakest possible terms. A public health nurse, for example, acknowledged that the teen mothers she knew would object to her portrait of their lives, but she dismissed this as mere defensiveness on their part. From "the outside," people such as herself see that "you [teen mothers] live in a cockroach-infested basement, you are on your own, you have no friends, you're living on welfare, you never have any money, and you have a baby that you're responsible for. How can you say it's not that bad?"

This bleak picture and the wider good choices discourse in which it is embedded gloss over alternative possibilities. As I will explicate below, material constraints and cultural contradictions shape each of the various choices that culminate in teen motherhood, and, therefore, becoming a teen mother may be a good choice or the best choice in circumstances not entirely of the individual's making. Even for those young women whose choices may have been coerced or made by default, motherhood may (and in my observations, often did) offer the possibilities of joy as well as responsibility, of satisfaction at displaying competence as well as hardship.

We are all caught up in the large social and economic transformations that currently shape our choices and lives, but we do well to remember that we are positioned differently based on age, gender, race, class, sexuality, and so on. Depending on our social and material circumstances, the choices we face may be severely constricted. A woman makes reproductive decisions within a specific network of *social relations* and social arrangements involving herself, her sexual partner(s), her children and kin, neighbors, doctors, family planners, birth control providers and manufacturers, employers, the church, and the state. (Petchesky, 1984, p. 9)

In what follows I analyze and place into social context the various choices that are involved in becoming an unmarried teen mother. I conclude that the discourse about choices, good and bad, ignores the unequal class, gender, and racial power relations that shape the lives of teen mothers; it works as a means of moral regulation that is ostensibly (but not really) neutral with regards to structured inequalities.

The Choice to Have Premarital Sex

Most adults, as noted in Chapter 2, do not approve of teenagers choosing to have premarital sex. Religious conservatives still preach that premarital sex between people of any age is immoral and, by extension, so is birth control, because it permits people to have sex without consequences. Some traditional Asian cultures constrain sexual activity among the young in order to preserve "the established social order," "family unity" (Chan, 1994, p. 92), and immigrant community and cultural loyalty (Dasgupta & Dasgupta, 1996). Others feel that teenagers are not emotionally mature enough to have sex; such concerns have intensified since the onset of the HIV/AIDS epidemic in the early 1980s.

Nevertheless, an emphasis on sexual pleasure can be discerned as part of the "dominant system of sexual meanings" in North America (Irvine, 1994, p. 20). Young women today are reaching puberty at age 12, down from age 15 in the nineteenth century (Harari & Vinovskis, 1993, p. 25), yet the average age that people marry has steadily increased. Can society reasonably expect young people to postpone having sex for so many years? The adults with whom I spoke, while they did not endorse premarital sex for teens, were pragmatic about the large number of young people making this choice—a choice shaped by culture and social class.

A national survey of 4,000 Canadian high school students revealed that 55% of the 15- to 19-year-olds were sexually active (a figure roughly comparable to U.S. data; see, e.g., Luker, 1996, p. 143). Rates ranged from 63% for Natives, 57% for both Whites and Blacks, to 42% for South Asians (students of Indian or Pakistani heritage), and 26% for East Asians (primarily students of Chinese and Japanese heritage) (Bibby & Posterski, 1992, p. 39). My interviews with students of Asian descent support the finding of lower rates of sexual activity among both male and female East Asian teenagers, as does clinical research in the United States. Chan explains "that Asians have stricter family expectations to refrain from being sexually active and less pressure from their peers to be sexually active" (1994, p. 92).

Premarital sex rates differ by social class, as well. Research done in North America suggests that young women from higher socioeconomic status backgrounds are less likely to become sexually active at an early age, are more likely to use contraception (particularly at first intercourse), and if they do get pregnant, they are more likely to obtain abortions (Alan Guttmacher Institute, 1994; Lu, 1997; Orton, 1999). Luker, however, citing "scattered data," speculates that these class differences may be diminishing (1996, pp. 91–92).

The Choice to Use Contraception

A surprisingly high percentage of teens report using contraception. For example, in a greater Vancouver region of British Columbia study, only 13% of sexually active teens reported that they did not use any contraception the last time they had sex (McCreary Centre Society, 1993, p. 42). Some of the methods they use, however, are relatively ineffective (withdrawal, for example), while others occasionally fail (such as condoms) or are used incorrectly (birth control pills) and inconsistently. Non-use of contraceptives is common among teenagers, particularly younger ones, when they first become sexually active (Zabin & Hayward, 1993, pp. 57–58). Some young women report getting pregnant "during transitions—either within a relationship, as they move from male methods to female methods, or between relationships, when they stop using a certain method" (Luker, 1996, p. 145).

One key factor in understanding why teenagers do not use effective contraceptives more often is the still-prevalent sexual double standard. As I explored in Chapter 2, people commonly assume that women are responsible for managing sexual activity, including the use of contraception, yet women have less power than men to regulate what actually occurs in a sexual relationship. The adult world sends youths profoundly mixed messages about sexual decision making. More than one teen mother, for example, told me that either or both of their parents had refused to allow them to go on the birth control pill because they felt it would encourage "promiscuity."

Research has shown the effectiveness of social policies that are consistent in sending young people the message, backed by material support, that if they do become sexually active, they should use contraception. A major study of adolescent pregnancy in Ontario between 1976 and 1986, for example, found that as the province implemented school sexuality education and, in tandem, provided clinic contraception services, the teen pregnancy, abortion, and birth rates went down (Orton & Rosenblatt, 1991, p. 2).

The Netherlands, which has the lowest teen pregnancy rate among Western industrialized nations, combines a major sexuality education program with a very liberal, non-moralistic contraception policy (Ketting & Visser, 1994). Sexuality education extends beyond the schools to the government-financed mass media campaigns; for example, "'Sex Is Natural, But Never Self-Evident,' addresses boys and men on the topic of coercive sex" (Drenth & Slob, 1997, p. 905). Although the rate of sexual activity is comparable to rates in Canada and the United States, the teen abortion rate in the Netherlands is over five times lower than in Canada and ten times lower than in the United States (Bibby & Posterski, 1992, p. 39; Ketting & Visser, 1994, pp. 167–168; Luker, 1996, pp. 143, 196; Wadhera & Millar, 1997, p. 12).

Throughout many parts of the United States and Canada, by contrast, community leaders are much more divided on sexuality-related policies for young people. The province of British Columbia, for instance, mandates 10 hours of "family life education" per year, but such topics as contraception and abortion, approved for discussion in grades 10–12, are optional. This means that many schools in British Columbia currently omit these topics (British Columbia Task Force, 1994, p. 11). At both Town and City Schools, condom machines were available in a couple of bathrooms, but many young women were unaware that they could obtain low-cost oral and other contraceptives confidentially at local health clinics. Even if they do know about these services, sometimes the charge of $10 per month for birth control pills is a barrier for young and low-income women. In addition, conservative religious groups picket contraceptive facilities in some areas (British Columbia Task Force, 1994, p. 17).

In sum, teenaged women do not make contraceptive choices in a social vacuum, and they become pregnant for many different reasons. Relatively few young women say they deliberately did not use contraception because they planned to get pregnant, although those caught off guard by the timing of a pregnancy may nevertheless want their child (Luker, 1996, pp. 151–154). Some young women are coerced into unprotected sex, others are ashamed to get birth control until it is too late, and still others are unwitting victims of contraception that did not work.

The Choice to Have an Abortion

Abortion is highly controversial in both Canada and the United States, where the anti-abortion, traditional "family values" movements are active and visible. "Pro-life" supporters, for example, leafleted students in and around Town High. A few years before my study, they had gained control of the board of directors of the regional hospital, the only abortion provider in the area, and brought abortions to a halt. Although the situation had since changed, some young women I interviewed were convinced that a person would need to travel several hours to a major city to obtain an abortion.

Other young people find their way to supposedly neutral pregnancy counselors only to find themselves confronted with graphic "pro-life" propaganda. Manfred, age 18, told me, "I wanted my girlfriend to get an abortion. We were one day away from an abortion, but a [names organization] counselor made her watch baby movies that showed her life inside of her. So we changed our minds."

Well-publicized attempts to require young women to obtain parental consent for an abortion, although unsuccessful in British Columbia, confused April, a 17-year-old mother at City School. When she got conflicting messages on the telephone from health professionals about parental consent, she panicked at the thought of having to tell her "very strict" mother about her pregnancy and delayed action until it was too late. (As it turned out, her mother said she would have approved the abortion.) Fetal protection advocates have been more successful in passing anti-abortion policies in the United States, which may account for the recent increase in the proportion of young American women giving birth (see Luker, 1996, pp. 155–156).

Public schools throughout North America are often characterized by large silences with regard to issues of sexuality (see Chapter 7). The prevalent curriculum, for example, does not tend to weight all reproductive choices equally; students may get to hear from teen parents but rarely if ever from young women who have had abortions. "They do not hear that young women in Baltimore who have had abortions are personally and academically far more successful than those who have had babies in their teen years" (Phillips & Fine, 1992, p. 247). They do not hear about the

Canadian study based on in-depth interviews with 70 unmarried White women between 18 and 25 (the largest group seeking abortions) 6 months to 1 year after they had abortions. "Soon after the abortion, most women [78.6%] felt relief and satisfaction," wrote the study's author, social work professor Paul Sachdev. "Long-term psychological reactions of guilt or depression were rare" (Parsons, 1993, p. A1).

In the face of the silence in the official curriculum and the controversy raging outside of the schools over abortion, what attitudes do young people hold about it? Bibby and Posterski's (1992) national survey of Canadian teens found that almost 90% felt that it should be possible for a woman to obtain a legal abortion when rape is involved; they felt similarly if the mother's health is in danger or there is a serious defect in the fetus. Just 41%, however, agreed that a woman should be able to obtain a legal abortion "for any reason," a proportion "almost identical" to that of Canadian adults polled in 1990 (pp. 43–44). Canadian adults have split evenly in polls asking whether they approved of women seeking an abortion because of inadequate income, being single, or simply not wanting to have a child (p. 44). Similarly, "about 40 percent of Americans think that a young woman should not be permitted to have an abortion even if pregnancy would cause her to drop out of school" (Luker, 1996, p. 92).

The students I interviewed at Town and City Schools, both parents and non-parents, expressed similar patterns of opinion; their views about abortion were highly situational. Only one of the Town School teen mothers, for example, mentioned a strict pro-life position; the rest could be categorized as pro-choice, although five of these ten said they did not personally believe in abortion and only favored it for others in certain situations (e.g., rape, health of the mother or fetus). Four of the teen mothers said they would have considered an abortion if they had not been in a serious love relationship with the father-to-be, and one said she waited too long to have an abortion because she was under the mistaken idea that she would have to travel a long distance from home to obtain one.

One out of every two teen pregnancies resulted in a live birth in Canada in 1994 (Wadhera & Millar, 1997, p. 12). In the United States in 1990, 60% of pregnant teens gave birth (Alan Guttmacher Institute, 1994, p. 44). The higher proportion of pregnant teens giving birth in the United States can be explained partly by the greater number of barriers to abortion services, including the financial cost and the proliferation of states requiring parental consent or notification.

Cultural beliefs appear to influence the decision to have an abortion. School counselors at City and Town Schools reported that relatively few young Asian women became pregnant—and those who did become pregnant opted for abortions—because if their pregnancy became known, they faced expulsion from the family home. Indeed, the two teen mothers of Asian origin whom I knew had been disowned. In contrast, young First Nations mothers often said they did not believe in abortion, and this belief is apparently widely shared in their communities. For example, a task force looking into access to contraception and abortion services in British Columbia concluded, after a province-wide consultation process, "that in First Nations Society, conception is a celebration of life, and abortion is not widely approved, although it is understood that it is a woman's own decision" (British Columbia Task Force, 1994, p. 13).

The Choice to Marry

Young women are much less likely today than they were two decades ago to get married once they become pregnant. In Canada in 1975, 37% of all births to teenagers occurred to single women; this figure rose to 71% in 1985 and 81% in 1995 (Statistics Canada, 1997, p. 34). Still, it is important to remember that about one out of every five babies born to a teen was born to a married mother in Canada; the figure is about one in three in the United States (Luker, 1996, pp. 142–143).

This trend toward single motherhood holds regardless of the age of the mother. In Canada, almost as many children are born to single women 30 years and over as are born to teens; 60% are born to single women in their twenties, while 20% are born to teens (Vanier Institute of the Family, 1994, p. 58). Only 30% of all non-marital births in the United States occur to teenagers (Moore, 1995, p. viii).

There is no clear or simple explanation for the rise in out-of-wedlock childbearing. Some of the most frequently mentioned factors include the growing acceptability of premarital sex and common-law relationships, continuing barriers to effective contraceptive methods for youth, the increasing value of higher education, the rise in women's labor force participation, high unemployment rates among young men of color, changes in the structure of the youth labor market, and the fragility of teen marriages. Increasingly, the general public realizes that "shotgun weddings" are not the answer: Pregnant young women who marry are more likely to leave school without graduating, quickly have another baby, and eventually divorce; these circumstances make it difficult for them to obtain further education or a paying job with potential for advancement (see Harris, 1997).

All of these changes have been accompanied by an increasingly toler-
ant attitude toward non-marital childbearing in general (Moore, 1995).
The women's movement provided alternative accounts and concepts that
helped to shift the meaning of "illegitimacy"; feminists, for example, drew
attention to the sexism of the term "unwed mother," which defined women
by whether they had a man to look after them and their children.

Tolerance, however, does not necessarily mean approval. Many people
still believe that, ideally, children should grow up with two loving, heterosexual parents. Their concern about the side effects on children of being
raised by unhappily married couples may lead them to see single parenthood as simply the lesser of two evils. Single teen mothers are likely to
rely on government assistance to support their children, which is widely
frowned upon. Even some feminists are at pains to declare themselves
against teen parenthood, because they fear it tars the entire category of
single mothers: Syndicated newspaper columnist Ellen Goodman (1993),
for example, wrote: "I share the national dismay at cultural messages
glamorizing unwed motherhood. I share a deep frustration watching teenage girls turn from Barbies to babies" (p. A3).

Opting for Adoption versus Keeping the Baby

Today an estimated 95% of unmarried teen mothers in both Canada and
the United States decide to raise their babies rather than place them for
adoption (Daly & Sobol, 1994, p. 4; Rhode & Lawson, 1993, p. 2).
Realizing that they cannot buck this trend, even religious conservatives,
such as Jerry Falwell, and pro-life advocates have stopped focusing on
adoption for fear that they might push young women toward abortion
instead. This point came home to me during an interview with a Town
School teacher, Ms. Martone, who told me she was "really angry" at the
Roman Catholic Church "for making girls feel ashamed" for getting pregnant, because it led women to have "abortions when they didn't really
want to." But, she reported, the Church had changed its emphasis for the
better: "Now they are . . . saying that having a child out of wedlock is not
a shameful thing." She was not so happy with the "pro-life" group to
which she had belonged: "If you're going to counsel a 13-year-old girl out
of having an abortion, then you've got to be able to counsel her about
how to be a good mom and to find resources to help her be a good
parent. Pro-life wasn't doing that at the time, and so I withdrew my
support."

Many people do not realize that throughout most of U.S. and Canadian history, both Black and White single women who found themselves

pregnant kept their babies (Solinger, 1992; Ward, 1981). After World War II, adoption became more widespread. From the mid-1940s until the 1970s, single White mothers were expected, even coerced, into placing their infants for adoption. Psychological theories of the day suggested that the White "unwed mother" could be redeemed through a three-step treatment: "remorse; relinquishment of the infant for adoption; and renewed commitment to fulfilling her destiny as a real woman [through marriage]" (Solinger, 1992, p. 94).

Although the evidence is scanty, the adoption campaign seems to have been aimed mainly at middle-class Whites, broadly defined. "Lower-class whites," like most Black single mothers, were "more likely to be advised to keep the child than to have it adopted and [were] more likely actually to keep an illegitimate child than to have it adopted" (Rains, 1971, p. 165). A few of the teen mothers I got to know told me about older, working-class relatives of theirs who became pregnant as unmarried teens in the 1960s; their children were kept in the family but raised as if they were their siblings rather than their own children.

Black single mothers were often excluded from maternity homes, and there was no demand among White families to adopt Black babies (Solinger, 1992; cf. Cahill, 1992, p. 58; Petrie, 1998, pp. 151–152). In addition, it seems that many in the Black community looked upon formal adoption outside of the extended family as immoral. Like the title character in Alice Walker's *Meridian,* an African American mother who relinquishes her child even to this day may experience incredible psychological pain "[k]nowing that she had parted with her baby when her enslaved maternal ancestors had done anything and everything to keep their children" (Collins, 1990, p. 135).

Traditionally, "no child is ever considered illegitimate" among First Nations peoples. "If a girl gets pregnant, the baby is still part of the family, and the mother is too" (Allen, 1986, pp. 49–50); young First Nations women can expect their extended families and communities to accept their children and help with child care (Keetley, 1981). Yet the ideological expectations held by members of the dominant Anglo, middle-class culture that a mother must be "self-reliant," has led the courts to devalue "the participation of extended family members in the care of children in First Nations communities" (Kline, 1993, p. 331). Many First Nations children in Canada, in what has become known as the "sixties scoop," were taken from their communities and adopted into non-Aboriginal (mainly White) homes during the 1960s and 1970s (Fournier & Crey, 1997). This experience, which some Native leaders have described as "cultural genocide" (Boyko, 1995), has understandably left many First

Nations peoples suspicious of adoption. A formal moratorium against the adoption of Natives by non-Natives has been in place in British Columbia since 1992 (Ouston, 1997).

As abortion became more available in the early 1970s, more and more middle-class teens terminated their pregnancies rather than opt for adoption. Women who felt they had been coerced into placing their children for adoption began to speak out about the emotional trauma they had endured (e.g., Strom, 1993). Today, it appears, "those young women who do give their children up for adoption resemble young women who have abortions more than they resemble young women who choose to rear their children. They are more affluent, have higher aspirations for themselves, and are performing better in school" (Luker, 1996, p. 162).

Those who decide to keep their babies must still face the criticism that they have made a "selfish" choice. In the dominant discourse, informed largely by White, middle-class mores, the "good" mother decides to give her baby up to a dominant-culture, middle-class nuclear family. Indeed, such feelings have shaped many teen parent programs. At City School, for example, young parent program planners in the early 1980s faced resistance from adoptive parent groups concerned that there were not enough babies to adopt. Community-based advocates of the proposed program charged publicly that approval of its day care license had initially been denied because government officials worried it "would encourage the teenagers to keep their infants." Ultimately, the day care got approved, but advocates gave up their original plan to enroll pregnant girls. In this way, City School did not have to contend with critics arguing that the program provided an incentive for pregnant girls to keep their babies; it could point out that it was serving only those who had already made their choice.

The Choice to Have a Second Baby

If people can "forgive" a teen mother for keeping her first baby, they are not nearly so understanding about a second. Experts have referred to this using terminology—"recidivism" (Schlesinger, 1979), "excess fertility" (Miller & Moore, 1990), "repeat pregnancy"—that makes a second pregnancy sound like a criminal act. If the views of teachers can stand in for the dominant-culture, middle-class perspective, then the choice to have a second baby can be read as "making the same mistake twice," being "irresponsible," "deliberate," "immoral," and even "repulsive." A subsequent pregnancy seems to confirm in many people's minds nearly all of the negative stereotypes about teen mothers. One teacher, for example, saw it as "alley-cat morality," while another interpreted a second pregnancy as "taking advantage of the system" for a "free ride."

It is this choice that most challenges the professionals who work in young parent programs or with teen mothers. A school administrator in Midland told a teacher ("in jest") who had two students pregnant a second time, "I'm going to fire you, because obviously you're not doing your job." City School had devised a maternity leave policy for program participants having a second baby that came under criticism by one of its Advisory Committee members for appearing to support a bad choice. Similar concerns arose at another young parents' program in British Columbia, and, with the aim of discouraging "multiple pregnancies," it began prohibiting students from enrolling more than one child at the school-based day care.

Other professionals echoed what a few of the teen mothers told me. "Some of them have made choices to marry young," explained a counselor. "Some people feel that it's healthier and happier to have children young." They may want their children to be close together in age or to limit the time of intensive mothering. Another counselor confided that she used to feel like a "failure" when one of the teen mothers she was working with got pregnant again. But she had come to see that the "illusion of control" that had "permeated everything" she did was, in a sense, "very disrespectful" of the choices of others. In addition, most young parents' program staff members with whom I spoke felt that a high proportion of teen mothers have been abused, often sexually, and that this is associated with "promiscuity" and "repeat" pregnancies. From the perspective of many outside of this field, however, the teenager who decides to have a second child is the epitome of the person "who makes bad choices."

Subtexts of the Good Choices Discourse

The good choices discourse is particularly insidious because it works to obscure unequal power relations based on age, gender, class, and race. Sociologists have speculated that as it has become less socially acceptable for social groups to create or reproduce boundaries based on "ascribed characteristics" such as gender or race, they may do "boundary work" based explicitly on moral, cultural, or socioeconomic status in order to implicitly or "euphemistically draw gender, race, or ethnic boundaries" (Lamont & Fournier, 1992, p. 14). Similarly, the good choices discourse focuses explicitly on the decisions or non-decisions one makes; that the individual being condemned for having made bad choices is often female and poor, a member of a racialized "caste," or both, and that the standard of assessment reflects a White, middle-class ideal remains largely implicit and unspoken.

I was particularly struck by this silence in the good choices discourse in an interview I had with Ms. Hoyle, a teacher at Town School. Based on the fact that Native women were overrepresented among the teen mothers at Town School, Ms. Hoyle asserted: "I think, unfortunately, Natives are seen as not being able to make good choices." I tried gently to suggest that this might be a "stereotype," explaining, too, that many Native people do not believe in abortion. As we wound up our conversation, I asked Ms. Hoyle if there was anything she wanted to ask me:

Ms. H: In terms of the number of teenagers that have abortions, how many of their parents are towards the middle class and up?

Deirdre: Very high. I think it's disproportionately middle-class people who have the expectation and the resources to send their children to university, and they're very motivated not to have something like a baby interfere with that.

Ms. H: *Or they're capable of making better decisions instead of dealing with emotions* [italics added].

Deirdre: Well, yeah, I guess that's one way of putting it. I tend to look at it more as a sociologist, more structurally, like what do they have to lose. And I've talked to middle-class parents—some in this district—who've made a point of telling their daughters, "We don't want you to be pregnant, we want you to protect yourself, but if you do get pregnant, you should consider abortion. . . ."

Ms. H: And I think those comments relate right back to the number of Native girls that are pregnant or have babies or who refuse to have abortions. They don't have the role model to help them make the decision that there are things in life more important than bringing a baby in at this time.

One does not choose to be born female or Native; more and more, these are illegitimate grounds for discrediting a person. One's socioeconomic status occupies murkier territory. To the extent that people believe that society is roughly meritocratic and characterized by equality of opportunity, for instance, one can be blamed simply for being poor and receiving state aid. As I will show in the next chapter, contrary to conventional wisdom, teen motherhood in and of itself does not cause poverty. Yet for those who assume it does, it makes sense from a middle-class, taxpayer's perspective to stigmatize the "bad" choices that seem to result in more welfare-dependent, single mothers. A teacher at Town School put it this way:

> I often say to people, if poor people have a tough time all their life or whatever, then don't be poor. And they say, "No, no one's poor on purpose." Well, that's not true. You know what I mean? So if it shows that these single moms are just going to go on welfare and then, what's worse, have children who are going to [repeat the cycle of teen pregnancy and welfare dependency], . . . then *don't do it* [get pregnant and become a mother].

As the good choices discourse slips between the decontextualized choices and the people who make them, it is not uncommon for those with institutional power to see certain groups as being prone to bad decision making and therefore not worthy of social investment. A state official in Wisconsin, for example, justified cutting benefits to welfare recipients pursuing post-secondary degrees by characterizing them as people who "tend to make a lot of poor choices" (quoted in Schmidt, 1996, p. A29). The Personal Responsibility and Work Opportunities Act passed by the U.S. Congress in 1996 enshrined this attitude and "prompted most states to adopt policies that discourage welfare recipients from attending college for anything but short-term job training" (Schmidt, 1998, p. A34).

In the realms of popular culture and the academy, experts use the good choices discourse to advance suggestions that hark back to the eugenics movement and coercive sterilization and contraception policies. Jasmine, a teen mother of color at City School, reported seeing part of a television show discussing Norplant—an implanted, long-acting contraceptive that was being promoted at an inner-city school for pregnant girls and young mothers—while a repair person was fixing her TV set.

> And he goes, "Oh, I agree with that totally. They need that because those teen mothers, I don't know what they're thinking." He's going on about this *in my home*, telling me all this, and . . . I'm getting really pissed off, because I don't feel like anyone has the right to say anything about anyone that way: "That's the way *they* live." I thought to myself, "It's not your life; it's theirs."

A professor of psychology at the University of Minnesota proposed in the pages of the widely read *Chronicle of Higher Education* that "society think about limiting the reproductive 'rights' of our citizens." Specifically, the government could require people who want to become parents to get a license. They would have to show that they did not fall into the following categories: unmarried, under 21, unable to support themselves or "have serious criminal records or incapacitating mental illness" (Lykken, 1996, pp. B1-B2. A similar plan has been proposed by Canadian academics; see Laucius, 1999). Professor Lykken left unstated what to do about violators, but it does not take a big leap to imagine the Newt Gingrich option (place the "unlicensed" children into an orphanage), coercive contraception (Norplant cannot be removed without help from a health care worker),[1] or even forced sterilization.

The individualistic good choices discourse, then, serves paradoxically to lead those with relatively more power in society to think about limiting or controlling the choices of those with the least power while appearing on the surface to be neutral with regard to gender, race, and class.[2] A coalition that spans the conventional conservative-liberal divide now appears to agree that teen mothers (and low-income single parents generally) epitomize people who make bad choices, especially if they rely on government aid. This consensus, in turn, rests on the assumptions that teen mothers represent a significant drain on government coffers and that teen mothers cause poverty.

In the next chapter, I critique these assumptions, first by examining the relevant scholarly literature through a feminist lens, then by analyzing the competing discourses about teen mothers, welfare, and poverty circulating in the mass media and academic work. I aim to debunk the idea that if only more young women made "good choices," then the social problems thought to be caused or made worse by current teen pregnancy and birth rates would disappear.

Notes

1. A past president of the American Educational Research Association, in submitting a "vision" statement to the widely circulated *Educational Researcher*, elected to write on the "problem of teenage pregnancy":

   I propose that teenage girls be encouraged to use long-term, maintenance-free contraceptive methods such as Norplant, IUDs, or Depo-Provera and that they be *paid* regularly to continue doing so up to age 20 or so. Instead of paying a girl if she has children, as we currently do, I suggest that a reverse-payment procedure be tried. (Stanley, with Parrish, 1998, p. 34)

2. An example of the paradox can be seen in an interview with a vocational education teacher at City School. He very much supported the Teen-Age Parents Program "because [teen mothers] are the type of young lady that, in addition to needing help most of the time, I think take the wrong direction if there's a choice, because . . . they come from problem situations in their homes." When asked to clarify, he replied:

   Not that they're not capable—a lot of them *think* they're not capable. . . . And a lot of them will say they're going to do things and don't follow through. And that is what . . . bothers me, because if I had the chance to follow them out the door of this school when they graduate and take them down to the Technical Institute and register them and say, "You are going to do this," then I think that maybe they would have more success sooner in their lives than they do.

   Thus, an emphasis on making individual choices can go hand in hand with a paternalistic desire to impose control when the choice makers in question are perceived to "take the wrong direction" when given the opportunity.

Chapter 4

Stigma Stories in the Media: Four Discourses about Teen Mothers, Welfare, and Poverty

That [newspaper] lady totally twisted what we said because she wanted it to sound worse. I wrote her a letter and said, "If you weren't going to write what we said, why did you waste your time and our time? You might as well just have sat home, made up the story yourself—not even bother us if you weren't going to use the facts."

—Molly, mother, age 17, La Fuente[1]

Feminist and other critical researchers have produced studies that have challenged conventional wisdom about teen mothers causing, and being produced by, poverty. But critical feminist research has been taken up infrequently by the mainstream media—and rarely as authoritative. Although ideas about teen sexuality and "alternative" family structures may have become less rigid over the last 25 years, the mainstream media's representations of teen mothers remain for the most part stigmatized, albeit within updated constructs.

Although the social stigma about teen pregnancy is popularly perceived to have lessened in recent times, I have shown in Chapters 2 and 3 that it is still quite prevalent, although its manifestations are evolving. Over the last 25 years, the forms taken by the stigma have been far more openly contested by various social and political groups. This contest is waged among those who continue to believe that adolescent pregnancy should be stigmatized as a deterrent to early sexual activity and welfare dependence and those with rival interpretations of the meaning of teen pregnancy and motherhood. This contest is making headlines in the United States at a moment when teen pregnancy and birth rates are leveling out at non-epidemic proportions after a slight increase in the late 1980s, although the percentage of teen births that are out of wedlock has increased steadily since 1960. The same debates rage today in Canada, where, with the exception of the past few years, teen pregnancy and birth rates have declined in almost every province over the last 20 years.[2] This contest can be seen as a clashing of discourses, an ongoing struggle over public definitions of deviance.

In the waging of this "stigma contest" (Schur, 1980), the mass media constitute a key arena. Within this arena, print media—newspapers and magazines—are key cultural texts. The print media frequently provide broadcast journalists with story ideas, and politicians and other members of the elite favor the quality newspaper as a source of news (Ericson, Baranek, & Chan, 1991, pp. 31–32, 45). It is within the print media, then—and at a moment when teen mothers are increasingly portrayed as the nexus of most major social ills—that I have focused my analysis of the discourses about teen mothers.

In this chapter I will present: (a) a framework for analyzing the discourses around teen pregnancy and motherhood and (b) reflections based on an analysis of print media coverage of teen mothers in Canada since 1980. As I compare and contrast discourses, I attempt to reveal the ideological agendas inscribed in particular representations of teen mothers.

Media and Discourse Theory

I focused on newspaper and magazine articles that addressed the topic of teen mothers, located through a search of the Canadian News Index for the years 1980–1992, the Alternative Press Index,[3] and a personal clipping file collected from the mainstream, alternative, and right-wing press (both in the United States and in Canada) over the last 8 years. As I analyzed the over 700 articles, I found a pragmatic model of discourse theory to be useful. Drawing on Foucault, among others, Fraser (1992, p. 185) describes the pragmatic model thus:

> Discourses are historically specific, socially situated, signifying practices. They are the communicative frames in which speakers interact by exchanging speech acts. Yet discourses are themselves set within social institutions and action contexts. Thus, the concept of a discourse links the study of language to the study of society.

More specifically, Griffith and Smith (1991, p. 90) define discourse as an organization of relations among people participating in a conversation mediated by written and printed materials. A discourse has a social organization of authorities, sites, production processes, etc. . . . The term does not just refer to the "texts" of this conversation and their production alone, but also to the ways in which people organize their activities in relationship to them.

These definitions direct attention not just to statements and texts but also to the variety of discursive practices, their interconnections, and the many ways people make sense of texts in everyday life. Experts in universities and policy think tanks conduct research that provides categories and language that news reporters and magazine editors appropriate and popularize in their stories; these stories, in turn, encourage readers (not always successfully) to think about teen mothers, for instance, in certain ways and not in others.

A number of discourses coexist and compete with each other; there is no "single, monolithic 'symbolic order'" (Fraser, 1989, p. 10). But the discourses do not compete as equals; some carry little weight and are marginalized, while others are considered to be authoritative and dominant. In Canada, as in other late capitalist societies, social groups have unequal access to power, status, and resources, including the discursive arena of the mass circulation media (Fraser, 1989, p. 165).

Within each discourse, media writers, social activists, professionals, and researchers use various frames to help their audiences make sense of phenomena or events. Sociologist Amy Binder (1993) explains: "Frames and frameworks are 'schemata of interpretation that enable individuals to locate, perceive, identify, and label' events they have experienced directly or indirectly" (p. 754). These frames, composed of arguments and images, are selected and constructed from larger sets of cultural beliefs; they serve "an ideological function when the frames reinforce unequal social relations by those institutionally empowered to do so" (p. 755).

Ideologies are partial accounts of the world constructed from within particular historical contexts, and they operate to serve particular economic, political, and social interests. An anti-racist, feminist ideology, for example, would point to the gender and racial subtexts of the dominant discourse about teen mothers (subtexts are what remains unsaid that is often central to a text's meaning). Although dominant ideologies downplay conflicts of interest and perspectives that challenge prevailing power relations, I am not suggesting that a position exists outside of ideology that is "innocent." This does not mean, however, that all truth claims are relative. As Hawkesworth (1989) states:

standards related to the range of human cognitive practices allow us to distinguish between partial views (the inescapable condition of human cognition) and false beliefs, superstitions, irrebuttable presumptions, willful distortions. . . . informed judgments can be made. (p. 555)

A Critical Feminist Interpretation of the Scholarly Research on Teen Mothers, Welfare, and Poverty

My admittedly partial view is that teen mothers provide a convenient scapegoat for those who would ignore the structural causes of poverty. I thus participate in what I describe below as an oppositional discourse about teen mothers. Before turning to an analysis of the discourses constructed and disseminated by the print media, I will summarize here a growing body of research that calls into question a number of widely held assumptions about teen mothers, welfare, and poverty.

First, poverty is not a straightforward cause of early motherhood; there appear to be many other precipitating factors. Research done mainly in the United States suggests that "[l]iving in poverty is associated with both early sexual activity and early pregnancy" (Miller & Moore, 1990, p. 1030). This, however, begs the question of causation. Phoenix (1991a) reviewed the research in North America and England and concluded:

> While many young people experience poverty and do not have "proper jobs," most young women who lack money do not become mothers. Poverty is thus the context within which the overwhelming majority of instances of motherhood under 20 occur, rather than a causative factor. (p. 90)

Second, adolescent pregnancy and childbearing do not necessarily cause poverty. To examine the long-term economic outcomes associated with female adolescent marriage and childbearing, Grindstaff (1988) looked at women who were 30 in the 1981 Canadian census. As expected, he found that women who became mothers at a young age obtained less formal schooling, but in terms of income, the early-childbearing women did not have substantially less than the women who became mothers at a later age. The timing of marriage and childbearing was "secondary to the overriding issue of whether the woman has a child" (p. 54). In other words, today's economy does not easily accommodate women of any age who combine childrearing and paid work. The data also showed that at least some teen mothers eventually do quite well economically.

Third, studies do not show that welfare payments entice women to become pregnant. Most of the research in this area has been done in the

United States. Wilson and Neckerman (1987, cited in Phoenix, 1991a, p. 87) reviewed U.S. studies that explored the connection between welfare policies, levels of welfare benefits, and the incidence of teen motherhood and single motherhood; they found no relationship between welfare provision and low-income women's childbearing.

In Canada, a few provincial governments have investigated the claim that availability of welfare benefits encourages teen pregnancy and found it to be without merit (on Alberta, see "Study," 1989; on Nova Scotia, see Clark, Dechman, French, & MacCallum, 1991). In fact, an international study found that countries with some of the highest welfare benefits, such as Sweden, have the lowest teen pregnancy rates (Jones et al., 1986).

Fourth, researchers have not established that teen motherhood is a prime cause of welfare dependency. To show such causation, one would need to design longitudinal studies, which are costly to do and thus rarely done. More often, researchers conduct statistical analyses of large extant data bases; these studies have found strong correlations between teen motherhood, school dropout, reduced earnings, and welfare status. Yet new research suggests that these earlier cross-sectional studies may have overstated the negative socioeconomic consequences of teen childbearing (Geronimus & Korenman, 1992).

A common problem with non-longitudinal studies is that the researchers, the various consumers of the research (such as policymakers, advocacy groups, news reporters), or both go beyond the research findings to make unwarranted generalizations and predictions. On the basis of a non-random, snowball survey[4] of 79 teen mothers in Vancouver, British Columbia, for example, a researcher reported that only 20% had finished Grade 12 and that 46% had completed Grade 9 or less, while 77% were on social assistance (Fallon, 1979, Appendix A, pp. 22, 25). Citing only this study, a practitioner who worked with teen mothers concluded: "Eighty per cent of adolescent mothers never complete their education, become welfare dependent, and endure lives of desperate poverty and futility" (Billung-Meyer, 1982, p. 28). Thus, the fate of all teen mothers was discerned from a sample confined, by its design, to a disproportionately poor segment of teen mothers, who had been interviewed only once, at a point in their lives that was too early to show how they would fare.

The few longitudinal studies that exist tend to paint a much less bleak portrait of teen mothers and their children. Pozsonyi (1973) did a longitudinal study of unmarried, first-time mothers who kept their children and who were clients of a Family and Children's Services agency, checking back with the mothers at six-month intervals for the first eighteen months after the baby's birth. At the last face-to-face interview, only 30% were receiving welfare and 26% had married. Pozsonyi concluded: "The majority of unmarried mothers and their children were found to fare well in the community" (p. 59; see also S. Clark, 1999).

Studies in the United States have followed women who became teen mothers over decades; they have refuted the stereotype of teen mothers as chronic welfare recipients (Furstenberg, Brooks-Gunn, & Morgan, 1987; Harris, 1997). Over time, many of the women in these studies obtained paid work, achieved more education, and increased their levels of employment. The lack of affordable child care services, however, often hindered them (Harris, 1997).

Finally, reducing the number of teen mothers would not mean a big cut in welfare spending. According to a recent Statistics Canada report, single-parent families (male-led and female-led) made up only 13% of all families in 1991, and only 6.4% of families led by female single parents were led by young women (aged 15 to 24) (Mitchell, 1993). Further, if the ranks of teen mothers were to somehow thin significantly, that alone would not result in commensurate savings to taxpayers. Luker (1991) summarizes the findings of U.S. policy analysts Richard Wertheimer and Kristin Moore, who "have estimated that if by some miracle we could cut the teen birth rate in half, welfare costs would be reduced by 20 percent, rather than 50 percent, because many of these young women would still need welfare for children born to them when they were no longer teens" (p. 80).

This conclusion is underscored by a group of U.S. studies that have used innovative ways to assess whether young women who are already disadvantaged by having grown up in poverty and so forth (i.e., those most likely to become teen mothers) are further disadvantaged by teen motherhood in and of itself. Geronimus and Korenman (1992) compared a national sample of sisters and found no correlation between teen childbearing and high school graduation or subsequent family income. They cite a study by Corcoran and Kunz that

> found teen mothers to be no more likely to be welfare recipients after age 25 than their sisters who became mothers at older ages. So too, Joseph Hotz et al. comparing teens who gave birth to those who miscarried in recent data from the National Longitudinal Survey of Youth concluded that a teen mother is no more likely to participate in welfare programs, to have her labor market earnings reduced, or to experience significant losses in spousal earnings, than the same woman would have experienced if she had delayed childbearing. (Geronimus, 1997, p. 5; see Hoffman, 1998 for a more critical and cautionary review of this new literature)

To be sure, some women spend extended periods of time receiving government assistance. They tend to be those who have troubled childhoods, leave school before getting pregnant, and face multiple and severe barriers to paid employment—beyond those that result from teen motherhood. As sociologist Frank Furstenberg has written in the U.S. context, "State government can remove them from the welfare rolls but it will not help them make the transition into the labor force without intensive and extensive assistance that certainly costs more than the modest funding provided by AFDC [Aid to Families with Dependent Children], as we presently know it" (1997, pp. x-xi). Further, women who grow up in poverty, as many teen mothers have, face long odds against doing well later in life whether or not they become pregnant early in life.

Stigma Contest: Discourses about Teen Mothers

Given the research cited above, why aren't the same conclusions commonly drawn by liberal technocrats and social service providers, two groups cited often in most mainstream media accounts and a sector that usually places such faith in social science? The irony, as I explain below, is that this group of bureaucratic experts, one that contests the more traditional stigmatizers, has incentives to tell its own stigma stories about teen mothers.

People are not always so explicit about what should be stigmatized or denounced and what should be defended or advocated. Instead, they talk about "needs." Nancy Fraser (1989) has argued that when the late capitalist welfare state undertakes to satisfy social needs, the definition of the needs in question is often taken for granted. But let us consider the "needs" of a teen mother. Does she need earlier abortion and adoption counseling? Or does she need more incentives to keep her child? Does she need publicly funded day care and training? Or does she need it to be easier to stay home with her infant? Does she need more self-esteem that comes with independence or the support that comes with marriage or family ties? Perhaps her needs are not so self-evident after all—and which needs a person identifies as paramount locates that person politically within the stigma contest surrounding teen mothers.

Fraser calls for a recasting of the dominant policy framework to highlight the "politics of need interpretation." In her discussion of women and welfare policy, she identifies three major, competing "discourses about needs" that are associated with bureaucratic experts, conservatives, and oppositional social movements.[5] How, then, has the stigma contest over teen mothers been waged by each group in North America?

Bureaucratic Experts: The Wrong-Girl Frame

In the late 1960s, popular and academic journals began to frame teen pregnancy as less a moral problem and more a technical one related to the creation of intergenerational welfare dependency and poverty (Arney & Bergin, 1984). Rather than attend to the conditions of poverty and frame the social psychology as rooted in the problems of the powerless, however, "experts" have tended to focus attention on the psychological motivations of girls who become pregnant and decide to keep their babies. Once the "problem" is located within the individual, the technical solution often amounts to therapy and monitoring.

In the same vein as the "girl nobody loved" construct that I introduced in Chapter 2, the two most prominent psychological explanations of teen motherhood both infantilize these mothers and cast suspicion on their families. The first argues that these young women, many of whom are said to come from "broken" homes themselves, have babies out of an unfulfilled need for somebody to love them: "An adolescent's decision to raise a child, for example, is often determined by such egocentric desires as the wish to . . . receive unconditional love from a dependent object, in this case, the baby" (D. Gordon, 1990, p. 349). This expert discourse then gets translated for a popular audience as it was in the *Vancouver Sun:* "The teen mother is usually a child who looked for love or acceptance, and instead found herself thrown into adulthood before her mind and body were ready" (Krangle, 1980, p. A1).

The second psychological explanation holds that the young women have been abused (sexually or otherwise) and that motherhood may help them escape a bad family situation. Boyer and Fine (1992) investigated the links between prior sexual abuse and adolescent pregnancy. They hypothesize that the "developmental process" of children who are sexually abused may become arrested. Further, "a link between sexual victimization and adolescent pregnancy may also illuminate . . . child maltreatment by adolescent parents" (p. 5). Or as the Canadian Press (1990) put it: "Experts in child care worry about the ability of many teenage parents to put the needs of their children ahead of their own. . . . The children are seen as especially vulnerable to abuse, neglect and slow development, what child-care workers call 'failure to thrive'" (p. 12). (I challenged this view in Chapter 2.)

These two psychological explanations are not, of course, mutually exclusive. In both versions, the teenager's having her baby tends to be seen as a "personal tragedy," in part because "adolescent pregnancy breeds poverty" (e.g., Schlesinger, 1982, pp. 45–46); she has made a mistake—not so much a moral mistake in this discourse, as an error in timing—and she needs help to set it right. The difficulty, according to these experts, is that she may not realize she has made a mistake in "forsaking her childhood and jumping the adolescent bridge into adulthood too soon." Indeed, "she may be unable—simply unable—to see that she has made a mistake and that she could be helped to put it right" (Hudson & Ineichen, 1991, p. 55).

Defining teen mothers in this way, as girls from flawed backgrounds who are making tragic mistakes, leads quite naturally to the analysis that the wrong girls are having and keeping babies. This indeed is the view of many university-based researchers and people who staff the various programs that deal with teen mothers. As is common practice, these bureaucratic experts are the first people the mass media contact to explain the meaning of teen motherhood. The Canadian Press (1980a), for example, quoted Benjamin Schlesinger, a professor of social work at the University of Toronto, as saying, "It appears the wrong girl is keeping the baby. . . . It's babies having babies" (p. A17). Age is not the primary factor that makes these mothers wrong; the average age of the girls in Schlesinger's study was, after all, 19 years. What makes these the wrong girls is their family background, according to Schlesinger: "Teenage unwed mothers from broken homes are keeping their children while those from more stable backgrounds give theirs up for adoption" (p. A17).

In searching for solutions to the wrong-girl problem, bureaucratic experts, encouraged by theories produced within the academy, have identified adolescent emotional maladjustment as a root cause of early pregnancy and childbearing. Teen mothers must therefore receive constant help and therapy as well as monitoring. In advocating for an alternative school program for Victoria teen mothers, the school board chair argued:

> One reason we'd like a program where they could bring their babies and bring themselves when they're pregnant is so we can monitor them and help them with parenting skills. The statistics for child abuse show it is much more prevalent in teenage mothers because of all the frustrations they have and their inability to cope. (Canadian Press, 1980b, p. A19)

What distinguishes the bureaucratic experts from their conservative critics? Unlike conservatives, the experts frequently use theories and language that suggest teen mothers and their children are in need of protection—from themselves, from their families, from their male partners. Bureaucratic experts are, in general, strong proponents of sex education and birth control counseling as a means of preventing teen pregnancy. They rarely, however, view teen pregnancy and motherhood as positive. Yet because their premise is that many teen mothers are victims of abuse, they assert that society must address "the reality" and provide services to teen mothers (e.g., Rincover, 1991). Further, because their views are strongly contested by economic and social conservatives (discussed later in this chapter), experts—and the reporters who quote them—must frequently justify government intervention and spending by underscoring that its purpose is to "break the cycles of child abuse and welfare dependency." In short, this form of argument, although it destigmatizes extramarital, teenage sexual activity, it still stigmatizes a teenager's pregnancy and decision to keep her baby, albeit in an indirect way.

Reprivatization Groups: The Wrong-Family Frame

Economic, social, and religious conservatives, in contrast, are usually much more direct about what they think should be stigmatized or restigmatized. In a *Vancouver Sun* column, Les Bewley (1984), for example, pined for the days when

> any young, unmarried girl [who] allowed herself to become pregnant . . . was properly and publicly regarded as a fool, a tramp, or a slut . . . and she was ostracized by the community. If a young man knocked a girl up, he was expected to marry her and support her, even if it had to be at gunpoint, rather than leave her with a bastard child. (p. A11)

This approach, according to Bewley, accomplished three things: "girls had a powerful set of reasons for saying the simple word 'no,' young men had some powerful deterrents against knocking girls up, and the community was spared the very real threat of bankruptcy from social welfare programs."

Conservatives such as Bewley aim to exclude teen mothers from public places such as schools and return the responsibility for sex education to parents; they engage in what Fraser (1989) has termed "reprivatization discourse," that is, they seek "to repatriate newly problematized needs to their former domestic or official economic enclaves" (p. 157). Mass media stories about teen mothers do not usually build upon a conservative set of assumptions unless they appear in such right-wing publications as *Alberta Report* and *British Columbia Report* or on the editorial pages of mainstream newspapers. Yet reprivatization themes frequently provide the counterbalance to bureaucratic experts in mainstream news stories.

Teen mothers have become a touchstone for a number of reprivatization discourse themes. What unifies these themes is a concern over the fate of the traditional family—which conservatives define as a heterosexual, nuclear family made up of a sole breadwinner father, a homemaker mother, and children—as well as the changing relationship between families and the state. For conservatives, unmarried teen mothers not only symbolize the wrong family model, but through the government-funded services now provided for them and their children, they may pave the way toward official sanctioning of everything from universal child care to state-run adoptions.

More specifically: First, conservatives fear that public schools are taking away parents' rights to raise their children (Byfield, 1993) and they oppose liberal—or any—sex education in the schools. They would replace it with a program that promotes chastity. The conservative media present this as "an uphill fight" that parents face against the "liberal" public school system (Cunningham, 1992a, p. 28). These stories feature photos of teen mothers with such captions as "more teen pregnancies and more abortions" (Cunningham, 1992b).

Second, conservatives oppose teenagers' access to abortion and birth control. In the early 1980s in British Columbia, this became a point of contention between Health Minister Rafe Mair, who opposed abortion, and school officials who pointed out that "[Mair] is not prepared to put anything into prevention" (Canadian Press, 1980b, A19). A related and more recent example was conservative opposition to an amendment to the B.C. Infants Act that gave teens the right to obtain medical treatment (including an abortion) without parental consent (Brunet, 1992).

Third, conservatives oppose teen single motherhood. The editor of *British Columbia Report* (O'Neill, 1993) longs for the days

> when society wagged its collective finger at unmarried moms. It may have seemed cruel, but it served a greater usefulness (a recognition that a stable marriage was the best atmosphere in which to raise a family), and it certainly didn't preclude individual acts of compassion toward the unfortunate young women. (p. 2)

One underlying assumption of this analysis is that if these "unwed" mothers would only marry, then their husbands could assume financial responsibility for them and their children, thus sparing taxpayers the expense.

Fourth, conservatives oppose welfare for young people, believing it undermines the authority of parents and other adults and costs too much.[6]

Teen parenthood is but the most striking example of how "children are choosing, or being pushed, into handling adult responsibilities." Citing leaders of teacher organizations, a writer for the *Ottawa Citizen* (Dube, 1993) argued that students who live on their own with the help of welfare dollars exist outside of "parental authority," which has "produced a big change": "Granted so much independence, it's hard to conform just because a teacher tells you to" (p. A4).

Fifth, conservatives often oppose regular school programs for teen mothers. Some object to any help at all because, they argue, this lets adolescents off the hook morally and financially and encourages promiscuity. Bewley (1984), for example, noted disapprovingly: "Pregnant children are beamed upon in the classroom, and at least one Vancouver high school publicly prides itself on its free day-care centre for the children of unmarried student mothers." Others "might not like the addition of another costly social program, but"—in a nod to bureaucratic expert discourse—"they generally recognize that if the young moms can lead productive lives by graduating, they are less likely to become a burden on society" (O'Neill, 1993, p. 2).

Still, they worry that babies are becoming "status symbols" among school children. Thus the editor of *British Columbia Report* (O'Neill, 1993) suggests "that it makes sense to at least ensure that teen parent programs are not located in regular high schools, but in separate facilities" (p. 2). Presumably these conservatives would favor the old model whereby pregnant and mothering girls stayed at home or went to homes for unwed mothers, perhaps receiving an education by correspondence.

Some pro-life conservatives, however, are more concerned that pregnant teenagers be supported in their decision not to abort. Ridiculing O'Neill's suggestion that teen mothers be "isolated," two pro-life women demanded, "[W]hy not put the fathers of the children of teen moms in separate facilities so they don't impregnate more girls?" (Green & Steel, 1993, p. 3).

Sixth, conservatives worry that school-based day care centers for the children of teen mothers will pave the way for universal, government-funded, group child care. The founder of the "pro-family" Citizen's Research Institute, for one, is concerned that when schools provide on-site child care, they send a message that "institutionalizing infants in day care is a normal and healthy measure" (Saenger, 1991, p. 23). A member of parliament, Bob Wenman, went even further, calling day care centers "little more than temporary orphanages" and a "misuse of taxpayers' money" (Cunningham, 1993, p. 10).

Finally, conservatives favor teen mothers giving their babies up for adoption and want to minimize government regulation of private adoptions. During the House of Commons debate on Canada's abortion laws, pro-life conservatives began stressing adoption as the most sound choice a pregnant teenager could make (see Brodie, Gavigan, & Jenson, 1992, p. 65). Conservatives also worry that private adoptions be unfettered by government interference because, they argue, "many young mothers will choose to have an abortion rather than surrender their babies over to heartless bureaucrats" (Kerby, 1993, p. 3).

To sum up, conservative groups seek to stigmatize abortion, and so some find strong motivation to destigmatize a teen's decision to carry her pregnancy to term. But in the contest over interpretations of teen mothers, "reprivatizers" employ heavy stigmas to enforce their idea of family: a family where sex occurs only after marriage; a family of two parents and a male breadwinner; a family independent of state aid. An unwed teen mother who relies on any government program and doesn't give her child up for adoption is, in this construct, the epitome of the wrong family.

Oppositional Movements: The Wrong-Society Frame

Several oppositional social movements, following on the achievements of the civil rights movement for racial equality, gained strength in the late 1960s and early 1970s. In particular, the Aboriginal people's rights movement, the anti-poverty movement, and the women's liberation movement each provided arguments that could be marshaled in support of teen parents and created space for an alternative discourse aimed at reducing the stigma of teen pregnancy. Such an alternative discourse, however, rarely informs, let alone frames, mass media stories about teen mothers.

An exception came during an interview with Nobel Prize-winning novelist Toni Morrison (in Angelo, 1989), who tapped into an oppositional discourse (feminist,[7] class-conscious, and anti-racist) to argue that teenage motherhood should be more accepted. She asserted that much of the reprivatization discourse is a subterfuge: "I don't think anybody cares about unwed mothers unless they're black—or poor. The question is not morality, the question is money. That's what we're upset about. We don't care whether they have babies or not." The interviewer followed up with a familiar question, "How do you break the cycle of poverty? You can't just hand out money." In response, Morrison demanded:

Why not? Everybody else gets everything handed to them. The rich get it handed— they inherit it. I don't mean just inheritance of money. I mean what people take for granted among the middle and upper classes, which is nepotism, the old-boy network. That's shared bounty of class. (p. 122)

Usually, to find views such as Morrison's, one must turn to the alternative media. But even there, liberal feminist versions of the bureaucratic expert discourse are heard (e.g., Billung-Meyer, 1982). This is so, I would argue, because mainstream feminists have often ignored social class, race, and age, key structures that contribute to the ongoing stigmatization of teen mothers (cf. O'Neill, 1998).

Scarce as it is, where the oppositional discourse is found, the following themes emerge. First, don't blame the poor for poverty and its consequences. Katha Pollitt (1992), a socialist feminist, wrote in her regular column for the *Nation:*

When the poor are abandoned to their fates, when there are no jobs, people don't get to display "work ethic," don't feel good about themselves and don't marry or stay married. The girls don't have anything to postpone motherhood for; the boys have no economic prospects that would make them reasonable marriage partners. (p. 94)

Sometimes these and related views find their way into mainstream media accounts when a maverick bureaucratic expert or an advocate gets quoted. *Montreal Gazette* columnist Susan Schwartz (1991) approvingly cited a report that argued that teen mothers "need, among other things, a network to give them that voice, a revamped welfare system that takes into account their needs as young parents, organized community services to help young mothers to combat their isolation" (p. B4; see also, Bolan, 1993).

A second theme in oppositional discourse: Support "a woman's right to choose when, where, how, and with whom to give birth" (Maternal Health Society, 1982).[8] This means young women "need solid information and safe contraception that serves their needs," including safe, affordable, and legal abortions (Stevens, 1979, p. 11). Feminists have also stressed the need to change sex education. Susie Bright, for example, an important voice for the sexual-libertarian wing of the feminist movement (see Willis, 1996) and an on-line columnist for *Salon Magazine,* wishes she had "had someone mentor me about the absurd conflation of sex and love in young women's minds. . . . [Most young women] know how to say 'no' repetitively, but they're utterly at a loss as to what to say 'yes' to, or what form their own sexual initiative might take. Consequently, their refusals often wilt into guilty compromises and resentful ambivalence" (Bright, 1998).

The third theme of the oppositional discourse is respect and support for the diversity of family types. Feminists point out that there have long been moral attacks on single women with children, particularly those living in poverty. Given this historical context, it has been fairly easy to portray teen mothers as selfish, irresponsible, and so on, as is evident in the following *Newsweek* story (Ingrassia, 1993) about highly educated, single women with a fair income who decide to raise children on their own: "It's one thing to dismiss single parenthood as the act of petulant teenagers; it's another to ignore professionals having babies alone. But are these Murphy Browns any less self-absorbed than teens?" (p. 58). In this analysis, many feminists would see sexism: "There is an analytical link between moral attacks on single women on welfare and on women who achieved unusual degrees of educational success. In both cases, the women have displayed personal independence rather than dependence on individual men" (Wrigley, 1992, p. 13).

Critical feminists (whose stance is defined in Chapter 1), among others, have stressed, instead, the notion of *interdependence*. I develop this theme and a more systematic critique of the welfare system's treatment of teen mothers in Chapter 10. Curiously, I have found that little of this analysis has filtered into the alternative press reportage on teen pregnancy and motherhood.

Teen Mothers' Self-Interpretations: The Stigma-is-Wrong Frame

Teen mothers' self-interpretations draw from, resist, or transform the three major rival interpretations of their needs. Yet we rarely hear from teen mothers themselves in the mass media or, if we do, their remarks have been selected and edited in ways that can make them feel their main message has been distorted, as we saw in the case of Molly, the teen mother quoted at the start of this chapter. Recently, I have run across several first-hand personal accounts by young mothers or—more often— former young mothers (these accounts appear either as letters to the editor or op-ed pieces); they represent about 3% of the total articles about teen mothers (yielded in a search of the Canadian News Index, 1980– 1992). In addition, a few articles quote young mothers extensively or report negative reactions of a group of young mothers to stereotypes about single teen mothers.

Based on this analysis (which was confirmed by subsequent interviews with teen mothers at City and Town Schools), I have found that some stress themes of empowerment and reject messages that portray them as victims, childlike, welfare abusers, or morally tainted. Often they claim the need to be seen positively as mothers and emphasize the following themes.

First, the right to choose, including motherhood and adoption, is essential. In an op-ed by Kim Anderson (1989) subtitled "Happy Teenage Mother Backs Right to Choose," a former teen mother, whose baby was then 7 years old, says: "We are especially lucky in Canada because we have programs that pay day-care fees, living expenses and even tuition for young mothers who want to complete high school." A direct beneficiary of such support, the author claims now to have a "well-paying, satisfying job." Pondering from a pregnant teenager's point of view the options of abortion, offering the baby up for adoption, or keeping it, Anderson concludes:

> Experts and well-intentioned outsiders on all sides of the issue should put themselves in her shoes. . . . The main conclusion is that a mother should have the right to choose her own destiny. She should know all the choices and all the problems associated with each of them. She should have time and space to think clearly about what she really wants to do. The parents of these girls should support their child's decision. (p. H2)

Second, choosing to keep one's baby should not be stigmatized. Millie Strom married the father of her baby and gave birth at 15. In an op-ed article appearing in the *Vancouver Sun* (Strom, 1993), she recounts how she escaped her battering husband by retreating to a mental hospital, the only refuge she could find. There, with a diagnosis of postpartum depression, she was labeled "unfit," and authorities coerced her to remove her son from his paternal grandparents, where he was happy. He was placed in foster care and, unknown to Strom, he lingered another 8 months before being placed with adoptive parents. This was contrary to the wishes of all family members, including Strom's ex-husband, the paternal grandparents, and Strom herself.

> I had been told that I would forget him. Since I would forget, I was not warned about the depressions around his birthday and on holidays such as Christmas. . . . Social workers often say adoption offers something to the new mother—a chance for a fresh start. However, this adoption ideology omits some important realities. Adoption does not obliterate the unplanned pregnancy. (p. A11)

Third, choosing to give one's baby up for adoption should not be stigmatized. Anouk Crawford, 20, and Christie Cooper, 22, are young women who founded Birth Mothers Coalition after they gave their babies up for adoption. They were profiled in a Vancouver *Province* article (Grindlay, 1993) headlined "Proud of Their Novel Conception." "'We're not supposed to be proud that we were young women and we had the courage to go through a pregnancy,' Crawford said. 'A birth mother is not supposed to be happy or proud of what we've done. We are'" (p. A23).

Fourth, high school programs dealing with sexuality as well as mothering should carry less stigma. Writing a letter to the editor in support of school-based infant day care, a teen mother ("Vancouver," 1981) argued, "If at the same time [as providing school-based day care] the School Board provided better sex education and the Health Department made birth control more available to teenagers then possibly, in the future this problem could be controlled" (p. 4).

Fifth, teen mothers are each other's best support system, which schools can encourage. Kathleen, age 16, told a writer for *BC Woman to Woman* (Rathie, 1989) that her school-based program for teen mothers kept her motivated to graduate:

> Just being together with 20 girls in one room who've had so many similar experiences. . . . There's times the teachers will look at you and say, "You know it's time to be quiet now," and you've been talking about your kids. You've been sharing what the problem was that week: the new tooth they just got or did your kid do this when he was that age . . . it's great! (p. 10)

Sixth, teen mothers have matured and taken responsibility; they deserve to be treated accordingly. As Molly complained to me about the "Children Who Are Having Children" article that omitted her views: "I don't see myself as a child—I am practically 18. I'm almost old enough to vote, and I'm old enough to drive." In this vein, teen mothers often represent themselves as emotionally mature enough to raise a child well, countering the discourse of the bureaucratic experts of the "abusive" teen mother.

Seventh, teen mothers not only recognize stigmas against them, they also fight back. A *Montreal Gazette* columnist (Schwartz, 1991) watched a National Film Board documentary about teen mothers with some young mothers and reported their reactions: "What angered me was that these three women were portrayed as so vulnerable," said Nina Sale, a single mother, age 22, "as being taken advantage of by the courts, by the welfare system, by social workers. There was no empowerment, no talk of anything to give them self-confidence or help them take control." A teen mother is quoted: "I love my daughter. Not once in that film did one woman say she loved her child. I can't imagine looking at that film and saying I ever wanted a kid" (p. B4).

A teen mother in New Brunswick expressed her opposition to official stigma by filing a complaint against the school board with the provincial Human Rights Commission (Sussel, 1989). Bobbi-Jo Hanson was not allowed to continue as student council president because she became pregnant. As one official at Saint John Vocational High School put it: "When I saw her my mouth dropped. . . . She was supposed to be a role model, a leader. We weren't going to put her out there and say 'this is a typical vocational girl'" (p. 2). Hanson won her complaint and the school board sent her a written apology.

The Usual Winners

When the various representers of teen motherhood wage their stigma contest in the media, an example of what usually results can be found in this passage from *Chatelaine* (Maynard, 1982):

> What's to be done about the problem of adolescent pregnancies? One extreme view, offered by a retired social worker who chooses to remain anonymous, is that both welfare support and abortions should be made less accessible. "Kids wouldn't get pregnant so easily if they knew they'd have to pay the piper." Another extreme is [psychiatrist] Dr. [Anne] Seiden's suggestion that instead of fighting them we might join them, "accepting the legitimacy of adolescence as one part of a woman's life in which she might choose to bear her children," and offering full support. Most expert views fall somewhere in between. . . .
>
> Of course society's best hope is not helping girls feel better about premature parenthood; it's prevention, making sure that those babies who are born are wanted and can be provided for. (p. 129)

In this morality play we find presented as "extreme" frames conservative and oppositional views, with decisive weight placed "somewhere in between," that is, with the bureaucratic experts. The reporter winds up with no call to destigmatize the decision to become a teen mother.

When presenting a public face, even advocates for teen mothers— advocates who are generally not interested in stigmatizing their constituency—find themselves compelled to pitch their message to skeptics, using the language of those less inclined to, say, vote for funds for their programs. Youth advocate Cat Adler (1982), in *Towards a Caring Community*—published by the Social Planning and Review Council of British Columbia—identifies three kinds of audiences: one is receptive to a humanitarian approach; one prefers a reasoned, factual approach; and one responds best to a "dollars-and-cents" approach. When it comes to convincing the latter to support "programs to prevent pregnancies and provide support to pregnant and parenting teenagers," Adler, in essence, recommends reinforcing the image of teen mothers as drains on welfare:

> [I]t will be important to present teenage pregnancy statistics, the numbers of girls keeping babies, the many health and social services required, how much it costs to give public assistance, to say, an under-educated unwed mother, who may repeat pregnancy and become a dependent on the community. (p. 26)

One feminist I interviewed acknowledged that when she campaigns for public support for teen mother services, she drops the feminist discourse because it is too controversial. Were she advocating merely for herself, she would stick to her principles, even if that caused anti-feminists to label her "bitch or immoral," she said. But "if I'm trying to get a valuable service going [for others], I don't want to alienate."

Another factor in how the various representations of teen motherhood fare in the media is the storytelling framework that reporters and writers must work within. For example, reporters realize that if a story is to gain the interest of readers, it must affect them personally. Therefore, the liberal press often puts forward the message that teen pregnancy and motherhood could happen to anybody (e.g., Maynard, 1982, p. 91).

Although poverty has not been shown to cause teenage motherhood and having a child has not been proven to consign teen mothers to poverty, poorer teenagers are more likely to carry their pregnancies to term. Also, fertility rates are higher within certain ethnic and racial groups. Therefore, as Kristen Luker (1991, p. 81) has observed, the risk of teen pregnancy [and motherhood] does not occur with "equal frequency," and when people falsely universalize the issue, they mask and confuse disadvantages by class, race, and gender. When some attack teen mothers as a group, the class and racial bias in their argument is hidden; it appears on the surface that they are merely chastising irresponsible teenagers.

The media often build on the "it could happen to you" angle by telling an individual story full of personal choices and dramatic twists. Readers are invited to live vicariously the soap opera-like existence of a particular teen mother: We learn that fate caused her birth control to fail, we meet her dangerous boyfriend, we cry with her over dashed college hopes. Because the media like endings that affirm personal triumph, a few of the stories fall into a category I call the "Saga of the Teenage Supermother." Both *Jet* and *People* magazine, for instance, have carried stories about teen mothers who get straight A's and become valedictorians. Such

Supermom storytelling, while compelling and even destigmatizing, plays down structural constraints and the benefits of institutional supports like day care and school services, sending instead a signal that young women, given enough individual mettle, can do it all.

The familiar flip side to the Teenage Supermom Saga is the media fascination with sex. Individualizing this theme often means casting the story as one of a personal form of moral deviance. Cultural studies theorist David Buckingham (1987) has noted that, "[W]hile on the one hand the press is concerned to define and to police the boundaries of 'respectable' conduct, it is also fascinated with behaviour which in various ways is seen to violate them" (p. 136). In reporting alarm over teen pregnancy in British Columbia, the *Province* ("Pregnancies," 1980) ended its story this way: "[T]he matter boils down to a single point: Who should teach morals, the family, the church or the school?" (p. A5). In other words, the matter boils down to the rights and wrongs of individual behavior, rather than more political issues such as sexism, racism, and unemployment. Readers are not encouraged to make links between individual lives and broader social forces.

Constrained by time and resources, reporters who tackle a complex issue such as teen motherhood must rely on a path prepared by others. It is common for a reporter to interview only a few people and label as "typical" the girl who fits the dominant frame of analysis. It is also the case, however, that the groups who might make available to the press other girls with more oppositional views have incentive to avoid doing so. The goal of an advocate for a funded program, for example, is to present a client to the public who sounds reasonable, grateful, and perhaps even repentant. Teen mothers, themselves not formally organized or in a position to create their own advocacy groups, rely on others with mixed agendas to speak on their behalf.

Those who work most directly with teen mothers are divided in their priorities and so do not speak with a unified voice in defining the needs of teen mothers. Some feminists worry that by disentangling teen pregnancy from other social problems related to poverty, broader material support for young mothers will disappear. As research challenges conventional wisdom about teen pregnancy and poverty, Luker (1991) is concerned that "the most subtle danger is that the new work on teen pregnancy will be used to argue that because teen pregnancy is not the linchpin that holds together myriad other social ills, it is not a problem at all" (p. 83).

Implications

The mass media largely attempt to reflect and construct dominant cultural values about teen mothers. The viewing, reading, and listening public looks there to see a "continuous performance morality play" (Golding & Middleton, 1983, p. 236). This morality play, with its attendant stereotyped images as well as its silences, then has repercussions. The morality play that the media conveys helps to (a) frame the public debate about teen mothers, (b) shape the implementation of public policy, and (c) influence the daily lives of young mothers and their children profoundly.

Politicians, particularly conservative ones, throughout North America have used allusions to irresponsible teen mothers to whip up public support for cutbacks in welfare payments and social services. In Alberta during the early 1980s, for example, the provincial government reduced welfare benefits to teen mothers. Even so, by the decade's end, Minister of Social Services Connie Osterman told an audience assembled in Edmonton for a conference on teen pregnancy that teens were getting pregnant because welfare was too easily available. Osterman neglected to mention that she herself had commissioned a study 2 years before that concluded the opposite: social assistance did not significantly encourage teens to become pregnant ("Study," 1989, p. B2). Teen mothers make such good political scapegoats partly because they are relatively isolated and powerless and partly because they have come to symbolize multiple meanings, often contradictory, related to sexuality, adulthood, attitudes toward work, and ideals of family (see esp. Chapter 2). By engaging in such scapegoating, the state has reinforced and institutionalized the stigma attached to teen pregnancy and motherhood, especially in times of recession.

Negative stereotypes, so often publicly voiced, have permeated the institutions that control the fates of teen mothers. For example, in many districts of British Columbia—including those of Pacifica and Midland where City and Town Schools are located—the Ministry of Social Services now subsidizes day care for young mothers, regardless of whether they are on welfare. Although this is a valuable service for the mothers, the Ministry justifies this policy with the assumption that any child of a young mother is "at risk of neglect or abuse." Many teen mothers are poor and in need of material support, yet to receive it they get constructed as inadequate mothers. This occurs despite research suggesting that a mother's age is far less important than other factors in determining her parenting behavior, including potential abuse of her children (for a brief review of this literature, see Chapter 2).

In addressing the assumed inadequacies of teen mothers, special classes are offered; some of them, like "Parenting," are useful enough that every teenager might benefit from them. Others border on the absurd—even humiliating. At the Midland Maternity Home, I observed a workshop on "budgeting skills" in which a social worker read aloud from a typed list of money-saving tips, including: "Squash toilet paper rolls so the center is oval not round, the paper doesn't roll off 10 yards at a time! This will help to cut your toilet paper bill" (field notes, 5/11/92). This class did not much help the students cope with the contradictions and consequences of structural poverty.

The "cycles" that commonly come to mind when people speak of teen mothers are "cycle of poverty," "cycle of welfare dependency," and "cycle of child abuse." Perhaps it would be fruitful to bear in mind, instead, a "cycle of stigma"—a cycle helped along by experts and advocates who enforce negative stereotypes in order to attract funding and support; a cycle given a spin by politicians who ignore their own studies in seeking scapegoats; a cycle reinforced by a mainstream media that relays the stigmatized images it finds "somewhere in between" and largely ignores the discourses of opposition and of teen mothers themselves.

Notes

1. Molly is 1 of 12 teen mothers I interviewed formally as part of an ethnographic study of two public alternative high schools in California; La Fuente is a pseudonym of one of the schools (see Kelly, 1993a).

2. Statistics Canada reports that the teen pregnancy rate for Canada as a whole is lower than it was two decades ago, although it has increased a bit during 4 out of the past 5 years for which data are available (Wadhera & Millar, 1997). It remains too soon to tell whether these slight increases are just random variations in an overall downward trend or if they mark a new upward trend. In any case, the 1974 to 1994 period saw an overall drop in the pregnancy rate from 53.7 to 48.8 per 1,000 females aged 15 to 19 years (Wadhera & Millar, 1997, p. 11). In British Columbia the teen pregnancy rate per 1,000 declined from 70.3 in 1974 to 40.7 in 1994 (a 42.1% drop), including a 42.8% drop in live births and a 37.8% drop in hospital abortions (Wadhera & Millar, 1997, table 3).

    For the latest U.S. statistics on teen pregnancy and birth rates and a discussion of trends, see Henshaw, 1997.

3. The Alternative Press Index includes popular and scholarly magazines and journals and covers the following areas: African-American studies, anarchism, ecology, ethnic studies, feminism, gay-lesbian studies, international studies, labor, Marxism, radical democracy, and socialism.

4. Snowball sampling is a strategy in which a research participant suggests other potential participants, who then name or refer other participants, all of whom fit a particular profile established by the researcher.

5. Oppositional social movements include feminism, lesbian and gay liberation, Aboriginal rights, workers' rights, welfare rights, and other collective struggles of subordinated social groups.

6. In the late 1970s, for example, B.C. Human Resources Minister Bill Vander Zalm "overturned an arbitration board ruling that allowed two 17-year-old pregnant girls in Kelowna" to receive social assistance. Instead, he offered that the ministry would "attempt to have the parents of the girls support their daughters" (Canadian Press, 1978, p. 4). Similar debates were occurring in the United States at this time. Liberals were arguing that pregnant and parenting teens were families in need of services; new conservatives, in contrast, wanted to strengthen the family that included the teenagers' parents "and to discourage measures that increased the autonomy of daughters" (Luker, 1996, p. 79).

7. There are a number of feminist lenses through which to view the subordination of women. It is beyond the scope of this chapter to distinguish them. My analysis of oppositional discourse about teen mothers, however, revealed that alternative press writers seemed most often to use a socialist feminist or multicultural feminist lens (see Jaggar & Rothenberg, 1993, for discussion of these and other feminist frameworks).

8. More recently, feminists have framed discussions of reproductive health issues in terms of rights rather than choices. According to Solinger (1998), this "reflects a growing recognition among advocates that 'choice' is the ultimate marketplace concept. When we construct the abortion arena on the marketplace model, we justify the fact that millions of women in the United States cannot afford to purchase adequate or necessary reproductive health services" (1998, p. 9; cf. Roberts, 1997). *Maternal Health News* is written and produced by volunteers in Vancouver, B.C. to provide a forum for ideas regarding controversial issues in maternal and child health care. It is informed by the feminist self-help movement, which encourages women to see reproductive functions as natural and normal.

Chapter 5

Integrating Teen Mothers into City and Town Schools: Coping with the Dilemma of Difference

Can we invent other practices that treat difference as just the variety of human experience, rather than the basis for dividing people into the class of the normal and the class of the abnormal?

—Martha Minow

Stigma and the discourses that help to construct it are the means by which difference is made hierarchical and assigned a value that is either positive or negative. Historically, pregnant and mothering students have been defined as different in the sense of abnormal or Other and excluded from school on this basis. This chapter focuses on the efforts of teachers and administrators at City and Town Schools to promote the inclusion of teen mothers. An analysis of their goals, beliefs, actions, and strategies reveals the profound challenge of inventing practices that move beyond the normal-abnormal dichotomy by treating difference, instead, as variation in a set. The challenge amounts to nothing less than refashioning the institution of schooling so that it does not "establish one norm that places the burden of difference on those who diverge from it" (Minow, 1990, p. 94).

Compared with this tall and utopian order, the vision of Ms. Long and Ms. Connell—leaders of the young parent initiatives at Town and City Schools, respectively—was, by necessity, limited. Circumscribing their vision were the resources at their disposal and the more immediate goal of meeting the perceived needs of students who were also mothers. "The purpose," Ms. Long told me at the start of her tenure, "is to keep them well integrated into a normal school life and just provide for the differences, provide for their extra needs. We don't want to set up an alternate school situation." Ms. Connell, who had inherited the Teen-Age Parents

Program at a point when many student-mothers were spending most of their time in a special classroom, immediately began pushing "to get them into the regular school. That was 100% [of my effort]—110%. I didn't want them isolated." The benefits of integration, according to Ms. Connell, included the student-mothers "recognizing that they're not a unique group in most areas of their life." Thus, both women asserted that teen mothers were more like other students than not, and both women used language that revealed a schooling system still bifurcated into "normal" versus "alternate," "regular" versus "special."

Their role (and the goal of their respective programs) often amounted to helping student-mothers to fit into a largely unreconstructed institution. At other times, though, their beliefs and practices and those of their colleagues called into question long-standing assumptions about how schools should be organized, for whom, and with what content.

Because young parent programs represent an effort to meet the distinct needs of a particular group of students, they inevitably confront the "dilemma of difference." Minow (1990) poses the dilemma of difference thus: "When does treating people differently emphasize their differences and stigmatize or hinder them on that basis? and when does treating people the same become insensitive to their difference and likely to stigmatize or hinder them on *that* basis?" (p. 20).

Once students are identified as teen mothers and are provided with services based on that difference, school adults may begin to notice traits—both positive (e.g., "teen mothers are more mature than other students") and negative (e.g., "teen mothers use their babies as excuses")—that distill into stereotypes. Yet were these school adults simply to ignore the differences of the teen mothers from other students, then the teen mothers might not receive due consideration of their heavy responsibilities and, as a result, might fail their courses or be asked to leave school due to poor attendance.

City and Town Schools approached this dilemma from different directions; City School tended to emphasize the difference, while Town School was more inclined to ignore it. Teen mothers at City School received support in ways that contributed to group identity and solidarity as teen mothers (see Chapter 6). For example, even fully integrated students met daily in the TAPP classroom, which served as their homeroom, and TAPP students went on field trips and celebrated various holidays together throughout the year. This strategy, paradoxically, led a number of people outside the Teen-Age Parents Program to perceive teen mothers as still largely segregated, and features of TAPP—as well as friendships formed through participation in TAPP—were seen to symbolize their exclusion from the mainstream. One teacher, who had observed a group of teen mothers together at commencement, worried that they may have felt "separate from the grad class" or like "lepers" because they were "different." And a student leader (Chitra, not a teen mother) perceived teen mothers to be "isolated" because they had a "special program and a special day care—there's even a TAPP class list and then the regular class list, so we always think that they're a different group."

In contrast, teen mothers were more interspersed at Town School and less visible as a group. There was, for example, no class where they all came together and no teacher specially assigned to the Young Parents Program. Thus, particularly in the early days of YPP, there were fewer warning signs in cases where teen mothers found themselves unable to cope and fewer options to help them remain in school.

Despite the difference in emphasis across the two schools, similar issues arose as they coped with the dilemma of difference while pursuing a policy of supported integration. (I use the term "supported integration" to distinguish it from simply enrolling student-parents in regular classes without the provision of child care and other services.) The stories of how teen mothers were integrated into regular classes provide more general lessons for those interested in detracking and creating more inclusive schools. In what follows, I analyze the various strategies used to foster integration and assess how successful they were at transcending the difference dilemma.

Creating Community Buy-In

When supported integration was first proposed and later implemented at City and Town Schools, reformers had to take account of the relations between the schools and their wider communities and within the schools themselves, and these relations, in turn, shaped everything from the rationale for the initiatives to the location of the day care in a designated school.

In the local struggles to sell the idea of regular school-based programs for young parents, the voices of youths and their families have been largely silent. In general, teen mothers are not collectively organized; they do not participate in a political movement formed specifically around their needs, hopes, and desires. Throughout North America, and in the cases of Midland and Pacifica in particular, potential service providers—social workers, doctors, nurses, teachers, counselors, and other professionals—have been the key advocates for pregnant and parenting teens (e.g., Weatherley et al., 1985). Thus, teen mothers have often been "positioned as potential recipients of predefined services rather than as agents involved in interpreting their needs and shaping their life conditions" (Fraser, 1989, p. 174).

Professionals and front-line workers, as I showed in the previous chapter, are much more likely to speak as bureaucratic experts to propose solutions to problems that they define as largely technical. They tend to mobilize political support and funding using a prevention discourse that is persuasive to their own group and to those who hold the purse strings.

Arguments about prevention and long-term cost savings are more likely to eclipse civil rights arguments, particularly during times of economic recession, when the first incarnations of both TAPP and YPP came into being. Conservative federal and provincial governments were in power, and debates over abortion, women's labor force participation, and welfare were occurring across North America. Both TAPP and YPP resulted from the efforts of a coalition of community and government representatives, largely people with a professional interest in teen pregnancy and parenthood. Planning committees in both places were composed of relatively high-powered members. The planning committee in Pacifica, according to one member, had "tentacles into practically every social group in town," which was "a very dramatic and effective way of getting certain social changes activated."

When they sought funding, program planners often had to promise long-term tax savings. In Pacifica a "big selling point" of the program, recalled a planning group member, was that it would "help these girls get off of the welfare rolls." In Midland—where the provincial government's "Initiative to Strengthen the Family" funded the town's Pro-Life Society, the Midland Maternity Home, as well as the Young Parents Program—a co-author of the YPP funding proposal noted how it was "slanted to appeal to the Dan Quayles of the world." The "slant" was evident in the policy rationales put forward, namely, the prevention of "cycles of child abuse" and "welfare dependency."

Significantly, each program planning team had a key supporter on the elected school board, and both trustees were respected health care professionals with a keen interest in young children and child care (neither had worked in schools). In both Pacifica and Midland, the initial stumbling block proved to be child care policy writ large rather than providing services to teen mothers per se. In Pacifica, for instance, the B.C. Minister of Human Resources at first refused to issue a license for a school-based infant day care facility, explaining in a letter to the school board that "family daycare homes are a better resource for very young infants than group care." The Deputy Minister of Human Resources likened infant child care to orphanages. Day care licenses for infants aged 6 weeks to 18 months were few and far between at the time of these negotiations in 1981.

Over a decade later in Midland, initial school board "resistance" to school-based day care, according to YPP's first coordinator, had less to do with "being cautious about a young mothers program" and more to do with fear about losing control over the allocation of space: "They were very cautious and fearful that if they allowed day care spaces [on school property], they would then not be able to redeem them [in the future]." Community groups, including the Youth Society, had been pressing the district to use school sites for after-school child care, and the school board feared that the YPP would open the door to much greater demands.

The Midland and Pacifica school boards both had a minority of conservative trustees who were not supportive. According to supporters, opponents wanted to punish teen mothers for becoming pregnant but tended, instead, to give more widely acceptable reasons, such as not wanting to "overload the schools" or the high cost of infant care. One Midland school trustee, however, was more open about the reasons for his opposition. In his weekly newspaper column, he cited "single mother education" along with several other school-based "social programs", as costly and beyond "our primary educational mandate," adding: "But my real concern is for the lack of consequences for those in society who show no responsibility for their actions."

Despite such views, I found that the professionals lobbying for the creation of the school-based day care in Midland had some unlikely allies in conservative quarters. Prior to the establishment of YPP at Town School, I interviewed a woman who had been a longtime board member and past president of the Pro-Life Society, and she "endorsed" the integration model being proposed. "Anything would be better than having an abortion, because there is absolutely nothing in the school system [now]" to support young women who decide they do not want to have an abortion.

To recap, liberal-minded professionals were able to obtain resources and start up young parent programs during economic hard times by using largely conservative arguments. It is revealing to compare the resulting program rationales—which frequently construct teen mothers as potential child abusers and drains on the welfare state—with the arguments made about inclusive schooling for children with disabilities since service providers have been joined by parents of children with disabilities and now adults with disabilities to advocate on behalf of children. Increasingly, they frame the issues using a civil rights or equality discourse (e.g., Lipsky & Gartner, 1996).

Once the programs received funding, planners in both places sought to perpetuate community support in two ways. First, both programs were established as jointly funded ventures and as partnerships between prominent nonprofit organizations with expertise in child care (the Community-Based Organization [CBO] in Pacifica and the Youth Society in Midland) and various branches of government (the school board, the health department, and the social services ministry). This strategy was partly aimed at keeping the program "safe," according to a member of the TAPP team. The thinking was that "each partner only has a little bit. So if one pulls out, the others can stay." Second, both programs established advisory committees composed of interested "stakeholders," including teen mothers (current program participants as well as alumnae). An important advisory committee role in both Pacifica and Midland was to serve as an advocate for young parent programs, to ensure that suitable funding remained available, and to promote community awareness of the programs.

Fighting for Visibility: The Politics of Location

Location decisions (which school/s in the district should house the young parent program, where within the school should the day care be located, where within the school should the special classroom, if any, be located) go to the heart of integration; the outcomes of these decisions become daily symbolic reminders of who is included and to what degree.

Advocates who focus on students with disabilities have argued that for schools to be truly inclusive, they should have "a natural or normal proportion of students with disabilities. They avoid serving as 'centers' or 'cluster sites' for any category of students" (Stainback, Stainback, & Ayres, 1996, p. 36). The situation of pregnant and parenting students is more complicated. To take each category in turn: In the case of pregnancy, the *official* school district policy in both Midland and Pacifica was to allow pregnant young women to remain in their neighborhood school, where presumably they would retain the support of peers who already knew them. Put another way, the school districts did not want to "ghettoize pregnant moms" (to quote one administrator) by sending them all to one school.

Of course, teen pregnancies and births are not distributed randomly across neighborhoods for reasons related to class and racial inequalities (see Chapter 2). Added to this fact, public schools located in middle- to upper-class neighborhoods, particularly those with a strong university preparatory ethos, have *unofficial* ways of letting pregnant students know they are no longer welcome.[1] A number of teen mothers I met in Midland, for example, had attended Academic High (which served both low- and high-income areas) at the time they discovered their pregnancies:

> One of the school counselors made an appointment with me, and I was quickly and coolly informed that I would now be taking school through correspondence at the Home for Pregnant Teens across town. Thank goodness being pregnant does not weaken one's backbone; with equal briskness I informed her that I needed to be in the classroom to effectively learn and reach my potential, and that in no uncertain terms was I going to leave the school. (Elaine, pregnant at 17, written communication)
>
> A lot of the teachers weren't really supportive, because they . . . never really had to deal with anything like that. It seemed to me what they were trying to do was to get me out of the school. . . . A lot of the teachers that I had a decent relationship with—like you could talk and joke around or whatever—they would just kind of shy away from you, it seemed. (Rose, pregnant at 17)

Elaine, an academically strong student, succeeded in her effort to remain at Academic High, whereas Rose, an average student, ended up leaving for the remainder of her pregnancy. With the Roses of the world in mind, one youth advocate in Pacifica argued: "In theory, yes, all schools should be supportive, but the reality is that if you're one teen mom in a classroom, you may feel too uncomfortable to stay in that setting, so you need to have options."

Once young women become mothers, they often benefit greatly from school-based day care and other services. There were not enough teen mothers in either Midland or Pacifica to warrant more than one school-based young parent program. This then raised the issue of where within the district to locate the day care.

Studies have shown that young parent programs are often offered in alternative settings, low-income and racial minority neighborhoods, or both (Lesko, 1995; Weatherley et al., 1986; Zellman & Feifer, 1992). Thus, district administrators who want to avoid controversy appear to locate programs "where they will be invisible to dominant groups in the community" (Nathanson, 1991, p. 163). Both Town and City Schools were located in low-income or working-class, ethnically diverse neighborhoods (see Table 1.1), yet the process by which they were selected was, in both cases, quite circuitous and was affected by multiple, sometimes contingent factors.

In both cases, administrators looked for a location that would be both central (because the program would serve the entire district) and close to where most potential teen mothers were living. Originally, YPP was slated for Midland High, located in a mostly White, middle-class neighborhood, because it had the space and an enthusiastic principal and was close to the Midland Maternity Home. When the construction of the day care was delayed for a year due to technical problems, the district, in consultation with the Youth Society, decided to move the project to Town School, located in the neighborhood where most teen mothers on the waiting list lived.

One of the Native youth workers at Town School greeted this change enthusiastically. "Now the day care is in a central location. When I heard they were going to put it out at Midland, I said, 'Why are you hiding them?' Town School has more of a mixture of students. Other schools in the district are very snobbish—upper class" (field notes, 9/27/94).

Many other staff members and students at both Town and City Schools credited the diversity of the student body with helping to create an inclusive atmosphere. Faced with many social group differences, most students, although they did not necessarily embrace pregnant and parenting teens wholeheartedly, did seem to accept them as a given. It was not just diversity, per se, but the fact that a significant portion of students at both schools had experienced hard living of one form or another, and this enabled them to empathize. A related point, made by a teacher at Pacifica, is that so many other special programs existed alongside TAPP that it did not become a "sideshow."

The desire of administrators to avoid controversy did influence the location of TAPP's special classroom and day care within the school in its early years. A TAPP teacher recalled the principal confiding that "the more out of sight we were, the less complaints there would be." Keeping TAPP "low profile" made it easier to bend rules; for example, late-arriving teen mothers were less subject to scrutiny and disapproval. Also, in 1983–1984 the district was laying off teachers. "We thought if the people knew about the program, it might be cut." By 1990 TAPP had won an award and was well established; a new teacher (Ms. Connell) successfully lobbied for the TAPP classroom to be relocated from "the very outskirts of the school" near the automotive department to a bigger, more centrally located space.

City School's TAPP, an early program well known to practitioners throughout the province, paved the way for Town School's Young Parents Program to be more visible from the start. The YPP day care at Town School also opened in a more progressive political climate; the British Columbia Minister of Education was on hand for the ribbon-cutting ceremony and declared his strong support for such programs and his high regard for the determination of teen mothers to continue their education (field notes, 10/24/94).

Building Political Support within the School

Assessing the relations of teen mothers with their peers and teachers—a key dimension of inclusion—was a difficult process. When either I or my research assistant, Sheila, was observing as we shadowed teen mothers through their school day, we obviously were always mediating the interactions they had with others. Nevertheless, taking account of these observations together with individual interviews of all parties involved, I conclude that both schools had succeeded generally in making teen mothers feel included by the vast majority of their peers and teachers. The variation in the experiences of teen mothers can be explained by their particular identities—shaped by differences of race, ethnicity, class, gender, and ability—and how these were recognized and affirmed (or not) within each school and classroom, as well as by the range of their personalities.

Enabling Positive Peer Interactions
through Physical Proximity

At City School the interactions of teen mothers with their peers were mediated by unofficial ability grouping. Many of the teen mothers signed up for vocational and art electives, classes that were avoided by students preparing for university. Thus, Chitra, who had already been accepted into university by the time she was interviewed, rarely saw teen mothers in her advanced math and science classes at City School. (Recall that she was quoted earlier as perceiving teen mothers to be "isolated.") By contrast, in elective classes such as Family Management, teen mothers made friends with peers based on common life experiences. Angela, for example, discovered that, like her, a classmate had left an abusive family situation and was living on her own.

At Town School, where most tracking had been abolished and no special classroom for teen mothers existed, teen mothers were much more likely to befriend, or be befriended by, their age and grade peers. It was not always, or even usually, obvious who was a teen parent and who was not, non-parenting students told me; from what they observed, most teen mothers were "treated with respect" (to use a recurring phrase). Evidence of their acceptance by peers ranged from smiles to making good on offers to baby-sit for the teen mothers. At the beginning of the year, I noticed that those who had been at Town School before their pregnancy and those who tended to be extroverts, not surprisingly, interacted positively with many peers throughout the day. The more introverted teen mothers, although they tended to sit alone or with another teen mother early in the school year, had made friends outside of YPP by second semester. As at City School, the integrated teen mothers seemed to do as well at meeting new people as any other group of students might, except that they had fewer opportunities to bond with others through extracurricular activities.

An important factor that influenced peer relations, especially at Town School, was the high level of acceptance of First Nations students; Town School administrators, teachers, and students alike took pride in their school being a welcoming place. Native students were overrepresented in YPP (they comprised 30% of participants, 45% if biracial students are included) in comparison with the population of Town School as a whole, where 11% of all students were Native. As evidence of the accepting atmosphere, the Native teen mothers I interviewed cited the popularity of the school among Natives regionally, the presence of First Nations support workers, and the offering of a Native Studies course that attracted non-Native and Native students alike.

> This [First Nations 12] class talks about prejudice and a lot of problems that the Natives have and stuff like that. I thought it was just going to be an all Native class, but there's half Natives in there, and 5 White people. And when I walked in the first time, I looked at them, and I thought, "What are you doing here?" 'Cause I thought it was just all for Natives or whatever, and I thought, "Geez, they're going to feel really uncomfortable," right, 'cause I thought a lot of the Natives would try to make them feel uncomfortable. But it's just another class, and everybody gets along. (Rose, half-Native, half-White)

The strategies that are meant to encourage the idea that "everybody gets along" mainly consisted of simple integration. Teachers and administrators, by and large, assumed that if teen mothers had the opportunity to be in the same physical space, a sense of belonging would develop as a matter of course. The integration strategy was supplemented at City School by other activities designed with a dual purpose: to encourage minimally integrated teen mothers to interact with peers and teachers outside their special classroom and to inform non-parenting students about the lives of teen mothers and possibly dispel stereotypes. The most common such activity was the use of teen mothers as guest speakers (e.g., in family life classes) or helpers (e.g., cafeteria servers, tutors in a class for the "educably mentally handicapped"); play building and performance (analyzed in Chapter 8) represented another such activity. Dispelling stereotypes using these strategies alone, however, sometimes proved unsuccessful when too many differences existed between teen mothers and other students (see Chapter 6).

Managing Teacher Resistance, Cultivating Teacher Acceptance

Positive teacher responses to the young parent program were less taken for granted by planners in both sites. It is not that the teachers would behave "unprofessionally," explained a City School staff member:

> They wouldn't hold back or not teach the students [who are mothers] just as well. But a student[-mother], even a good student, will still miss more time than an average student because of the fact that if the baby gets ill, they usually have to stay home. And if they get ill, you've got double jeopardy. So you really have to look for a teacher who is prepared to give them some help with the extra work they need to catch up.

Ms. Connell tried to enroll teen mothers who were just returning to school after a long absence and had experienced living on the streets in regular classes with teachers who were "open-minded," "easy to talk to," "fair," "not easily rattled or offended," and "motivational."

Similarly, a Midland administrator foresaw that teacher resistance would stem from absenteeism related to caring for sick children, and his proposed solution involved handpicking teachers whenever feasible. He described teachers as falling along a continuum; at one extreme were the "hard-liners" who tend to "feel the students are not studying properly" and that their absences are ploys to get out of work. "The other type of teacher is the basic social worker; they want to save the child." He anticipated selecting teachers cast more in the mold of social workers, people who were "flexible and understanding" while encouraging students to achieve academically.

While these discussions may seem prosaic, program administrators were actually recognizing schools "to be *arenas of struggle*; to be riven with actual or potential conflict between members; to be poorly co-ordinated; to be ideologically diverse" (Ball, 1987, p. 7). Across ideological differences, virtually all teachers at both schools said they favored integration. The most common rationale for integration was that it promoted social development, although staff members framed this differently depending on their general worldview.

More liberal teachers stressed, as one put it, that "integration gives them [teen parents] a sense of belonging." Conservative teachers, fewer in number at both schools, valued integration as a strategy for normalizing teen mothers. This perspective came through, for example, in a City School teacher's discussion of the pros and cons of special classes for teen mothers versus integration into regular classes:

> Look at what happens when . . . you put the kith and kin all together with the same ilk. That doesn't always make for success. It reinforces a lot of, maybe, problems. They do get a support network. . . . But also I think it's important that they realize that there are other teenagers who are not in the situation that they are, and it was because of various circumstances. Maybe it's education, maybe it's their family background, the support they got from parents, the way they were treated as young people.

Not surprisingly, given this divergence of ideologies, the attitudes of the teachers about such issues as single motherhood and welfare and their pedagogy more generally mediated how student-mothers experienced integration in individual classrooms.

Teachers' attitudes, both positive and negative, affect the behavior of their students, an observation made by teen mothers as well as teachers. (Likewise, the attitudes of administrators affect the orientation of their staff to teen mothers.) Janice (age 18, City School) noted that "if teachers look judgmental, then the students think that they can get away with it, too." A technical studies teacher at Town School described how he tried to model acceptance of teen mothers by inviting them to bring their children to class and putting them in the role of educator by asking questions like, "How do you balance school and having a kid?" "Quite often," he observed, "if students see me accepting that person or that situation or whatever, they do it as well."

The most inclusive teachers I observed clearly communicated ground rules from the beginning. A science teacher at City School articulated a commonly mentioned rule: "I tell my students at the start of the year in here that I do not tolerate anybody putting anybody else down." Acceptance was conveyed through small kindnesses, which often entailed the teacher helping a student to navigate the school or some other bureaucracy. Ms. Woods wrote a letter to the provincial government requesting that it cover the special school fees for low-income students in her Town School career prep courses (field notes, 10/13/93) and sponsored an informal support group for teen mothers at Town School. When, just months shy of graduation, Rose was told she was short one course, her homeroom teacher intervened on her behalf to get her "standing granted" credit. A City School teacher volunteered to play Santa Claus at the annual party for the children of the teen mothers.

Most teen mothers at both schools perceived that many, if not all, of their teachers treated them with "respect" and "understanding." They most appreciated teachers who showed flexibility with regard to assignments and makeup work yet maintained high expectations and treated them like competent learners (e.g., Fran liked that her science teacher "assumes we'll get the answers").

In the relatively few cases where teen mothers perceived tensions in their relations with teachers, teacher resistance took several forms: ignoring or participating in hurtful comments (e.g., jokes about the profligate spending of people on welfare), refusing to give homework or makeup exams even when students' absences were excused, overgeneralizing about teen mothers, and spotlighting teen mothers in whole-class discussions of contentious issues (e.g., government social spending, abortion). These examples seemed fairly mild, though, compared with some of the stories of contempt and shunning that teen mothers told about their treatment in other schools: "I was ignored and ridiculed by teachers," recalled Elaine about her time at Midland's Academic High. "I remember one particularly clear instance in which my biology teacher attempted to get me on task by stating clearly and loudly in front of the whole class, 'Elaine, do something productive, not *reproductive!*'"

Some teacher resistance at both City and Town Schools stemmed from their perception that their workload was already too heavy. Three out of four teachers in a recent provincial survey said that "they do not have enough time to provide adequate help to students with problems" (Hume, 1996, p. D4). According to administrators, teen mothers were seen by some teachers as having "too many problems" and as creating "extra work" through their more frequent absences. Complained one City School teacher, "you're forever catching them up."

Seventy percent of the teachers and administrators interviewed at City School, and 89% of staff at Town School, said the attendance patterns of teen mothers was sometimes a "concern." About one in ten staff members at both schools worried that some of the teen mothers might be using their babies as "an excuse" not to attend school regularly.

Young parent program administrators employed several strategies aimed at least in part at cultivating teacher acceptance of teen mothers, the program that served them, or both. Because these strategies served more than one purpose, however, I will discuss them separately.

Monitoring Student Attendance and Progress

Both programs monitored student attendance and progress, although it was done in different ways, reflecting some organizational and philosophical differences between TAPP and YPP. Ms. Connell, the TAPP teacher at City School, put a high premium on identifying integrated teen mothers to their regular classroom teachers and creating opportunities for communication and early identification and resolution of problems:

> I send out an update [form] every month to each one of the teachers asking how it's going and for feedback, and all they have to do is fill in little blanks and stick it back in my box. And that keeps me updated as to how [the student-mothers] are doing, and I can keep on top of it. But I've also spoken to the school as a whole and said, "If you have any problems, please stop me in the hallway, I don't mind. Please phone me any time. Even if I look busy, bother me, because otherwise, if I don't know that something's going on, I can't do anything about it." So just constant PR and constant liaisoning. If teachers have a problem, I just make sure that it's taken care of immediately. If there's an attendance problem, I take care of it right away; it's not put on the shelf. So they know they'll get some action, they'll come back again.

This strategy of "constant liaisoning" also provided opportunities for Ms. Connell to create acceptance among resistant teachers.

Over time, TAPP staff developed a structured and well-publicized set of attendance and progress expectations. Student-mothers were expected to maintain at least 80% attendance (regardless of whether absences were excused or not) in all classes, and those in the equivalency part of the program were expected to complete a minimum of two units per month. Those whose attendance or work dipped below minimum standards in any given month were given a "verbal warning"; if they failed to reach minimum standards the following month, they were put on "written contract." Once on contract, students were required daily to have each of their teachers initial an attendance card, and Ms. Connell reviewed these cards frequently. Students who violated the terms of the written contract were transferred out of the program and City School. Of the 31 participants in TAPP during 1993–1994, 5 were asked to leave the program due to poor attendance and work habits. In a more positive vein, the names of students achieving 80–100% attendance were prominently displayed each month in the TAPP classroom, and an attendance award (named after a TAPP student who had achieved perfect attendance one year) was given to the student with the best attendance record at an annual ceremony.

TAPP's approach had its disadvantages. Not all teen mothers liked being identified to all their teachers or monitored so closely. In addition, a number of teen mothers complained that they were being held to an attendance standard when no clear minimum requirement had been set for their non-parenting peers and that they (teen mothers) faced severe consequences when they failed to meet the standard. (Administrators explained the discrepancy by saying that no students were lined up to get into City School per se, but they were waiting to get into TAPP, a comparatively expensive program where each placement needed to be used to fullest advantage.)

At Town School, where teen mothers were not identified as such on teachers' class lists, the students felt more in control; they could decide who to inform and when. Fran (age 18) explained: "Some mothers might not want their teachers to know; maybe they feel like the teachers would give them special treatment because of that. Or maybe they feel it's their job to say whether or not they have a child or whose business it is." Some teachers, however, felt strongly that they should be informed, and over time, a compromise was worked out: All counselors had a list of YPP participants, which they could share with teachers who expressed a concern about a particular student's attendance or work. Also, after two teen mothers were transferred out of Town School without anyone at YPP being informed, Ms. Long sought and eventually received "early warning" information on a "need-to-know basis" (field notes, 11/16/93). School administrators assigned a mailbox to Youth Society-YPP staff and began sharing monthly attendance records for all YPP participants as well as copies of all warning letters sent to teen mothers or their families (field notes, 9/21/94).

The system of monitoring attendance and progress was less formal at Town School and did not hold teen mothers to a different standard (although they benefited from the sick child policy, discussed below). Mechanisms for communicating attendance expectations included counseling, warnings, contracts, "round robins" (where teachers compared notes on a given student's behavior), recognition of good attendance, and "transfer out" of the school for chronic absenteeism and failure to complete school work. A U.S. General Accounting Office (1995) review of approaches that help teen mothers complete high school cited attendance monitoring and follow-up as key. (A danger of this strategy, in my view, is that it can slip from a philosophy of conveying realistic expectations and structures for achieving success into rigid formulas and coercive measures such as linking attendance to receipt of welfare.)

Providing Support and Accommodation

Teen mothers at both Town and City Schools cited the on-site day care as crucially important to their ability to handle the demands of integration. Both schools provided other kinds of support and accommodation, although these took different forms, given the different organizational structure of the two young parent programs. In the early years of City School's program, funds were not allocated for a full-time teacher (and later a full-time support worker) until it became clear that most participants would not be fully integrated. Over time, and as the inclusive schooling movement within special education gained momentum in British Columbia and beyond, Ms. Connell received more support for redefining her role as an "inclusion facilitator" and that of the support worker as a "resource locator" (Stainback, Stainback, & Ayres, 1996, p. 37).

Despite these changes, it still proved easier to provide counseling and support services to students involved in the equivalency part of TAPP. The CBO-employed coordinator of TAPP, for example, facilitated a weekly support group at a variety of community locations for interested students; fully integrated students could not usually attend because support group was held off campus and during regular school hours.

At Town School YPP program staff members were employed by Youth Society and were not based inside the school itself, which meant that nobody was ideally placed to take on the inclusion facilitator role. The YPP family support and outreach worker, however, had an office in the on-site day care; I observed her frequently offering student-mothers tips on parenting, referring them to a variety of support services available in the community, and providing informal, one-on-one counseling.

A fair number of teen mothers, particularly at City School, entered the young parent programs below grade level, short on course credits, approaching age 19 (when the Ministry of Education no longer provides schools with funding for students), or all three. Given the often rigid structure of regular schools (e.g., few opportunities to accelerate, attendance expectations, graduation requirements), teen mothers need more options.

At Town School the YPP day care was located adjacent to the Midland Alternative Education Complex. This gave YPP students the option of attending several alternative education programs. During the day care's first year of operation, one teen mother enrolled in the First Nations alternative program, and two teen mothers participated in the self-paced, individualized, computer-aided instruction program that led to a high school diploma through correspondence. The Youth Society also ran an equivalency program for women between the ages of 16 and 26 years. Like the TAPP equivalency component at City School, this program put more emphasis on teaching parenting and other "life skills" as well as providing social and emotional support. Of the 19 women enrolled in YPP-Town School during 1994–1995, 3 eventually transferred to this adult basic education program.

These supports and accommodations represent a minor redistribution of resources toward a disadvantaged group, and this was the source of some tension, particularly at City School. "The dilemma is," one teacher explained, "the program looks too good to the teachers and the public. The program looks like there's too much money and time being put into a few kids who seem to be getting a lot of extra benefits." A City School administrator made the same point, noting that "there's also a recognition that equality doesn't mean equal dollars for each situation, because some students are more at risk than others and they just need more support to level the playing field." Yet in many North American schools, "equality" is often the benchmark of what is fair, and a disadvantaged group provided with compensatory programming or "special treatment" can come to appear privileged.

Using Teen Mothers as Role Models: "Shining Stars" or "Communicators of Reality"?

Both YPP and TAPP staff used teen mothers as role models for a variety of purposes: to encourage teacher and public acceptance of the programs, to motivate students to set their sights high and work hard, and to develop self-esteem and leadership among teen mothers. The role model strategy is common in schools; holding up strong women for girls to emulate, for example, represents a major educational policy response to gender equity concerns (for critiques, see, e.g., Britzman, 1993; Coulter, 1996). Ms. Connell and Ms. Long pointed to some successes that were apparently produced by this strategy, but it was not without its tensions and contradictions.

Ms. Connell spoke of how two teen mothers on the honor roll helped to change the minds of two of City School's most "resistant teachers." One, a "shining star," found herself challenging his "very fixed ideas about people on welfare":

> He made some comments that she found very offensive, because here she was on welfare living on her own with a baby. But she was quite able to stand up and speak for herself, and I think he was thrown off track a couple of times.

This teacher "really did a lot of thinking" and eventually recommended the student for a university scholarship. This student, in turn, "paved the way for some others," according to Ms. Connell, including a popular, articulate "superachiever" (on the honor roll, in the choir, on an athletic team) named Ellen.

Clearly, Ellen (a White woman whose parents were professionals) brought a positive visibility to TAPP that some teen mothers were still basking in 2 years later (e.g., field notes, 4/12/94). But this role-model-as-shining-star strategy rests on an uncritical acceptance of the ideology of individualism, which equates success with hard work and takes little account of how race, class, gender, sexuality, and ability constrain—and indeed, help to define—success. As critical legal scholar Regina Austin (1990) notes, "Role models are not an adequate response to material conditions that limit the choices of young black [and low-income] women, both those who get pregnant and those who do not" (p. 575).

The strategy hides from view class, race, and other barriers to full school participation as well as the difficulties many teen mothers have fitting the superachiever mold. Most of the shining stars who emerged at both City and Town Schools had comparatively more family support (psychological and material) or greater access to other resources outside of school; many had been doing well in school—academically, socially, or both—prior to their pregnancies. Thus, the role model strategy does not provide a way out of the difference dilemma: According to Harvard Law School professor Martha Minow (1990), "Exceptional individuals who succeed in escaping the negative meanings of a trait they manifest make little headway in changing the institutional practices that continue to assign negative significance to that trait" (p. 80, n. 2).

In addition to being an inadequate response to the difference dilemma and to material inequalities, the shining star strategy produced some more immediate negative side effects. First, the strategy put pressure on integrated students. When a student at Town School mentioned to her counselor that a teacher had been making hurtful generalizations about teen mothers, for example, the counselor told me she had urged the student-mother to "prove that he is not correct" (field notes, 9/21/94). Thus, the burden of change was placed upon individual students rather than on the institution. Program supporters found themselves expecting stellar behavior from student-mothers because discipline problems threatened to assign them a "courtesy stigma" (Goffman, 1963) in the eyes of their peers and, more seriously, the loss of program funding.

> We have very high expectations as to their behavior within the school, because they're a little bit older, and also they do have children; they have to be more responsible. . . . [T]hey know that there's pressure on them to maintain a certain standard so that they don't embarrass themselves and other people within the program. (Ms. Connell, City School)

A second negative side effect produced by the shining star strategy amounted to dissension within the ranks of teen mothers. Ms. Connell described the "tensions" thus:

> The equivalency students think that the integrated students are more of a shining star and get more kudos because of being integrated and being so wonderful—which they do, because it is hard. And we do push it [integration] so that we can get lots of positive PR with the school.

Related to this, some teen mothers did not embody the traits of the "good student" (see Chapter 6), yet they were still admired by their peers for their pluck, even defiance against authority. There were pleasures as well as conflicts associated with being outside the norm (Britzman, 1993).

The shining star strategy also created the temptation to screen the "lesser lights" out of the program, a third negative side effect. All things being equal and given a program waiting list, a counselor explained, teachers would prefer "academic students" or "simply nice kids without a lot of emotional baggage." Agreeing that this was a danger, the TAPP coordinator told me she had to fight hard to keep Samantha, a young First Nations mother with a history of truancy, in the program. Over the year that Sheila and I were at City School, we observed Samantha making the most of her second chance, and she was cited by her peers and Ms. Connell as a role model (field notes, 1/26/94). Without some screening, however, administrators argued that high student turnover could pose problems and that it was reasonable to select those on the waiting list who might benefit most from the program.

I saw some evidence that the shining star strategy had created teacher acceptance, even among initially resistant people. A City School teacher explained:

> At first I had kind of a negative feeling about the whole program, especially being a taxpayer. . . . But over the last few years, I feel that the young ladies that have been in the program . . . have tried to do well in school. . . . I think they make good working citizens once they've finished this program.

An upper-level science teacher at Town School attributed his change of heart to the character of the teen mothers ("serious," "polite," "organized") he had come into contact with: "The ones who have been in my classes have been really nice people, and that makes it easier for me to understand the program, to buy in and to support the program, not only here at Town School but in the community as well."

Likewise, the role model strategy did seem to boost the self-esteem of teen mothers asked to do public speaking. Ms. Long, for example, told me about asking Rose to speak at a large Youth Society gathering, for which Rose received an honorarium. After the event, Rose asked Ms. Long if she would photocopy the canceled check, because her father wanted to put it in the family scrapbook (field notes, 10/4/95).

Despite these apparent successes, I found myself doubting how deep and enduring the effects of the role model strategy would be. The sense in which many (not all) people at Town and City Schools understood the term "role model" rested on a particular version of morality: that teen mothers had made a one-time mistake; that they were, by virtue of being in school, trying to redeem themselves; and that, by word or deed, they conveyed a prevention message. In essence, they were thought of as models of what not to do or what not to be.

Teen mothers emphasized, and I observed, that they did tend to play a preventive role in their schools. In a Grade 11 English class at the Town School, for example, I mentioned to students around me that I was studying the day care center that had opened at their school. This prompted a young woman to turn to the teen mother I was with and say, "I didn't know you had a baby, Anastasia." Anastasia replied, "Yeah. I have a daughter, Ashlie. She's 13 months old." The young woman joked, "I want a baby," to which Anastasia quickly and emphatically responded, "No, you don't! Believe me. I'd wait until you're 40" (field notes, 10/12/94).

Jane (age 20) spoke about the "strangeness" of the role she was frequently called upon to play at Town School:

Jane: A lot of girls aren't scared to come talk to you. [laughs] They just come right up to you and ask all these *strange* questions. I answer them and tell them how it is to have kids. . . like having sick babies [who] can't go to the day care, having all these money problems, and then they notice how hard it is. And we all tell them how rotten the fathers are [laughs]. . . . It's sort of like they're learning from our mistakes. One of the things, we're used as the examples.

Deirdre: Does that make you feel strange sometimes?

Jane: Sometimes, yeah. "Gee, leave us alone!" [laughs] But it's good, though, if they don't make the mistake, and they get that extra few years of freedom. I would rather have it that way than they get pregnant and not know what they're getting into.

Despite this prevention message, some teachers had misgivings about teen mothers as role models—either because they were too good or not good enough. In an ironic twist, a Town School teacher worried that although Rose did preach prevention ("she's definitely on our side as adults"), she was "so together" in combining her mothering and school responsibilities that the teacher feared Rose might prompt others to emulate her. In contrast, one of the teachers described earlier by Ms. Connell as having changed his mind and nominated a teen mother for a scholarship told Sheila in an interview that he had begun to have doubts about the long-term benefits of TAPP. He mentioned a teen mother who had become pregnant a second time a year or two out of high school, adding, "You'd think that after all the support and what she'd learned here that hopefully she wouldn't fall into the same situation again." Thus, the shining star strategy seems vulnerable to backlash; the occasional superachiever can be dismissed as the exception who proves the rule.

A more complex understanding of the role model strategy can be heard among the voices of some teen mothers and teachers. Elaine, the young woman who fought to remain at Midland's Academic High, wrote:

> I believe that students such as myself can do a lot of *good* for a school, in terms of being a communicator of reality: not to be epitomized as the best example of a bad example, but to demonstrate to the students that having sex *can* result in pregnancy (even when using birth control), that it *can* happen to anyone, and that it is not to be either glorified or degraded.

"Reality," according to Jane, included telling her peers "what you lose and what you gain" as a "young mother." This view complements a City

School teacher's definition of role models as "people who are dealing with a difficult situation, who are able to offer something to the people around them, who are showing some leadership."

This more realistic and open conception of who can be a role model begins to challenge the emphasis on academic achievement as the main criterion of success. Had this alternate definition held more sway, more teen mothers would have been seen as role models. Jane comes immediately to mind. I first met her in the YPP day care, where I often saw her nursing the younger of her two children during breaks in Town School's schedule. Jane, who had an easy laugh, proudly told me of her twin heritage, Gitksan and Wet'suwet'en (two Northwest Coast Nations), and of her ability to speak Shushwap. Over the course of the school year, I observed Jane to be a talented artist, an informal spokesperson for Native students, and a member of the graduation planning committee. When coping with her chronically ill son, a lack of money, and the drinking problems of her family members and ex-partner became too much for her, she had the courage to ask for temporary foster care for her children. Against the odds, Jane completed the school year but failed her provincial exam in English; this failure prevented her from receiving a high school diploma. Profoundly disappointed, Jane moved away from Midland that summer. Ms. Long hoped that one day Jane would see her tenacity as a form of success (field notes, 6/28/95).

Viewing a role model as a "communicator of reality" rather than "the best example of a bad example" or "shining star" affords more power and dignity to those called upon or choosing to act in that capacity. To the extent that role models like Jane live in poverty and face institutional racism and sexism, these inequitable material conditions "must be the subject of a sustained and forthright critique" (Austin, 1989, p. 575).

Advocating with and for Teen Mothers

Teaching teen mothers to advocate for themselves involved two substrategies: (a) helping them learn to "deflect" the negative judgments of others, and (b) teaching them about effective ways of communicating their views and concerns to those in positions of authority. Deflecting stigma, according to a TAPP Advisory Committee member, simply meant learning not to "internalize" or "personalize" discrediting remarks and actions. Some teen mothers took their cue from the ways in which staff members countered common stereotypes (discussed below), while others found the alternative discourses of visiting anti-poverty activists and First Nations mentors to be powerful resources (see Chapter 6).

When teen mothers voiced anger at a perceived injustice, staff members at both Town and City Schools usually offered to help the students brainstorm which authority figure to approach and how. Student-mothers were frequently encouraged to put their complaint or protest in writing; I heard about or saw letters that individuals had written to teachers, administrators, the manager of a grocery store, and the editors of various local publications. In most instances, staff members made editorial changes but stressed that they wanted to avoid being "the second parent" or "overprotective." Said a YPP staff person: "You can teach helplessness if you're too helpful" (field notes, 11/30/94).

Although they wanted teen mothers to learn how to advocate for themselves, staff members in different arenas also felt compelled to advocate on behalf of teen mothers. This took at least three forms. First, they countered common stereotypes and reframed the issues in both one-on-one conversations and at staff meetings and workshops. Ms. Connell described her approach, often practiced face to face with teachers:

> I think when you want to win anyone over, you have to listen to their side first, because they're not interested in listening to you at all. And so once they have given you their side, and also you get some ideas of where they're coming from . . . then [you start] just very slowly giving as much as they can absorb, which isn't very much at the beginning quite often, because they have such set views. You just want to plant a little seed.

Ms. Long did not have the day-to-day access to school staff that Ms. Connell did, but she used periodic appearances at Town School staff meetings to answer questions and address recurring misperceptions. For example, at the start of a new school year, she spoke to teachers and administrators about "why it's not the same for you as it is for teen mothers, even if you happen to be a single parent," making the following points: (a) "teen mothers don't have their own transportation," (b) "they don't have the same material resources; most of them are on income assistance," (c) "they don't have family support in many cases," and (d) "they don't have the years of experience that you do as adults, so they can't problem-solve and don't have the same emotional control as adults do" (field notes, 9/19/96).

A second form of advocacy for teen mothers involved showing program effectiveness. This ranged from highlighting "success stories" to arranging testimonials by teen mothers to publicizing relevant statistics (e.g., attendance, achievement, completion or graduation, transition to work or post-secondary institutions). Given the academic underpreparation of many teen mothers upon entry into the programs, TAPP and YPP staff also had to educate the school and wider communities about meaningful and reasonable measurements of, and expectations for, success. For example, Ms. Long discovered that a 65% attendance rate was not uncommon among new mothers attending school in British Columbia, and she told her staff they could take pride in the fact that teen mothers at Town School had exceeded this average (field notes, 2/20/95).

A third form of advocacy was lobbying for changes in school policies that disadvantage teen mothers. Ms. Long's successful efforts to get Town School administrators to accept caring for sick children as an excused absence provides the prime illustration. Depending on the philosophy of the teacher or administrator with whom they were dealing, teen mothers had more or less difficulty negotiating the consequences of absences related to sick child care. Skye (age 18), for example, was told she could not make up a test, even though the reason she missed part of it was that the day care called her out of class to attend to her feverish daughter (field notes, 11/23/94). Her teacher later explained to me in an interview:

> I accept the reason for being absent, but they've still missed the work, and I can't pay them for that day. You can use an analogy of working at a job. You had a heart attack and you're away, so I can understand it, but I'm not going to pay you for the 8 hours, though it was a very good reason.

When teachers are negotiating policy one on one with students, misunderstandings can arise, particularly when they differ by race, culture, and class from their students. Tracey (age 20 and Native) suspected some of her teachers of "prejudice" because she was "darker" than they were.

> They'd be like rude. They don't answer my questions, or if I'm absent and I go ask them for homework, they just say, "No, you get it from one of the students," and then I go to the students, and they don't know what to do either. I just feel like I'm just this totally different person, like I'm not even there, type of thing.

In the absence of a schoolwide policy excusing absences for sick child care, individual teen mothers had to ask for special treatment. When they were not accommodated by individual teachers or administrators, they had a number of reasons to refrain from complaining. Making a complaint cast them as victims and brought attention to their difference once again; it could conceivably have earned them the label "troublemaker" without necessarily bringing about any improvement in their situation (Minow, 1990, p. 92). In such circumstances, Ms. Long, as coordinator of YPP, was well placed to advocate in their stead and, indeed, played a key role in changing school policy.

Conclusion

Compared to other recent accounts of pregnant and parenting teens in school (reviewed in Chapter 1) and to stories told by participants in my study about their earlier experiences in other schools and districts, City and Town Schools could both claim success at promoting integration and inclusion. My focus on the pros and cons of various strategies that were used in this chapter emphasized that creating inclusive schools is an on-going process. There are inevitably detours, pitfalls, and tensions whenever controversial school policies are implemented, and most of the dilemmas encountered—and strategies for coping with them—at City and Town Schools were found in other young parent programs I visited or heard about.

Not all strategies were equally effective at coping with—or in some cases, transcending—the dilemma of difference. Norm-challenging institutional practices were superior to both individual adaptations and isolated, one-on-one arrangements between a teacher and her colleague or between a teacher and a student. Minow has suggested that broad "[s]trategies for remaking difference include challenging and transforming the unstated norm used for comparisons, taking the perspective of the traditionally excluded or marginal group, disentangling equality from its attachment to a norm that has the effect of unthinking exclusion, and treating everyone as though he or she were different" (1990, p. 16).

Minow's categories provide a typology of ways to move beyond the difference dilemma facing school-age mothers. In Table 5.1, I have illustrated each category with examples of strategies discussed in this chapter or elsewhere in the book and have provided some suggestions that are beyond the power of any one school or district to implement but that are nevertheless relevant to destigmatizing teen mothers and creating inclusive schools.

The suggestions that flow from the idea of broadening the definition of difference range from those that are commonly done now to the more visionary and global (Table 5.1, col. 1). The former, such as locating young parent programs in schools where other special programs already exist, runs the risk of a hierarchy developing among the programs, based

Table 5.1 Strategies for Including and Destigmatizing Teen Mothers

Broaden the definition of difference (make more traits relevant to the distribution of a particular benefit)	Consider the perspective of the marginalized group	Broaden the definition of who is the same	Treat everyone as though they were different (unique)
Examples:	Examples:	Examples:	Example:
requests from teen mothers that parents traveling with small children be given priority bus seating	advocate on behalf of teen mothers; challenge stereotyping, policies that disadvantage teen mothers	recognize that many students (and school staff members) need flexibility about attendance, workload	locate program in a school with a diverse student body where diversity is valued
locate program in school with numerous special programs	teach teen mothers to advocate for themselves; act with teen mothers to bring about needed changes; include teen mothers in governance	recognize that all students would benefit from a curriculum that addresses their social, emotional, and intellectual needs	
define teen mothers as citizens rather than non-taxpayers	provide opportunities for other students to interact with teen mothers	recognize that all students would benefit from inclusive pedagogy	
broaden eligibility for income support, child care services	provide on-site child care services		

on each one's adherence to or deviance from the competitive academic curriculum (see Kelly, 1996). The latter challenges two unstated norms: (a) that high school students do not have family obligations that will interfere with their school attendance and work, and (b) that high school students are neither taxpayers nor adults with full citizenship rights. Feminist, anti-racist, anti-poverty, and youth rights activists have all proposed policies that would, for example, move in the direction of social democratic states such as Sweden and Norway and would broaden eligibility for income support and child care services. Closer to home, the Quebec government announced an ambitious plan to expand and integrate publicly financed day care centers into the school system, beginning with children living in poverty and gradually extending "to all families on a geared-to-income basis" (Seguin & Unland, 1996, p. A4).

Consideration of the perspective of the marginalized group—in this case teen mothers—generates a range of suggestions, all of which had been tried at both Town and City Schools (see Table 5.1, col. 2). Opportunities for other students to hear from teen mothers and get to know them can potentially dispel fears and challenge stereotypes. As their peers learn about what they have in common with teen mothers as well as the particular challenges of teen mothers, empathy can grow. Of course, for this to happen, teachers and administrators must convey that individual and group diversity in general contribute positively to the classroom and wider community. (See Brantlinger, 1997, p. 435, for an excellent summary of "beliefs that undergird inclusive schooling.")

One strategy that might have fit here (Table 5.1, col. 2) that I have left out is using teen mothers as role models. As often practiced in schools, the role model strategy fails to challenge or complicate the idea that if individuals simply work hard enough, they will succeed—regardless of context. In contrast, if the experiences of teen mothers were explored in the classroom and if institutional practices that both enable and obstruct success were examined and understood, then teen mothers would be less likely to be stigmatized. Taking to heart the interests of some of the least advantaged students might also lead to reconstructing the mainstream of schooling.

The most likely path to such reconstruction lies in broadening the definition of who is the same (Table 5.1, col. 3). Students at City and Town Schools with young children needed flexibility with regard to attendance expectations, pacing of instruction, nature of assignments, and workload. But in both schools, they were far from alone in their need for greater flexibility. Some students were living independently, either with social assistance or away from their reserve (reservation). Still others were working long hours, either to supplement their family's income or to care for younger siblings. Still others were sometimes needed by immigrant parents to serve as translators in important matters affecting the family. Some school staff members, although relatively materially advantaged, also found it a struggle to meet family and work obligations around the rigid school timetable.

Besides changing the timetable, improved flexibility would mean changing classroom practices to accommodate heterogeneous groups of students. (Clearly, handpicking teachers to work with teen mothers does not challenge more traditional pedagogy, which many students, not just teen mothers, find alienating.) "Classroom practices that have been reported as supporting inclusive education include cooperative learning, activity-based learning, mastery learning, use of instructional technology, multi-level instruction, and peer support and tutoring programs" (Lipsky & Gartner, 1996, p. 781).

In addition, broadening the definition of who is the same as teen mothers would lead to a reconsideration of the competitive academic curriculum. By competitive academic curriculum, I mean the university preparatory courses in language, mathematics, social studies, and science, which derive their high status from their links to the society's wider system of rewards. Planners of young parent programs often assume that teen mothers need classes in parenting and "life skills." More than one staff member involved in what was seen as the non-academic aspects of the curriculum wondered, as a health educator put it, whether "these young women had more opportunities to come out of this [young parent] education [program] as better rounded people than your average student going through an ordinary schooling experience." Yet exposure to this curriculum usually meant segregation in a special classroom. Recognizing that *all* students would benefit from a curriculum that addressed them as multidimensional people with social and emotional as well as intellectual needs would help to challenge the hegemony of the academic curriculum, narrowly defined.

Treating everyone as though they were different (Table 5.1, col. 4) appears to be the most utopian means for generating ways out of the difference dilemma. The idea appeals to the liberal notion that we are all unique beings. Yet Minow notes the apparent limits, including the propensity of humans to think in categories and the issue of finite resources (1990).

The gap between the vision and current school practices remains substantial, as passionately noted by a special education teacher at City School:

The biggest problem I have with integration and public, and even teachers', perceptions is, they say, "Well, these kids are different, they're special, they have different needs," and my biggest complaint or belief or whatever is that *every-body* is different, everybody has needs, and everybody's different needs need to be met. And I'm sorry if you think that this is a big burden for you, but we really need to be more flexible. The high schools are doing such a poor job for *every-*

body, not just teen moms or special education kids. We need to be flexible and provide for people's needs, and we're not doing that.

Locating the young parent programs in schools with diverse student bodies did appear to contribute to a comparatively accepting climate for teen mothers at Town and City Schools. Yet in cases where too many axes of difference exist between groups, it remains difficult to convert prejudice into tolerance, let alone respect (cf. Minow, 1997).

Notes

1. Private schools can simply expel young women whose pregnancies become known to authorities. The Midland Christian School had such a policy and acted on it during the time of my study. The principal later explained to me that in most cases of "premarital sex," he felt that sending the students a message that this was "wrong behavior" outweighed "teaching them about God's forgiveness" (field notes, 9/23/94).

Chapter 6

Therapeutic Haven Versus Real-World Microcosm: How Citizenship Challenges the Dichotomy

City School staff members found themselves steering between two guiding visions for the Teen-Age Parents Program. One guiding image of the program was that of a *microcosm of the "real world,"* where the student and future worker identities took precedence and teen mothers were expected to give birth, return to school, and adjust to the status quo. The other image of the program was that of a therapeutic *haven*, where the mother identity took precedence and students were provided a safe space, albeit sometimes at the expense of the confidence and skills they needed to succeed in the wider world. These visions coexisted in tension with one another.

The microcosm-haven tension was not unique to City School. In fact, all secondary schools grapple with it when they simultaneously attempt to prepare youth to take on adult responsibilities and nurture their intellectual and social potential in a sheltered environment. Yet the tension was particularly evident at City School because of the bifurcated structure of its Teen-Age Parents Program: some teen mothers were fully integrated into regular classes (like all teen mothers at Town School were), while just over half at any one time spent all or most of their time in the TAPP classroom. For this reason, I will concentrate in this chapter on my observations and interviews at City School.

The haven and real-world microcosm visions are best thought of as ideal types representing opposite ends of a continuum of programmatic approaches. The haven model focuses on the "special" needs of pregnant and mothering girls and risks stigmatizing them, while the real-world microcosm model often fails to support students adequately and risks losing them. Haven and microcosm can also describe differences in teaching philosophies, and thus the tension between them can arise within a separate program or across an entire school.

The haven vision rests on the idea of difference, in this case pregnancy and motherhood. One of the clearest expressions of this perspective came from the principal of a high school in Pacifica, who had this to say about teen mothers:

> I do not see them being reintegrated into regular high school. These kids are no longer teenagers with the same carefree attitudes and sense of themselves—they are totally changed people. They are women who have children, and they sense that difference themselves; it's they who would not be able to reintegrate.

Based on her perception of teen mothers as "totally changed people," she recommended that such students transfer to City School where they could support each other and learn "mothering skills." Thus, in the haven vision, the mother identity was frequently paramount because it marked a set of special needs.

Conversely, the microcosm vision rests on the idea of sameness or commonality with other students. According to a non-parenting, female student at City School, teen mothers were "just normal human beings who had babies, and you have to accept them as that and not treat them like, 'don't touch me with a ten-foot pole' type of thing." This assertion of the essential normality of teen mothers underpinned a belief that they should be fully integrated into the mainstream. In the microcosm vision, the student identity—and its close affiliate, the future worker identity— were paramount.

The haven-microcosm dichotomy I observed at City School was an enduring one, one that I have seen in many such young parent programs, and I doubt there is a way to resolve that tension once and for all. But what if each approach—or better, the two in combination—made an enlarged notion of democratic citizenship a more central curricular theme?

By this I mean putting more emphasis on the idea of collective empowerment and fostering in people the understandings and dispositions necessary to critique the existing society with the goal of improving it. This conception departs from the understandings of citizenship prevalent in both the haven and microcosm approaches. In the therapeutic haven, the emphasis was on personal development; it was implied that a healthy society would *follow* from creating well-adjusted individuals. In the real-world microcosm, the emphasis was on promoting individual conformity with mainstream norms and social practices; it was implied that society was basically just.

In contrast to these individualist notions of citizenship, a social change-oriented conception would not gloss over the deeply embedded economic, political, and social barriers circumscribing the life choices of TAPP participants. It would, instead, address them as valued members of a larger polity with rights and entitlements. It would not neglect their obligations as citizens but would define such obligations more broadly than the achievement of economic self-sufficiency. It would recognize interdependence as the hallmark of their lives and the importance of developing collective identities as the basis for effective organizing for social change.

Teen-Age Parents Program as Haven

The parts of the Teen-Age Parents Program most associated with the haven vision included the day care (located on campus, adjacent to City School), the support group, and the TAPP classroom. Not coincidentally, these were the parts of the program most directly influenced by the Community-Based Organization, which operated the day care and provided a program coordinator, Carol Roberts, who also facilitated weekly support group meetings.

Carol, as the program participants called her, agreed with Ms. Connell on the importance of integration into regular classes for "teen moms who can handle it." But she was clear that young women who had been out of school and were coming back needed options:

> It's really important for them to have the safety of a classroom, where they are with other young moms, where they get that support. Teens—well, like any of us really—like to not always travel alone and be sort of the one teen parent around. And I think they get a tremendous amount of support from one another: moral support, emotional support, real basic sort of needs met. And I think the same thing happens in support group. It's a place where people can talk about, "Oh my God, my child didn't sleep last night, and I was up all night. How do you get these kids to bed?"—to share that kind of information with one another. There aren't many places where they can do that without anticipating judgment.

Ms. Connell agreed on the importance of a "safe space." To this end, at the beginning of the year, she worked with program participants to formulate rules, such as a prohibition on swearing or "put-downs" in the TAPP classroom. Each day in the classroom began with "circle," where everyone present formed into a circle and had the option of relating a recent experience or passing to the next person. According to Ms. Connell, circle provided the opportunity

> for someone to share their experiences of their child growing up, to meet some-
> one who wants to hear about what's important in their life. They can share those
> experiences with other people, and they get a lot of support within the classroom
> from each other. They're not so isolated.

Yvonne Dalton, TAPP's youth worker, stressed that teen mothers needed "safety," "stability," a feeling of accomplishment, and contact with others "in a similar situation."

Sharing personal experiences with others, safe space, mutual support: these themes are common to both feminism and therapy. Yet as the haven vision was enacted, feminist principles sometimes came into contradiction with therapeutic practices; at other times, they fused informally into what Jillian Sandell (1996) calls "therapeutic feminism." Therapeutic feminism rests on the "belief that society per se *cannot* be changed and it is futile for us to think that it can be. We have control over only our own individual acts of transformation" (Sandell, 1996, p. 23).

To varying degrees, TAPP staff espoused the belief that many, if not all, teen mothers had special "emotional needs" and were coping with issues of codependency, addictions, and sexual abuse. Their belief was buttressed not only by their direct experiences with teen mothers but by experts. For example, psychologist Judith Musick asserts:

> The teenage mothers I know are a heterogeneous group, yet they share certain
> common qualities that cut across geographic, ethnic, and, to some extent, eco-
> nomic lines. Chief among these qualities is a profound psychological neediness,
> the legacy of severe and often protracted emotional deprivation, beginning early
> and continuing through the adolescent years. (1993, p. 100)

TAPP thus aimed to address the emotional needs of teen mothers. Further reinforcing their identity as therapeutic subjects, teen mothers were required by the Ministry of Social Services to receive "life skills" and parenting education as well as emotional support from TAPP, a condition agreed to by the Community-Based Organization (CBO) in exchange for an extra day care subsidy extended only to "high-risk" populations (field notes, 2/8/94).

The term "life skills" was widely used and expansive. At the time of my study, Dale-Johnson (herself a teacher in a program similar to TAPP) surveyed nearly every young parent program in British Columbia on the meaning of the term and derived this inventory:

Content in lifeskills courses may include such varied topics as relationships and mental health, anger/stress/time or money management, goal setting, communication skills, child care and development, alcohol and drug education, parenting skills, personal health, eating disorders, first aid, abuse issues, conflict resolution, nutrition and cooking, childsafe, crafts, recreation (tennis, parent and child swimming), child custody issues, making wills, car maintenance, community resource exploration, career awareness and more. For a large percentage of students in these programs, there is a *critical need for intensive restorative and therapeutic work* [italics added] in many of these areas. (1995, p. 30)

TAPP's life skills curriculum closely mirrored this inventory. During the 1993–1994 school year, for example, guest speakers addressed such topics as health issues that affect young parents and their babies; drug abuse and rehabilitation; family services and financial assistance; social assistance regulations; laws pertaining to child custody, sexual harassment, and sexual assault; dating violence and battered women support services; child abuse and neglect; and job training options. The guest speaker series was part of TAPP Family Life, a 3-hours-per-week, noncredit course; other features included a weekly class with the public health nurse, a weekly support group meeting, occasional craft projects, discussions about group dynamics, and special events (e.g., seeing a movie together).

Many of these topics and activities spoke to the young women's lives in all their complexity. The life skills curriculum acknowledged the reality of violence and abuse and the importance of interpersonal relations. By contrast, these subjects were largely ignored in most regular City School classes, an ironic fact given that advocates for the microcosm approach criticized the haven vision for not reflecting, or preparing participants for, the "real world."

Yet I detected some dangers associated with the therapeutic dimension of the haven model. An informal criterion for success appeared to be a willingness to take the "talking cure" of therapy. In the course of my formal interview with Yvonne Dalton, for example, I began to notice how she spoke about students she considered problematic. Samantha was "not willing to open up. She's a closed book, and she doesn't want anyone to know what's inside, who she really is. . . . But part of learning is opening up and sharing." For her part, Samantha volunteered to me in her usual laconic style that "Yvonne just asks so many questions."

Bonnie was another "closed book" to Yvonne. Bonnie was fully integrated and about midway through the school year unenrolled herself from TAPP; she did not like having to report to the TAPP classroom before the start of every school day, and she felt support group was not useful:

I found that I didn't have a lot to say, and for 2 hours in the afternoon every Tuesday, I could find a hundred better things to do academically than sit around on a couch and talk about problems that I don't really have and that don't really bother me.

Commented Yvonne: "We couldn't get Bonnie to connect [with TAPP]. She didn't want that closeness. . . . If they can remain at that level where they never get intimate, then they don't ever have to share their deep troubles or their worries." Yet Bonnie's portrait of herself as untroubled jibed with what a number of her teachers said about her. One described her as "a super-enthusiastic student," while another said that compared to other TAPP participants, Bonnie was "stronger, has more money, [and] has a wider circle of friends." Still a third teacher painted her as "a happy individual—I've never seen her crying or upset."

While some teen mothers liked the counseling aspects of TAPP, others felt, like Bonnie, that they did not have "deep troubles" to reveal. Still other teen mothers did not feel safe revealing too much personal information; they did not want to make themselves vulnerable to breeches of confidentiality. A student representative to the TAPP Advisory Committee noted in a meeting: "There is a fear that your child could get taken away" (field notes, 1/19/94). Their concern about being monitored through the program was well founded: Yvonne's position was funded by the Ministry of Social Services. She was in regular contact with social workers assigned to the teen mothers and obliged to report any hints of child abuse and neglect.

Thus, the haven model offered peril as well as promise. How to provide support, for example, to teen mothers who had been sexually abused without spotlighting them or treating them like therapeutic subjects? As I discuss below, the history of TAPP shows that its place on the margins of mainstream schooling has allowed room for alternative curricula and pedagogy to emerge. As expert discourses have been translated into social services, however, TAPP's history also reveals a tendency toward normalizing the identities of the participants as mothers, students, future workers, and citizens (Fraser, 1989), whereby efforts are made, in the words of one teacher, to "return" them to "a respectable way of life."

Mother as Full-Time Caregiver?

The normative (White, middle-class) view of mothering in North America holds that the good mother is someone who always puts her child's needs above all else, meaning, for example, making sacrifices in order to provide full-time, stay-at-home caregiving. In the 1990s, this ideal has become elusive because the majority of mothers are employed for pay outside the home. Yet it continues to shape behavior, for example, when women choose part-time over full-time jobs or prepare for careers that pay less but offer flexibility in order to accommodate continued primary responsibility for child care. Thus, the White, middle-class ideology of mothering still "categorizes employment as oppositional to mothering" (Glenn, 1994, p. 16).

"Developmental texts create a view of 'normal' mothering in which mothers are constructed as sensitive and child-centered[,] and taking their own needs into account is selfish and 'unmotherly'" (Woollett & Phoenix, 1996, p. 98). The good mother is always there for her child, always subordinating her own purposes and desires to those of her child. Feminists have called this the ideology of "exclusive" and "intensive" mothering (Glenn, 1994; Hays, 1996).

The haven approach within TAPP both maintained the ideology of exclusive, intensive mothering and challenged it. Those City School teachers most committed to the idea that teen mothers should be learning first and foremost about parenting and "home management skills" were also those most likely to espouse a normative view of the good mother. A consumer education teacher, for instance, said in an interview: "I really feel children need their mothers (that's a personal bias) and especially from ages one to six. They're well looked after over there [at the school-based day care], but . . . I worry sometimes that there is not enough of the bond with the mother."

The haven part of the program was also gender segregated, which seems to have encouraged a more therapeutic feminist focus and may have inadvertently reinforced the idea that mother-child bonding was all important. Although TAPP was open to young fathers, the program to date had only served teen mothers. Some reasons for this were beyond the program's control: most of the men who fathered children born to the teen mothers were older, sometimes no longer in their teens, and they were often out of school.[1] In addition, roughly half of the teen mothers were no longer romantically involved with or living with the men who fathered their children, and the mothers had retained custody of the children.[2]

Yet the absence of young men in TAPP was partly the by-product of the program's structure, namely the need to balance the number of student-parents in the educational part of the program with the number of infants and toddlers in the day care part. On one occasion, for example, there was room to accept one baby into the day care but not enough room to accept both student-parents into the TAPP classroom. In this rare instance of a couple wanting to apply together, they were told that only one could be accepted for financial reasons, and eventually neither applied (field notes, 5/9/94).

Because of the therapeutic component of the program, it was hard for TAPP staff members to imagine the presence of teen fathers in the classroom. Said one: "I don't know how they would manage in a room full of women; it might be very complicated." Perhaps most complicated would be how to address the issue of male violence against women. According to Ms. Connell, TAPP participants were "quite often badly treated by these men" who had fathered their children. Her strategy for helping them recognize and leave violent relationships was to appeal to the young women's new identity as mother:

> I quite often get girls that when they first come into the program go, "Well, it doesn't matter, I've been on the street, I've been used by this guy and this guy and this guy and this guy. I've done this, I've done that, who cares anymore?" [I say to them] "You should care. You've got a child, your child cares, you're his mom. And regardless of anything else, you are his mom."

Because she viewed the experiences of teen mothers through the lens of abuse, Ms. Connell sometimes constructed them as passive victims. "They talk," she told me, "about why they let themselves become sexually active." This statement assumes a lack of autonomous sexual desire on the part of teen mothers and inadvertently feeds into a model of mothering that ignores the sexuality of the mothers. Missing generally in TAPP discussions about men's violence against women was an understanding of how economic and social structures help to create situations in which abuse occurs.

The dominant ideology of mothering was also maintained by the official emphasis on parenting education. Many City School staff members supported this goal. In stressing the importance of a parenting class for all teen mothers, one teacher stated that "a *teen* mom is almost like an incomplete thought." Teen mothers often intuited that they were being positioned as inadequate mothers when they were told they needed a parenting program, and they resisted this assumption. Many said they found the "family management" texts frequently boring, abstract, and out of touch with what goes on in real families. Most said they preferred learning how to mother informally, from each other and by interacting with family members and early childhood educators in the day care.

Over the years, early childhood educators in TAPP have moved away from overt, didactic teaching of "parenting skills" to a pedagogy of mothering based on informal observation, participation, and what the coordinator of the day care called a "partnership" between caregivers and mothers. Explained another caregiver, "We don't sit there and *lecture*. We don't set ourselves up as the people who know everything. So I think that that offers an opportunity, then, for them to ask questions." Before and after school and during lunch, each TAPP participant was, to cite another caregiver, "welcomed as a mother" into the day care.

The caregivers to whom Sheila and I spoke agreed that most of the TAPP participants were doing "a wonderful job of parenting": they were praised for being "dedicated," "focused," and able to "communicate really well about where their children are developmentally and about what their children might need during the day." The head caregiver contrasted their overall success as mothers with their status as students. In the school system, students were constantly being evaluated and not always measuring up, whereas in the day care, "we've seldom had anyone that I didn't think was doing really well":

> We have this relationship with their children, and they can see the care we give. And we tell them about what the child did, and they can see the enthusiasm and the caring *we* have that we *share* together. They don't get that at the school, do they? I mean, not unless they're getting *great marks* and the teacher is saying, "Great!"

In the competitive academic environment that is school, relatively few students are recognized as excellent, and only some will go on to higher education and the high-status work that an advanced degree makes possible. By contrast, in the TAPP day care, the message was that everyone could be or become an excellent mother. Explained the head caregiver:

> A baby is so strange when it's very young, and they [the new mothers] are very nervous, just like I was when I was a new parent. I can hear staff just now in my mind, encouraging, "No, you're doing just the right thing, keep that up, that's really good. You can see he's responding to that." So, encouragement to do the things they're doing now, the things that are working, and then if they aren't working, they're asking questions, so you can say, "Well, have you tried this, or have you tried that?" So they're bound to improve, because they're at it all the time.

Although the day care part of the haven certainly drew on and reinforced the identities of TAPP participants as mothers, its informal, respectful, and collective approach to teaching and learning how to parent seemed at odds with the tenets of the ideology of exclusive, intensive mothering. Teen mothers said they appreciated the "break" they got from knowing their children were well cared for close by while they attended classes, and they liked that their children were "learning to interact with other kids."

The haven orientation in TAPP helped to create solidarity among many of the teen mothers at City School. Noted Amber, "All my friends are in the same situation and have the same problems, so we can help each other deal with things." Whether out of a sense of shared interests, protection against judgments, or both, teen mothers at City School tended to band together (in contrast to what I observed at Town School). "Because they're in a group, they travel together around the school," remarked Carol Roberts, TAPP's coordinator. "That does give them more sense of power, a bit more sense of their right to be who they are and to be vocal about that in a way that 25 years ago was not possible."

For others, the mother identity still marked them as an "outcast" and made it difficult for them to assume the (integrated) student identity. At the annual review of TAPP, Janice revealed her fear about leaving the safety of the haven:

> I am afraid to be integrated because I think every other student is a student, but I am a mom. A lot of people ask, "How is it to be a mom? Do you regret having your baby?" So many stupid questions! So that's why I'm struggling with integrating. In my Spanish culture, they put you down so much, so I wish they could accept that I have a baby, but they can't, and they treat you very bad, so I am staying in the [TAPP] classroom.

Yvonne Dalton inadvertently fed Janice's fear by commenting that Jasmine (an integrated student admired by Janice) also "has the pressure of so many [regular class] assignments," while a visiting Advisory Committee member (herself a woman of color) addressed Janice's fear and gave her a coping strategy: "Let your attitude change their attitudes" (field notes, 5/26/94). While encouraging, this advice shares the weaknesses of the role model strategy (analyzed in Chapter 5) and fails to directly challenge institutional and cultural barriers to integration. The haven-microcosm tension had revealed itself once again.

Student as "Needy"

TAPP staff members tended to see the participants working inside the TAPP classroom as "needy" students, whereas those who were integrated into regular classes were "shining stars" or "high functioning." The needier students required more life skills, whereas the high-functioning students could concentrate on academic courses. Thus, fully integrated students were exempt from attending weekly support group meetings.

Within the TAPP classroom, the good student was measured by her attendance, punctuality, and productivity. By this measure, many of the TAPP participants had been "borderline" students before they got pregnant. Three quarters had either left school or were chronically truant prior to pregnancy. This overrepresentation of formerly disengaged students has its roots partly in the demography of who becomes a teen mother and partly in the policies that shaped TAPP at its inception.

In the early years, the Ministry of Social Services (then called Human Resources) would only fund day care for young mothers on welfare, and it often rejected social assistance for teens living independently unless they could show that their parents had been abusive. As a result, the first TAPP cohort included a disproportionate number of teen mothers who had been abused and were living on the streets. One month into the first school year—on the heels of a physical fight between two teen mothers and as a result of overall poor attendance—a counselor assigned to TAPP recommended a switch in emphasis from full integration to what she called the "closed classroom" (i.e., the TAPP classroom).

This counselor estimated that two thirds of the teen mothers exhibited traits of the "unsuccessful" student, namely poor attendance, "weak home support," "low academic ability," and "no apparent immediate goals for attending school." She recommended, therefore, that they be scheduled for self-paced, individualized instruction under the guidance of one teacher and that emphasis "be placed on teaching study skills, goal setting, and life skills."

Although funding restrictions have since eased and TAPP has become more selective in its recruitment, City School teachers in 1994 still perceived a significant proportion of teen mothers as having learning and emotional or behavioral disabilities. These perceptions lay behind their support for the bifurcated structure of TAPP. Teachers overwhelmingly favored the integration of teen mothers in principle, but to the extent that teen mothers were underprepared academically or had learning disabilities, teachers favored an alternative setting that, in essence, operated as a lower track. A math teacher put it this way:

They're not lepers. *They have babies!* This is such a big deal? I mean, they should be separated from the population because they have babies? Who are we kidding! We know that many of these kids that we teach are sexually active—they just didn't get caught. Now, one of the things that I have noticed is certainly the academic abilities of these girls is much lower, by and large. And I think it's very important that those are pulled up *before* they are integrated, because who needs more failure?

This perspective seems reasonable, until one considers that the City School students who were not teen mothers exhibited a wide range of academic abilities and preparedness. Many of these students had academic abilities no higher than those of the teen mothers, yet they were integrated into the mainstream. Seen in this light, the teacher's comment can be read as a rationale for TAPP as a lower track, a safety valve for an overtaxed "regular" system rather than a safety net (see Kelly, 1993a).

For their part, the teen mothers in the TAPP classroom often laid claim to the good student identity less as something meaningful on its own terms and more as a counter to various stigmas: namely, "stupid slut," "welfare mom," "dropout," "neglectful mother," and "person who makes bad choices." Isabel, for example, told me, "I want my education to get a proper job and to support *my* kid without being on welfare." Asked Ashley rhetorically, "If you don't get your own education, then what is your kid going to learn? You can't teach them."

According to some TAPP participants, when they failed to live up to the image of the good student, staff members drew on the stereotypes associated with the bad student in an attempt to discipline them. It was well known that Nicole, for example, had a poor attendance record, due at least in part to her caring for her infant son after he had undergone a series of minor operations. The day before her formal interview, Nicole reported that Yvonne had admonished her, saying: "I don't see the point of me paying taxes for you not showing up for school."

In one sense, the TAPP classroom was a proving ground, and if participants showed they were ready, they could enter regular classes. The schoolwork itself was seen as a pale imitation of what went on in integrated classes. A number of students at the annual review said that the individualized, self-paced format was "boring" (field notes, 5/26/94). Kevanna explained in her formal interview:

There's like no lesson to it. Usually in integrated classes they give a lesson before they give work, right? So I thought Ms. Connell would give a lesson the week before, but then everyone works on their own out of a book and does worksheets. . . . I do this *all* day, just writing and reading this book. It's like, "Oh, give me a break!"

From the outside looking in, the TAPP classroom seemed "soft" and less rigorous. Amber, a partially integrated student, said, "It's harder to go to normal classes than to sit here [in the TAPP classroom]. Teachers don't care if you have a kid. It's a lot harder. Here, you get a little slack. She's [indicating Ms. Connell] still tough. But it's more at your own pace" (field notes, 5/26/94). From the inside, a number of non-integrated students argued that the haven protected them from themselves, that is, the temptation of getting in with the "wrong crowd" and returning to old habits like "skipping school."

For Jasmine, "being in the TAPP classroom reminds me that I'm a mother" with heavy, adult responsibilities. "It tells me, I'm a mother and I'm studying for a reason: to graduate." With many of the social aspects of learning stripped away, schooling in the haven came to be seen mainly as a means to an end, rather than the site of something inherently meaningful or fun. "Before I thought of school as a place to learn, take your time, have fun, hang out, skip," explained Nicole. "Now 'cause I have the baby and I want to do a lot of things with him, it's different, like I'm more rushed. I want to get everything done with: get an education for a career so I can get a job, save up to put a down payment on a house, and stuff like that."

Worker as Deferred Identity

Given that in the haven approach the student role was frequently overshadowed by the mother role, what was being conveyed about worker identity was unclear. To the extent that TAPP participants in the haven were constructed as poor students, their prospects for paid work seemed less bright. To the extent that they were constructed as therapeutic subjects, they were thought to have important emotional needs that would require addressing before they could (or should) think about work.

In the microcosm approach, academic achievement was stressed in terms of helping students obtain jobs; in the haven approach, academic achievement was seen as important to building self-esteem. A former TAPP teacher explained: "I always felt that if a student got a Grade 10 certificate, that's as good as any counseling in the world—that that makes them feel very good about themselves."

Unlike many of her colleagues, this teacher defined success for TAPP participants more broadly than their eventual economic self-sufficiency, including whether they were "happy with their lives":

On occasion I used to think, even if they're still on welfare, if they're making the best of it, if they're making a good life for their kid, if they're eating well and [are] healthy—so they're on welfare. . . . It [success] may not necessarily be being off welfare, depending on what stage they're at. If their kids are at home, if they're little, maybe they shouldn't even try to get them off welfare.

I asked this teacher if she felt she could voice these views to her colleagues, and she replied, "No, not very many of them anyway, a few. . . . I think being a mother is a full-time job, and if you're the only parent, it's tough."

Citizen as Personally Empowered Individual or Social Change Agent

The path toward citizenship means many things to different people. In the haven vision, it took on two specific meanings, one dominant, the other present but subordinate. The prevailing meaning was personal development, which flowed from the therapeutic, life skills curriculum discussed above.

The second meaning of forming citizenship focused on collective empowerment and the need for social change. It acknowledged that, historically, certain groups have been excluded from full citizenship, including women, Aboriginal people, and the poor, and that as a society, we are still struggling with the legacy of these exclusions. In this conception, a good citizen would rightly be concerned about social problems such as sexism, racism, and poverty, seek to understand more about them, and take social action.

In this section, I tease out the elements of the haven approach that were suggestive of this more subordinate meaning of citizenship and contrast it with the personal development meaning. In contrast to most City School staff members, I conclude that the citizen-as-social-change-agent perspective offered the best chance to TAPP participants to avoid self-blame for political, social, and economic problems beyond their individual control and to develop a constructive critique.

There was not much explicit talk about teen mothers as citizens in the haven part of TAPP, although the CBO had attempted to include them in the ongoing evaluation of the program in two ways. First, two TAPP participants served on the Advisory Committee, which met six times during 1993–1994; the non-student members often invited the views of the students and, from what I observed, listened respectfully to their responses. Second, the Advisory Committee organized mid-term and annual reviews of the program, which involved all TAPP participants in both written and verbal evaluation of the various components of TAPP.

TAPP staff, as I discussed in Chapter 5, made an effort to teach teen mothers to advocate for themselves, usually as individuals. Occasionally, TAPP participants were exposed to alternative discourses and directed to outside resources that addressed them as members of disadvantaged groups. International Women's Day was celebrated (field notes, 3/8/94). The feminist issue that interested TAPP participants most, judging from informal conversations and the books they sought out to read in the TAPP classroom (e.g., Say "No!" to Violence: Voices of Women Who Experience Violence), was violence against women.

Nearly one in three of the TAPP participants during 1993–1994 described their ethnicity as Native or as Native and White, and TAPP staff encouraged them to join the First Nations Club at City School, sponsored by a district-employed First Nations support worker. Three did so during 1993–1994. According to the sponsor, the club participated in activities aimed at raising awareness about cultural identity and racism. The previous year, two Native teen mothers attended a conference in New Mexico with Native students from around North America; they returned feeling "empowered," according to Yvonne Dalton, and made a full oral report to fellow TAPP students (field notes, 6/9/93). Material on restoring Aboriginal self-determination (e.g., Liberating Our Children, Liberating Our Nations) was available in the TAPP classroom.

Perhaps the most powerful alternative discourse TAPP participants were exposed to was that of an anti-poverty activist, who was invited to speak to them about "welfare rights." The speaker, a middle-aged White woman dressed casually and wearing a peace sign necklace and lots of rings and charm bracelets, addressed us (eleven students, Sheila, Yvonne, and myself) in a direct and humorous style. She encouraged the TAPP participants to see themselves as citizens, with a right to welfare; they were doing valuable work as mothers and, by working hard in school, they had the potential to become even better mothers, wage earners, or both.

The anti-poverty activist alluded to her organization's belief that high levels of unemployment and low wages are not inevitable. Her talk was peppered with statements like "Make the system work for you" and "Power moves downward in the welfare bureaucracy; you have upward power." The speaker urged the young women on welfare to resist viewing themselves as stigmatized recipients of public charity:

> Welfare is not charity; it's not something for nothing. It's like medicare [Canada's universal health care system]. With medicare, you're in the hospital because you need to be there. It's the same with welfare. Welfare is about your well-being; it's to help you be well—socially, physically, and economically. (field notes, 11/1/93)

Most of her talk consisted of "rules" to follow when dealing with the welfare bureaucracy and areas where the Ministry of Social Services could not legally dictate the behavior of welfare recipients. In contrast to the conventional wisdom at City School, the anti-poverty activist emphasized the present-day rights of the TAPP participants, which were not something off in the future that they had to earn somehow. She addressed the students present as citizens, not adults-in-training. The teen mothers with whom I spoke, especially those who were receiving social assistance, described the presentation as "excellent" and the speaker as an inspiring "social activist." Karry-Ann commented, "I feel more powerful now" (field notes, 11/1/93), and months later, Karry-Ann noted in our formal interview: "Everyone should know as much as her. The welfare system couldn't screw people around then."

In the months following this talk, a few students confided to Sheila and me their feelings of anger that time allotted to TAPP Family Life class could not be spent learning "social activism." Samantha and Jasmine were upset that, instead, they were learning "childish" craft projects (they described as particularly "meaningless" a project in which they were asked to create and decorate name cards for themselves; field notes, 1/19/94). Recalling how inspired she had been by the anti-poverty activist, Jasmine asserted at lunch one day that it was important for students to learn "to stand up for their rights," and Karry-Ann and Mina agreed (field notes, 1/26/94).

Thus, TAPP participants were occasionally exposed to people, literature, and organizations that offered an alternative, more participatory model of citizenship, one aimed at developing in people "a sense of collective influence over the social conditions of one's life" (Young, 1997, p. 89). This model was not espoused by TAPP staff, however, who stressed a more individual notion of empowerment.

A key difference between these two models of citizenship and empowerment became clear to me one day during a conversation with Carol Roberts and a support group facilitator from another young parent program. They agreed that schools needed to teach more about "addictive behaviors," which prompted me to ask whether this would not lead to blaming people, for example, who are stuck in low-paying, mind-numbing jobs or who are coping with stress related to living in poverty. Perhaps, I wondered aloud, a focus on rights (e.g., welfare rights, tenant rights) and channeling anger into collective action might be therapeutic in its own way and empowering at the same time. Carol and her friend disagreed. In their view, individuals have to change first, because even if they succeeded in changing economic and social structures, the same "addictive person-alities" would still be in charge and nothing would really change (field notes, 2/17/94).

TAPP did not ignore the private lives of the teen mothers and the identities that flowed from these experiences as have other young parent programs studied by qualitative researchers (Burdell, 1995–1996; Holm, 1995; Horowitz, 1995; Lesko, 1990). TAPP participants were exposed to some alternative discourses about citizenship but in an unsystematic way, which largely failed to challenge the discourses beyond and within City School that positioned teen mothers as second-class citizens.

Teen-Age Parents Program as Real-World Microcosm

Ms. Connell, TAPP's head teacher, pushed to integrate program partici-pants as much as possible, contrasting her vision with a critique of the haven model. Previous TAPP teachers, all with backgrounds in home economics, had preferred to have the teen mothers "separate and pro-tected." Arguing against this, Ms. Connell asked rhetorically, "So what are they [teen mothers] going to do, have a separate site all through their life? A separate work site, separate stores?" Ms. Connell, who has a back-ground in math and science and is a single mother herself, felt TAPP participants would be better served by meeting, or even exceeding, the level of attendance expected of non-parenting students and by focusing on academics. "How can they get a job if they can't make 80% atten-dance? The whole idea," she continued, "is to get them off welfare and producing and feeling good about themselves."

Ms. Connell's emphasis on preparing students for the transition from school to work was the central theme of the microcosm approach at City School. This theme was taken up by one of City School's administrators, who spoke on behalf of some staff members who questioned the level of support given to TAPP participants:

> They think perhaps that it's not very realistic for the students in the program, because then they leave here and don't have those kinds of things available to them. And so maybe we aren't being very realistic in terms of teaching them the skills that they do need to survive.

The question, of course, arises: Which vision of the "real world" was TAPP supposed to be a microcosm of? My analysis of how the identities of mother, student, worker, and citizen were formed within the microcosm approach stresses that TAPP participants were largely being asked to adapt to the status quo, without much accommodation of their differences.

Mother as Economic Provider

City School staff, including Ms. Connell and Ms. Dalton, emphasized the importance for TAPP participants of schooling as a means to a job that would allow them to provide financially for their children without government assistance. Staff members were asked to articulate what they surmised the main goals of TAPP to be; the following was a representative reply:

> To be able to carry on with their education and hopefully get their Grade 12 equivalency so they can go on and become "productive members of society," better mothers because they're better educated, because they can go out and get a job, because they are less dependent.

TAPP's goals of continuing education and career exploration—embodied in its 1992 mission statement—are common to school-based young parent programs. As a former facilitator of a teen mothers support group asked pointedly, perhaps from a haven perspective: "Does this not conflict with the statement that 'parenting is an extremely valuable occupation'? By encouraging another occupation, are we not devaluing motherhood as not 'doing something'?" (Victor, 1995, p. 41).

Student as Child or Adult-in-Training

Although City School, like many high schools, emphasized readying students for adult responsibilities (read: paid work), the student role it assigned was a fairly powerless and dependent one. "Students typically have little control over what they study, how time is spent in school, or with which students and teachers they will interact" (Lesko, 1996, p. 48, citing Pallas, 1993, p. 413). So although in the microcosm approach teachers and administrators generally rationalized the official and unofficial curriculum as preparation for adulthood, most students were treated like children.

At the heart of the microcosm vision and the push for integration, therefore, lay a paradox. On the one hand, teen mothers felt they could reclaim "lost childhoods" by becoming part of "regular school activities," as Karry-Ann put it. Integrated TAPP students discovered that, although ostensibly harder than the TAPP classroom, many "regular" classes allowed them more room to "goof around," socialize, and "giggle." Jasmine said she liked being integrated because "I feel like a teenager":

> I lose total responsibility about being a mother, all that. I still concentrate in school and all that, but I act like I did when I was going to school before I ever had a baby. It's so weird. I goof off, I get in trouble for talking too much. And it's not like I ask for these things, it just happens. But it's so much fun.

On the other hand, integrated TAPP students had to lay claim to adult status—based on their responsibilities as mothers and, often, their experiences of living on their own—in order to achieve enough independence in the integrated school setting to balance their various roles. Most teachers interviewed said that teen mothers generally had the same types of needs as other students but that they required more flexibility and emotional support. There were limits, however, to how much the difference of teen mothers could be accommodated, given the conventional organization and culture of City School.

The disembodied student role in the microcosm rests on the idea that the student's life focuses on schoolwork and activities; it is assumed that family members provide for the student's personal needs. When the real student is also a mother, she often is solely responsible for caring for her own and her child's personal needs as well as for doing schoolwork. Thus, the teachers most committed to the idea that school should mirror the expectations of the "real world" were those who many TAPP participants felt were in danger of denying their identities as mothers.

Mr. Fisher (a science teacher), for example, was clear that teen mothers "don't get treated any differently than anybody else in here. We have a curriculum to do. They have to meet the responsibility like any other student." Mr. Fisher had set rules regarding attendance, homework, and the like and clearly communicated his expectations. Students were each allowed 15 absences before they failed his year-long course, and, according to Ms. Connell, the year before my study began, he had failed six TAPP students for exceeding this limit (field notes 10/21/93).

Mr. Fisher's approach polarized the TAPP students. The newer mothers, some of whom were breast-feeding and coping with higher rates of illness, found him infuriating. Charity had been away for one day caring for her sick son; when she returned to class, she was told she could not turn in her homework for credit because she had not phoned Mr. Fisher personally to explain her absence. According to Charity, she told him,

"You are really discouraging young moms from coming to school. You are making me think I really should not be here." She continued, "Mr. Fisher thinks we should be treated just like the other kids, and I do not think we should. What if my kid is screaming all night? I don't think we should be treated better, but differently; we are more responsible, we live on our own" (field notes, 10/23/93). The TAPP students whose children were older saw Mr. Fisher differently. Jasmine explained, "What he was trying to say was, he's not going to do us any favors because we're mothers. We're all trying to do the same thing: pass [his class]. . . . I don't feel because we're mothers that we should all be felt sorry for."

Amidst a 50% turnover rate of TAPP participants during 1993–1994, Carol Roberts asked, from her vantage point outside the school system: "How do school staff define success? Are there goals beyond attendance, exam scores, and graduation?" (field notes, 1/24/94). Shelly noted how the priority put on attendance was a double-edged sword:

> They really want your attendance to be good, and that really helps because it's sort of getting you ready for college and a job . . . but I think they pressure some people too much. . . . Like with Ms. Connell, I called her and told her my grandfather died, and she didn't say, "Oh, I'm sorry" or anything. She just said, "Make sure you get back to school quick."

City School did have alternative arenas where students could experience success, such as sports, the arts, social activities, and student government. Yet these involved time outside of regular classes, and given the day care's short hours of operation and the limited means of family and financial support of most TAPP participants, many teen mothers were effectively excluded. April had been a good baseball player but felt she could not play at City School: "It's at 3:45 and I have no friends here that would take care of my son." Mina wanted to join the choir but between practice before school and during lunch and time spent away on field trips and touring, she felt it was impossible.

There were a number of ways the good student role could be performed at City School, but they were all predicated on behind-the-scenes, extra-school support that was frequently lacking for teen mothers in TAPP.

Worker as Conformist

In the real-world microcosm vision of TAPP, staff made a continual analogy between the good student and the good worker, between school and work. Ms. Connell explained to me, for example: "If they have a grumpy teacher who is unfair, I tell them, 'That could be your first boss. You need to learn to get what you need to from that person without alienating them'" (field notes, 10/23/93). This analogy made sense in light of what many school adults saw as the main mission of TAPP, to (as Yvonne Dalton put it) "get these young women off welfare and get them into jobs, something that pays." It implied, however, that the meaning of work and the relevance of education were both narrowly defined; the authoritarian work relations characteristic of capitalism were left unquestioned, and critical thinking about existing labor market inequalities was not encouraged.

City School's career preparation classes mirrored the sex-segregated labor market, and most of the job possibilities they suggested for women did not appear to pay a living wage or allow for advancement. The career prep programs that enrolled the most TAPP participants were tourism, human services (including child care), fashion merchandising, and office skills. With children to raise on their own, TAPP participants nearing graduation had begun to look at the bottom line. Jasmine concluded that interior design made no sense, but maybe she should seek paralegal training. "I want to get into something where I can move up," she explained. "If I'm working with lawyers as a paralegal, I can move up, right?" (field notes, 2/10/94).

Angela was enrolled in the fashion merchandising career prep program but had begun to question the soundness of this option. She had looked into the entry-level wages of typical jobs in this area and discovered they did not pay much more than what she was already receiving on welfare, and she wondered how she would be able to afford this and pay for full-time child care, even if she received a government subsidy. Angela's attitude "worried" her career prep teacher: "I'm perceiving that many of these women who are accessing welfare expect it as their right."

In the past, Ms. Connell had encouraged TAPP participants to think about work in the higher-paying, male-dominated trades. She persuaded some students to enroll in technical studies classes (electronics, drafting, woodworking, automotive mechanics), but they reported feeling uncomfortable because of the "sexist atmosphere." Explained Ms. Connell, "The remarks that are made, 'Well, try it; even though you're female, you might be able to get it done.' Or there was a girl who was taking mechanics, and she had someone say something about, 'Oh, be careful your boob doesn't get caught.'"

Counselors had stories of a few "tough girls" who persisted and landed high-paying construction jobs. One said that post-secondary or apprenticeship opportunities for young women in the trades would occasionally come up, but he had difficulty finding any female students (teen mothers or not) who were interested. Liberal feminist assumptions about social change permeated all of my discussions with City School staff about occupational segregation by gender; that is, teachers assumed that a few strong-willed women would lead the way toward greater gender equity. Nobody puzzled over the institutional barriers that prevent women from entering certain occupations or discussed collective (versus individual) strategies that might overcome these barriers.

TAPP participants did hear the message loud and clear that they needed to form their own identities as (future) workers; they could not count on marrying a man who would earn a family wage. One teacher, herself a single mother, stressed with her students that "education is power, and economic power is emotional power":

> There is no question in my mind that any young woman today, and any young man, should have their own economic situation, their own goals, their own jobs. It's very nice to have a relationship, and, yes, that sort of completes the whole thing. But one should be an independent thinker and be able to independently support themselves, *regardless*.

Drawing on their own experiences and, in some cases, those of their mothers, a number of teen mothers echoed this message. Jasmine, whose mother had endured years of physical abuse at the hands of her husband, asserted:

> I want to be financially and emotionally and everything, independent. I don't want to have to rely on a man. That's why I don't want to think about marriage . . . because I want to know that I can do it on my own. My mother's problem, one reason she didn't leave him, was because she didn't think she could do it on her own. I want to prove to myself that I can do it.

A painful gap lay between the desires of the TAPP participants for financial independence and their knowledge and ability to prepare for and obtain work that would both pay a living wage and be flexible enough to accommodate a single parent's domestic and child care responsibilities. Because women, on average, earn significantly less than men across North America, marriage still emerges as the most expedient way for single mothers to lift themselves and their children out of poverty. A number of the teen mothers seemed aware of this, despite their rhetoric about not wanting to depend on a man. Jasmine laughingly said that if she came to the university with me, she would be on the lookout for "cute guys." This prompted Mina to joke that she planned to join the chess club in order to find Mr. Right (field notes, 3/16/94).

Citizen as Good Student and Taxpayer

In the microcosm vision, whether or not teen mothers were "good citizens" was evaluated by City School staff in *immediate terms* by how closely they approximated the institutional definition of the good student. "Their citizenship here in the school wouldn't have anything to do with them being a parent," explained an administrator. It would be judged based on "reasonable attendance, reasonable work here in the school, willingness to become involved with the whole population in terms of their needs and provide events and activities for them."

On the one hand, City School staff members, with few exceptions, strongly endorsed the hypothetical participation of teen mothers in school leadership positions and extracurricular activities generally. Although they had not observed this happening much, they thought it would be positive for teen mothers and their peers:

> The teen moms are awfully busy with their own children, and to be able to devote that kind of time to Student Council would be amazing. If they could pull it off, it might even stand to show other kids, "Gee, I don't even have a child and I can barely keep up, and here this lady has a child and she is doing all this stuff."

On the other hand, because school-based citizenship was defined conventionally and because of the practical constraints on the lives of most teen mothers, many TAPP participants did not have the opportunity to display good citizenship. Yet given a more expansive definition of citizenship, some of the teen mothers might have received more recognition. The caring work they did, not only for their children but for other members of their extended families as well, could be seen as contributing to the social good (Young, 1997, p. 128). Samantha had taken in her partner's younger brother, who had fetal alcohol syndrome. Angela devoted a lot of energy to caring for her partner, who suffered from epilepsy, arthritis, and chronic depression.

In *future terms*, the citizenship of teen mothers was often evaluated by their determination to get off or stay off welfare. In interviews, over half the City School teachers mentioned getting teen mothers "off welfare" as a primary goal of TAPP. One described this goal as giving "these young parents a perspective on their future as employable, as trainable, as fully functioning citizens who are giving to the system, not taking from it." This discourse (coming from beyond the school but commonly articulated within it, as well) was not lost on students.

While I was shadowing Karry-Ann one day, her English teacher, Mr. Howe, invited me to read through drafts of students' essays, and I was struck by the anti-welfare statements contained in several essays on the topic of poverty. A few described people on welfare as "lazy bums" and on the basis of this assertion made the case for "workfare" (field notes, 2/8/94). When I mentioned this later to Karry-Ann in our formal interview, she replied:

> Mr. Howe has a real big thing about welfare, and it kind of chokes me a bit. He's not aiming it directly at me, it's just generally, he's on this whole big trip of, "Well, we work, and almost half our paycheck is taken off because of taxes, and a lot of them go to support programs like welfare." I mean, he has mentioned that the programs are okay when they're there to support somebody, but he looks down on it really badly.

Certainly Karry-Ann (and I) had heard similar opinions expressed by other teachers. What hurt Karry-Ann in the case of Mr. Howe was that he was her favorite teacher and she had learned a lot from him: "If I had teachers like him for all my classes, I'd be a straight-A student." Despite this connection (or perhaps because of it), Karry-Ann told me she did not feel safe enough to challenge Mr. Howe's anti-welfare views.

During the time of my study, a new definition of citizenship was taking hold across North America. The older concept of social citizenship (expounded by Thomas H. Marshall) contained the ideas that individuals might be poor through no fault of their own and that "in a welfare state citizenship includes an entitlement to social provision—the guarantee of a decent standard of living" (Fraser & Gordon, 1992, p. 45). These tenets are abandoned in neoliberal discourse, which "targets" government resources only to those committed to "self-help"; at the same time, "the targeted are pathologized as non-citizens" and dependents (Brodie, 1996, p. 20).

The equation of citizenship with independence and paid work put TAPP participants in a double bind. Although many had concluded that it was dangerous to be financially dependent on men through marriage, their immediate prospects for landing jobs that would lift them and their children out of poverty were slim. Young (1997) provides a potential way out of this bind by distinguishing between two meanings of "independence": self-sufficiency, defined as a high-wage job (which she rejects as the basis for citizenship) and autonomy, defined as the ability "within the bounds of justice . . . to make choices about one's life and to act on those choices without having to obey others, meet their conditions, or fear their threats and punishments" (pp. 125–126). In this alternative vision of citizenship, schools would be an important site for fostering the capacities of students "to be autonomous—to choose their own ends and develop their opinions" (p. 126).

Conclusion

In this chapter I have discussed the haven (closed classroom) and real-world microcosm (full integration) visions for the Teen-Age Parents Program at City School, comparing and contrasting the identity formation of TAPP participants within each. Table 6.1 presents an elaboration of the haven-microcosm division in terms of a set of hierarchical oppositions. This series of tensions is enduring. Each side has its strengths and weaknesses. When a program pursues one set of goals with one set of strategies, some problems are solved while others are created. I conclude that both the haven and microcosm strategies are necessary, and neither alone is sufficient. Rappaport has called this the "pursuit of paradox":

> If it is correct that solutions create problems that require new solutions this should be of some interest to us, but not because we can expect to find a solution once and for all. Rather, it is the paradox itself that should be of interest because that should tell us something about the fact that *a variety of contradictory solutions will necessarily emerge* and that we ought not only expect but welcome this, because the more different solutions to the same problem the better, not the worse. (1986, pp. 148–149)

Table 6.1 Competing Visions of the Teen-Age Parents Program

Haven	Real-World Microcosm
special	normal
feminine	masculine
private (hidden)	public (exposed)
soft/easy	hard/rigorous
student as child (yet adult?)	student as adult (yet child?)
student as different	student as mainly the same
separate and protected	integrated and unprotected
support without judgment	coping skills for "real world"
"I'll do it for you"	"You do it all yourself"
(fostering dependence)	(strict to point of non-nurturance)
attachment	detachment
breaking confidentiality	ignoring life outside school
teacher as mother	teacher as technician
elementary school	secondary school
social/emotional	academic
individualized, personalized	standardized, impersonal
intimate (small, closed)	cosmopolitan (big, open)
friendly	intimidating
homeplace	workplace

Similarly, in the context of ethnic minority students, Rosaldo has argued the need for both mainstreaming and a "safe house of separateness" (1993, p. xi).

One approach must not be allowed to preclude the other, however, and this is a constant danger. Some teen mothers, for example, feel different and want a haven where they can develop solidarity with other young mothers; the danger is that they may have unfounded fears about taking regular classes, which would then go unchallenged. Jasmine spent part of her first year in the TAPP classroom, but with encouragement, she decided to try integration. "I was very nervous going to my first class," she said, but found immediately that she "loved being integrated" (field notes, 5/26/94).

Once a haven exists and the students it serves are deemed different, it can encourage teachers and students in regular classes to see teen mothers as more different than they really are and discourage them from seeing commonalities. Satisfied that the needs of teen mothers (especially those who are academically underprepared) are being met in the haven, regular classroom teachers have less incentive to rethink their curriculum and pedagogy in ways that might be more inclusive.

What I perceive as potential problem areas in each of the two program approaches could be mitigated by an explicit focus on democratic citizenship built around the values of participation and autonomy. In the haven approach, there is a tendency to treat participants as in need of therapy, sometimes forcing them to submit to the judgments of professionals about what they learn and how they live their lives. Instead, they could be encouraged to participate more in their own learning and problem solving. Participants, with staff help, might articulate their concerns and collectively theorize about their experiences, much as they began to do in the script-writing phase of the play-building workshop (see Chapter 8). Participants and staff could join in small or large arenas (in the classroom, the school, and beyond) in an effort to improve their lives and develop a sense of collective efficacy.

In the real-world microcosm approach, there is a tendency to treat as second-class citizens those who fail to conform to institutional norms or who rely (or appear likely to rely in the future) on government assistance to meet some or all of their needs. Instead, participants could be encouraged to recognize the value of the caregiving they already do. Caring for children and other dependent people "makes a vast and vital social contribution" (Young, 1997, p. 128) and should not be seen as secondary to obtaining well-paying, secure jobs.

Cultivating the capacities of participants to make important life decisions and to formulate their own opinions—whether in the haven, the microcosm, or preferably a combination of the two—would entail more emphasis on critical thinking. For example, teachers could open up an ongoing dialogue about the meanings of being a mother, a student, a worker, and a citizen in today's society. Students could explore the competing images of the good mother—full-time caregiver, economic provider, someone who balances multiple roles and responsibilities and wants her child's life, too, to be balanced—and discuss who benefits and who is marginalized by such images. Students could debate who the good student is. Is she someone who is punctual, attends class regularly, completes assignments, and gets good grades? Or is she someone who thinks for herself, connects what she's learning in the classroom to the world beyond it, poses difficult questions, and challenges conventional wisdom?

Notes

1. At City School during 1993–1994, 2 of the teen mothers conceived their first babies with young men of the same age; in 3 cases the information was missing. In the 19 remaining cases, the fathers were between 2 and 15 years older; the median difference in age was 6 years. At Town School during 1994–1995, 1 of the teen mothers conceived her first baby with a young man of the same age; in 4 cases the information was missing. In the 6 remaining cases, the fathers were between 1 and 7 years older; the median difference in age was 2 years.

2. At City School during 1993–1994, exactly half of the teen mothers were still living with or in almost daily contact with the biological fathers of their children around the time they were formally interviewed. Of those fathers no longer in a romantic relationship with the teen mothers, 1 had worked out a co-parenting arrangement, while the remaining 11 did not see much of their children. These findings were not atypical. A random sample survey of 105 young mothers in 36 school-based young parent programs across British Columbia found that 44.7% reported that the biological fathers were not at all involved, 24.3% of the fathers were involved in some ways (e.g., providing baby-sitting, financial help), and 31.1% were involved in most or many aspects of child rearing. Further, 21.8% of the young mothers were living with a boyfriend or husband at the time of the interview (Rivers and Associates, 1995, p. 27).

Chapter 7

Inconceivable Conceptions:
The Politics of Silence at Town School

. . . silence is meaningful when it represents avoidance of an issue that is divisive
if mentioned.
—Murray Edelman

Feminist and other progressive scholars have noted the "layers of silencing" in North American public schools around issues of sexuality (Fine,
1988; Sears, 1992; Belyea & Dubinsky, 1994). In both Canada and the
United States, "plumbing and prevention" (Lenskyj, 1990) themes continue to dominate the curriculum. Neither government takes an active
role in providing public information about reproductive health, and sexuality education programs vary considerably by province or state and by
school district. Divisive issues such as contraception, abortion, and sexual
orientation are routinely ignored.

In this context as well as within British Columbia, Town School represented an ordinary high school. In a province-wide survey on adolescent
health, students at Town School ranked in the middle on the range of
behaviors asked about, and, according to a researcher on this project, the
school was selected as a follow-up case study because it was so "average"
(field notes, 11/29/94). Town School was also ordinary in the sense of
veering between two sets of polarized attitudes in British Columbia. In
large urban centers such as Pacifica (where City School was located),
sexuality educators were given fairly wide latitude to address controversial
topics in a progressive manner. Other towns and small cities had adopted
abstinence-only guidelines for sexuality education. One small indicator of
Town School's middle path was its decision to allow condoms to be sold
but only in one set of out-of-the-way washrooms.

In an ordinary high school, where little that is innovative is happening
in the area of sexuality education, would it make a difference if teen

mothers—who serve as a graphic reminder of teenage sexuality—were to become fully integrated and their needs for child care met within the school? Would such a policy of formal recognition begin to unfurl some of the layers of silencing? Would staff respond by liberalizing the sexuality curriculum? Would a dialogue between parents and the school open up? Or could a young parents program coexist alongside—or even reinforce—a sexuality curriculum largely based on scare tactics, and if so, how?

To answer these questions, in this chapter I examine two plays about teen pregnancy and motherhood (one written by Grade 9 drama students, the other a featured school performance) for their messages and silences. I compare these with the official sex education curriculum, as seen through the eyes of students I interviewed in Grades 8–12 and as I observed in three "family life" classrooms, both before and after the Young Parents Program was established at Town School. I then assess the impact of teen mothers on the lived sexuality curriculum, relying on the observations I made while following teen mothers through their school day and on formal and informal interviews with them.

The Play's the Thing That Silences

One way to take the measure of what can and cannot be said about sexuality within a particular school culture is to examine the plays that its members can perform publicly for other members. At Town School I was able to observe two plays that dealt centrally with issues of sexuality, both performed the year before the Young Parents Program started. One was "built" by students, while the other was a commercially available script selected by the drama teacher. Yet despite the freedom students had in the former case to select their topic and message, the resulting play contained many of the same silences about sexuality as the one selected by an adult. (For a feminist poststructuralist analysis of play-building as curriculum, see Chapter 8.)

Teen Pregnancy emerged from a play-building unit in the Grade 9 drama class, a popular elective course that attracted an equal number of boys and girls across a range of ethnic groups. At the start of the semester, the teacher, Ms. Bosworth, assigned students to groups, who then chose their own topics. The group that elected to focus on teen pregnancy consisted of four girls (all White) and three boys (one White, two South Asian). As it was initially drafted, the play's plot was fairly simple: the protagonist, Caitlin, despite asking her boyfriend, Dev, to "go slow," finds herself pregnant. Although Dev is slow to express his feelings, by the end of the play, both he and Caitlin have revealed their love for each other and their desire to keep the baby. Ms. Bosworth and I were struck by the silence around contraception and the other two pregnancy options, abortion and adoption.

Adult concerns got registered through responses to the evolving script and in the course of the group's research. For example, the students interviewed the Grade 9 counselor, who had earlier expressed opposition to the proposed on-site day care, because he feared it would encourage students to get pregnant and keep their babies at public expense. Although he mentioned all three pregnancy options, he was most enthusiastic about adoption and provided the drama group with a brochure from the Midland Maternity Home. According to one student, "He was ready to drive us out there."

Alerted to the presence of the Midland Maternity Home, the students, together with Ms. Bosworth, invited three young pregnant women from the Home to see and comment on an early draft of the play. As it happened, none of the three were still with their boyfriends; in fact, one confided that her boyfriend had threatened to sue her for custody if she ever asked him for financial support. One, who had gone against her mother's wish that she have an abortion, was contemplating placing her baby for adoption. As a result of her story, the students decided that their female protagonist, still firmly supported by her boyfriend, would place her baby for adoption, and much was made of the fact that Caitlin's family received "welfare," while the adoptive parents-to-be were both "rich" lawyers.

The following semester, Ms. Bosworth, in consultation with the counseling department and with permission from the principal, selected *Dolls* (McDonough, 1988) to be Town School's featured spring drama. The play is unabashed in its negative portrayal of teen motherhood: Anisa, at school by day and at work by night, never gets to see her baby; Samm is indicted for child abuse; Renee divorces and rejects her child shortly after giving birth; Jana, a heroin addict, dies of AIDS, as does her baby. Only Yoli enjoys some happiness and a college scholarship, but these rewards come only after she decides to let a well-off couple adopt her child. *Dolls* contains only one vague reference to contraception, and celibacy until marriage is strongly endorsed. Sexual orientation is not mentioned except to link AIDS partly to the "gay world." Abortion is touched upon only indirectly, and in highly stigmatizing ways, through characters who voice "pro-life" sentiments.

When I suggested that *Dolls* was a cautionary tale that used scare tactics, several adults assured me that it was about "choices and consequences, not right and wrong," a line echoed by students involved in the production. Yet in other contexts, adults volunteered that the play was about preventing teen pregnancy. Ms. Bosworth did not feel the play was "didactic," but she offered that its "message" was "to abstain" and that it presented adoption but not abortion as an option. The author of *Dolls* explicitly concurs when he states in his preface to the script, "A kid having a kid doesn't do either kid any good" (McDonough, 1988, p. vii).

Given this clear moral, it should have come as no surprise that the play would upset the young women from the Midland Maternity Home, whom Ms. Bosworth had invited to an early performance. In the discussion period following the play, one rose to say that *Dolls* did not address her situation and that her pregnancy had inspired her to make positive changes in her life. The counselor who was facilitating the discussion acknowledged the point but then cut the young woman off by asking for reflections on the "choices shown" in the play.

The Grade 8, 9, and 10 students I interviewed enjoyed the play, although they all said they would not personally choose to place their baby for adoption if they or their girlfriends found themselves pregnant by accident. Lisa, age 15, told me that, as a result of the play, a friend had abandoned the idea that having a baby would improve her relationship with her boyfriend.

Meanwhile, though, "choices" that were left relatively unexplored in *Dolls* were unfolding offstage among the cast and crew, the students whom Ms. Bosworth thought would most take the play's message to heart. While *Dolls* was touring at other high schools, a male actor's girlfriend discovered she was pregnant and decided quietly to have an abortion. Angry at her decision, he began spreading rumors around Town School that she was a "slut." Shortly thereafter, two other students involved in the play accidentally conceived; by the following school year, they had moved in together with her parents and announced their plan to keep the baby.

In sum, the publicly staged dramas—*Dolls* and *Teen Pregnancy*—delivered several collective messages: teens should not have sex outside of a long-term love relationship, preferably a relationship that will happen when they are older and married; if sexually active, teens should use "protection" but not expect shame-free access to safe, affordable, reliable contraception or abortion (a "don't ask, don't tell" subtext of both plays); if pregnant, the preferred resolution is adoption; if teens decide to keep their baby, they should expect no support from society.

Although contradictory, the messages of the plays are in line with prevailing adult views in North America and, apparently, in Midland (the fears of Town School administrators of community disapproval were unfounded; not a single parent complained about the content of *Dolls*). Most adults, for example, do not approve of teens having premarital sex (Bozinoff & MacIntosh, 1992; Laumann et al., 1994, p. 322). Many take a moralistic stance toward contraception and abortion (see Chapter 3).

The "Emperor's-New-Clothes" Approach to Sexuality Education

These prevailing adult attitudes helped shape Town School's conservative, if typical, sexuality education curriculum. As evidence of the curriculum's resilience, I noted that very little changed once Town School was chosen by district administrators to house the new Young Parents Program. The YPP, as proposed and implemented, consisted mainly of an on-site day care, which was run by a community service organization and backed financially and philosophically by a progressive provincial government. Teen parents in need of child care services, regardless of where they lived in Midland, could apply for 1 of 12 day care spaces, and most were eligible for a full subsidy. Planners anticipated that YPP participants would be fully integrated into regular classes and school activities, and in the first year they were.

One might expect that the formal recognition of teen parents—in the form of material support and full integration—would prompt a liberalization, or at least a rethinking of, the existing sexuality education curriculum at the school. But this did not happen. A day care for teen parents, one obvious reminder that at least some youths engage in heterosexual intercourse, could stand alongside the semi-official promotion of abstinence and a general silence around contraception and abortion and other sexuality-related topics at Town School. One might expect that the increased visibility of teen parents might prompt inquiry into the underlying causes of teen pregnancy and renewed efforts at prevention. Yet I found generally that the presence of individual teen mothers (no teen fathers participated in YPP) paradoxically, and often unintentionally, reinforced the preexisting sex education curriculum. What silences were maintained, and how and why did this emperor's-new-clothes situation persist?

Contraception and Abortion: "Don't Ask, Don't Tell"
In British Columbia, the desire to prevent health risks, especially HIV/AIDS, provided the impetus over a decade ago for mandating 10 hours of "family life education" per year across the province. But such topics as contraception and abortion, approved for discussion in Grades 10–12,

are optional. This means that "many schools" in British Columbia currently omit these topics (British Columbia Task Force, 1994, p. 11). At Town School the topics were not so much omitted as pushed to the margins. Physical education teachers were responsible for teaching "family life," and whether and how they took up the issue of contraception depended on the individual. Mary (age 15) voiced a common student experience: "It's only if you ask what you can use [to prevent pregnancy] that they'll volunteer anything."

I observed a similar "don't ask, don't tell" policy at work in an elective class, Human Behavior 11. The teacher had invited a public health nurse to speak on contraception, and she relied on an up-to-date and comprehensive fact sheet prepared by Planned Parenthood. But the teacher announced that it was too difficult to get school and parental permission to distribute the brochure, and the samples being passed around would have to be collected at the end of class. Only one fact sheet made it back to the teacher, however; the rest were quietly slipped into student backpacks. The facts that contraception was available through a local health clinic without parental consent for those 14 years and older and was free to low-income youths and for a minimal cost to others were neither publicized nor widely known.

Abortion seemed to be an even more taboo topic. The only context where I observed it being raised was in a short unit on pregnancy options, again in Human Behavior 11. The teacher had students watch an educational video called *Baby Blues,* in which the main female character, Kristen, finds herself pregnant. The video is supposed to prompt a discussion of "responsible sexual decision-making," yet we learn that Kristen feels she could not go through with an abortion. This had the effect of eliciting only anti-abortion statements from several young women in class.

Outside of class, students who wished to research pregnancy had access to anti-abortion materials, deposited, with the principal's consent, in the school library by the local Pro-Life Society. *ProLife News,* for example, contained articles designed to appeal to young women, such as a first-person account by a teen mother who was happy she had chosen not to have an abortion. A brochure graphically described various abortion procedures. One student I interviewed, herself a teen mother, drew upon this brochure to explain her pro-life views: "There's one where they have this injection they put into the mother's stomach. Then the baby violently thrashes around, turns and spins around, just freaking out, and then she dies slowly in mom's tummy. Then they pull it out of her." Not surprisingly, given the school's general avoidance of this divisive issue, some students erroneously believed that minors could not obtain an abortion without parental consent or that the procedure was not done in town.

Gendered Power Relations

Unequal power relations between girls and boys constituted another muted topic in Town School's sexuality education curriculum. In fact, the failure to name and examine gendered power relations reinforced the silence surrounding contraception and abortion. The *Teen Pregnancy* play illustrates these points well in its uncritical depiction of the still prevalent sexual double standard. If Caitlin, the protagonist, feels any sexual desire herself, it remains hidden. Dev, her romantic interest, initiates and controls their relationship and then boasts to his male friends when he "hits a home run." Caitlin's role is relatively passive; despite her request that they "go slow," the couple has unprotected sex and she finds herself pregnant. Feminist-inspired questions were not asked: Why is male sexual desire celebrated and female sexuality suppressed? Why are men seen as virile when they initiate sexual activity and responsible when they insist on contraception, while women in either case are seen as "sluts"? Why do some men resist wearing condoms, and why do women find it difficult to insist that they do so?

Most of the girls and young women at Town School appeared to be aware of the double standard but resigned to it. Their close linking of love with sex and their inability to imagine themselves as initiators within heterosexual relationships proved repeatedly to be a heartbreaking combination. Rose (age 19) spoke for many teen mothers at Town School:

> When you're in a relationship, right, and you're young, a teenager or whatever, you're really vulnerable almost. . . . When a guy tells you that he loves you and he'll do anything for you and everything, it's easy to believe. And then if, when you start having sex, then the questions always comes up: "What if I get pregnant?" The guy's first response, "Oh, I won't leave you, I'll always be there for you, I'll be there for the baby." Most of the girls that I know, that's not the case; [the guys do leave].

The fact that young women continue to consider sex mainly in the context of romantic love may provide a partial explanation for my finding that young women at Town School were more likely than young men to oppose abortion. Young women may fear that abortion would encourage young men to see them as sexual playthings. A conception creates a moment for the young woman to gauge her boyfriend's love and the seriousness of his intentions. To the young man, a quick decision to have an abortion is a "clean" solution to the "problem," while the young woman may feel compelled to contemplate her potential as a mother.

These gender differences arose when I asked Caitlin why her group's play did not mention abortion. She explained that students were divided on the morality of this choice, and only one person, a male, felt it was unequivocally the "right" choice, given the circumstances:

> Not to sound sexist or anything like that, but he would prefer abortion, 'cause I think then he could be out of the situation. . . . By having an abortion, he could keep doing it, [having] sex. He thinks all the girls are going to do that, have abortions, but it doesn't always happen, 'cause they [girls] all have different minds [on the issue].

Rather than explore this gender-based conflict in the play, students chose to omit any mention of abortion.

Likewise, in an informal discussion in a Human Behavior 11 class, I overheard one young woman say that "a down side to abortion is you feel guilt." "Just the girls feel guilty," replied another female student, "The guys never feel guilty." The two young men present in class both said they favored abortion in cases of accidental pregnancy, because having a child while still in school was "too much responsibility" (field notes, 10/20/93). There almost certainly were young women in the class who agreed with this attitude, but they did not voice it. Recall that the actor in *Dolls* succeeded in tarnishing his ex-girlfriend's reputation by publicizing the fact that she had obtained an abortion.

The Human Behavior 11 teacher did not attempt to explore or challenge the attitudes of the students. In fact, the following year (after the Young Parents Program had begun), she decided to shorten the pregnancy options unit, because, she told me, "the boys don't like that stuff." Further, because the course was seen as an "easy" elective and a "dumping ground" for students with "discipline problems," she had redesigned the unit around worksheets and eliminated all group discussions, because the students "get too carried away." This type of "defensive teaching" (McNeil, 1986) has been documented in other sexuality education classrooms in North America (Trudell, 1993).

The Teen Mothers Enter: Muted and Conflicting Voices

What effect, if any, did the teen mothers have on the various silences that characterized Town School's formal and informal sexuality curriculum? My sense, based on fieldwork and interviews, was that their impact was minimal. Many of the teen mothers were a storehouse of practical information and seemed eager, individually and as a group, to share their knowledge. For example, some had learned the hard way the circumstances under which the Pill may be less effective, such as when it interacts with antibiotics. But they were not given a forum to impart their experiences.

When a sizeable group of teen mothers chanced to be at the same extracurricular session on parenting, they hit upon the idea of speaking to a school assembly about the "realities" of teen pregnancy and parenthood, including the importance of using contraception if sexually active. But they speculated that parents would not agree to let their children attend, because teen mothers would be perceived, wrongly, as deviant and as "promoting sex." Two teen mothers broached the assembly idea with a few people, but despite some interest by a student council member, no school adult stepped forward to sponsor it.

In their informal, one-on-one conversations with peers, the teen mothers generally underscored the prevention messages featured in the official curriculum. Based on my interviews with other students, I concluded that teen mothers helped to provide a reality check, especially for the younger high school girls who sometimes fantasized about having a baby. Mary, age 15, told me:

> I used to think [in Grade 8] that, "Oh wow, she's so lucky, she has a kid"—that's how I used to see it. But now, when I hear what they have to go through, I feel sad for them, too, because they have to put up with it for their whole life, and they can't . . . have their childhood anymore.

Still, some school adults worried that the teen mothers, by their very presence, prompted other teenagers to think about having and keeping babies. Some school adults at Town School took steps to counterbalance this supposed effect: no official mention of the day care to parents or students; discouragement of teen mothers from bringing their children into the main school building from the day care; and stigmatization of welfare, including the day care subsidies.

Most of the teen mothers were not well placed to challenge the welfare stigma. Their stories often attested to the pervasiveness of poverty, child abuse, racism, and class inequality, factors that constricted the choices they had made. Fearing that such explanations sounded like special pleading or invited stigma, though, in public settings like classrooms, they usually elected either to remain silent or to emphasize the importance of getting an education now in order to avoid long-term "welfare dependency."

Similarly, the teen mothers were not well positioned to break the silences surrounding abortion and gendered power relations. Given the choice they had made, they could not usually draw on their own experiences to challenge common beliefs about abortion, for example, that it is medically dangerous or emotionally damaging. Not all teen mothers were strongly anti-abortion; in fact, of the eleven I formally interviewed at Town School, all but one believed in a woman's right to choose. Yet in explaining their personal choice, many drew on anti-abortion discourse.

Irene (age 19), for example, had been on the Pill but found herself pregnant. Nevertheless, she told me she chose to carry her pregnancy to term not out of religious conviction but because of her belief that "you shouldn't use abortion for a means of birth control." Those pregnant because they were not using contraception consistently often said they did not want to compound their "stupidity." "I didn't take the responsibility during the time when I was having sex with [my boyfriend] to say, 'Okay, well let's use a condom,'" explained Fran (age 18). "I could have prevented it from happening, and this is my responsibility. I want to take care of it."

Although students like Fran could speak about the pain she felt when her boyfriend did not return her phone calls once he learned of her pregnancy, she could only puzzle over why so few young men showed an interest in co-parenting. Such cautionary stories merely underscored the scare tactics used in the official curriculum to encourage abstinence rather than open up a discussion of gendered power relations. Fran did not perceive that she had been coerced into having unprotected sex, despite the fact that her boyfriend was 7 years her senior and that she was "scared" to ask him to use a condom. What remained largely hidden and unchallenged was the extent to which Fran's boyfriend had structured her sexual decisions by asking for sex while remaining silent about his feelings.

In summary, far from being catalysts for the opening up of the sexuality curriculum, the teen mothers became cautionary symbols within Town School. Their own initiative, to talk collectively about contraception among other things, was not taken up. They were not ideally placed to break the silences about abortion and unequal power relations between men and women, and in some cases they may have reinforced them, however unwittingly. Topics that were ignored completely in the formal and informal curriculum included the pleasures of sexuality and sexual orientation.

Thus, the stories of the teen mothers did not, as one might expect, prompt a comprehensive and in-depth discussion of the full array of choices students might make about contraception and after conception. The patchwork sexuality curriculum at Town School suggested that their conceptions were inconceivable. Equally unimaginable were the ideas of sexual desire (including same-sex desire), accessible contraception and abortion services without stigma, and an exploration of the material and cultural factors that complicate and constrain the negotiation of choices in the realm of sexuality.

The curriculum proved to be hegemonic in the Gramscian sense of the word; it expressed the "advantaged position of dominant social groups with respect to discourse" about sexuality (Fraser, 1992, p. 179). It was not just that oppositional ideas were excluded; traces of an alternative discourse (e.g., "reproductive rights") were present but marginalized, which, paradoxically, may have strengthened the hold of the existing curriculum by making it seem more inclusive than it was.

Chapter 8

Warning Labels:
Stigma and the Popularizing of the
Stories of Teen Mothers

We know that the forces that silence us, because they never want us to speak,
differ from the forces that say speak, tell me your story. Only do not speak in a
voice of resistance. Only speak from that space in the margin that is a sign of
deprivation, a wound, an unfulfilled longing. Only speak from your pain.

—bell hooks

Those who are interested in critical, feminist, and anti-racist pedagogy
search for means to counter dominant ways of speaking about stigmatized groups. Some see promise in popular theater, which starts from the
experience of those on the margins. Popular theater can become a site for
enacting identity and challenging stereotypes.

In the face of widespread misconceptions and given their relative lack
of power, teen mothers are an unlikely group to succeed in disputing the
stereotypes. But what if they were given the chance? What if they were
allowed to mount a production to tell their "own story" to the rest of the
world? That is just what was proposed at City School, where a group of
teen mothers was invited by community and school adults to write a play
based on their experiences and then perform it for fellow students at City
School and three other high schools in Pacifica.

School authorities made no overt attempt to silence the play that the
teen mothers eventually produced. Yet the voice—or voices—that emerged
from the play proved to be, if not silenced, more conflicted and compro-
mised than the play-builders ever intended because of the forces shaping
the play's production, performance, and interpretation. In the end, the
stories of the teen mothers proved generally easy to "recuperate"; that is,
the dominant discourse was able to subsume the challenges of the teen

mothers by "negating and defusing" them (Barrett, 1985, p. 82; cf. Alcoff
& Gray, 1993), primarily by portraying them as victims. In this chapter, I
show how this occurred and explore the implications for pedagogical theory
and practice.

The Appeal of Play-Building and the
Pitfalls of Experience as a Building Block

The use of popular theater techniques such as play-building with young
people—as authors, performers, and viewers—holds much promise (see,
e.g., Griffiths, 1990). Drama teachers and popular theater directors have
used the medium to help students, particularly those on the margins, give
voice to their experiences. The play *Canadian Stories*, for example, was
based on the personal accounts of English-as-a-Second-Language students and sought to promote multiculturalism and fight racism (Griffin,
1991). A broad consensus exists that immigrant students who are struggling to succeed in Canadian society should not be stigmatized.

In the case of teen mothers, however, society remains sharply divided
over how far to go in humanizing this "other." Many continue to believe
that adolescent pregnancy should be stigmatized as a deterrent to early
sexual activity and welfare dependence. The dominant discourse today is
that of the bureaucratic experts, who have framed teen pregnancy as less
a moral problem and more a technical one related to the creation of
intergenerational welfare dependency and poverty (Arney & Bergin, 1984;
Chapter 4).

For those interested in countering or reframing the dominant discourse,
a form of popular theater like play-building, which starts with the experience of those on the margins, holds appeal. How do teen mothers, for
example, make sense of their lives? What stories might they tell that have
not been told within the dominant ways of speaking and conceptualizing?

Yet there is a danger in seeing the experiences of teen mothers as
somehow more authentic and able to transcend the dominant discourse
to a new point of clarity. Increasingly, poststructuralist feminists and other
theorists are seeing this view of unmediated experience as naive (see,
e.g., Grant, 1993). They have redefined experience in light of a more
complex understanding:

> Experience is the process by which, for all social beings, subjectivity is constructed.
> Through that process one places oneself or is placed in social reality, and so
> perceives and comprehends as subjective (referring to, originating in, oneself)

those relations—material, economic, and interpersonal—which are in fact social and, in a larger perspective, historical. (de Lauretis, 1984, p. 159, quoted in Scott, 1991, p. 782)

The "stories" of teen mothers consist in their continual reflecting on their experiences and actions, talking about them to others, and reconstructing them after the fact. Thus, the stories are always representations. In making sense of their experiences, teen mothers, like all of us, inevitably draw on existing ideologies. Therefore, rather than accepting their accounts at face value, we need to "examine collectively the central role social and historical practices play in shaping and producing these narratives" (Fuss, 1989, p. 118).

Social, economic, and political relations inevitably shape what stories get told and how they are interpreted. In the case of the stories of teen mothers, for example, the "stigma contest" (Schur, 1980) currently being waged over the meaning of teen pregnancy and parenthood in the wider society provides an important context. The purposes of the play's sponsors, the intentions of the teen mothers in agreeing to participate, the concerns of authorities in the schools where the play was performed, and the play's intended audiences, therefore, all need to be examined. As Alcoff and Gray, writing about the discourse of survivors of incest, rape, and sexual assault, point out:

Before we speak we need to look at where the incitement to speak originates, what relations of power and domination may exist between those who incite and those who are asked to speak, as well as to whom the disclosure is directed. (1993, p. 284)

Is it possible for marginalized groups to counter the dominant discourse? How might such change come about? According to Scott (1991, p. 793), "change operates within and across discourses": "Subjects are constituted discursively, but there are conflicts among discursive systems, contradictions within any one of them, multiple meanings possible for the concepts they deploy."

As I will show, the teen mothers used both strategies: they used one discourse against another, and they took advantage of the contradictions within the dominant discourse in an effort to forge a positive identity for themselves. They began to represent themselves, but the ultimate success of their effort would depend on others taking up their way of speaking, too (Davies, 1991, p. 52). It would also depend on whether the teen mothers were able to fashion a reasonably coherent representation which they recognized as their own, and this in turn would involve coming to terms with differences within the group and even with shifting self-identities.

Enter the Ethnographer, Stage Left

While I was looking at potential sites for my study of school responses to teen pregnancy and parenthood, I learned that for the past few years, teen mothers at City School had participated in a week-long play-building workshop. Ms. Connell, the TAPP teacher, invited me to observe the next workshop and subsequent performances of the teen mothers' play as a pilot study for my subsequent year-long ethnography, contingent upon my receiving permission from the students.

Thus, prior to the play-building workshop, I made a presentation to students enrolled in the Teen-Age Parents Program about my broader interest in studying the politics of interpreting their needs and lessening the stigma attached to teen motherhood. I answered questions about myself, the proposed study, and the discipline of sociology. Students voted unanimously to allow me to participate in the workshop as well as to continue with my wider study.

In the winter of 1993, I observed a meeting at which the idea of play-building was introduced; I also observed the workshop and all subsequent performances. I audiotaped all question-and-answer sessions following each performance and noted the sex, race, and age of the questioner as well as the nature of the interaction between the questioner and the teen mothers. Afterward, I interviewed four of the teen mothers in the play, ten student audience members, and seven adult audience members (mainly teachers). I also obtained written responses to the play from twenty student audience members in two classes (one for Grade 8 students who were considered "at risk" of dropping out, the other a Grade 11 English class) and three teacher audience members. Questions focused on the play-building experience, perceived educational benefits, and concerns about the play's intended and unintended messages.

Prior to the workshop, I spoke with the director from a popular theater company who was to lead it, a White, middle-aged woman who had previously worked as a high school teacher and actor. I learned that she was interested in gender equity issues and believed in reproductive rights for women.

Building the Play

Purposes in Tension: Creating Empathy, Issuing Warnings

"The purpose of the workshop," read an annual report put out by the community-based organization that sponsored it, "was to produce a piece of forum theater which would depict aspects of the life of a young mother and encourage the prevention of unwanted pregnancies." This purpose proved to be double-edged. In seeking volunteers to participate in the play-building workshop, the director emphasized to the teen mothers that the play would give voice to their experiences, thereby enhancing other people's understanding of their lives. In the invitation to school administrators and teachers to bring their students to see the play, though, its sponsors made clear that the dramatically framed experiences of young mothers would "encourage the prevention of unwanted pregnancies." The play, therefore, carried two, likely competing, purposes: a warning to other teenagers as well as a vehicle for teen mothers to tell their stories and counter prevailing stigmas.

Tensions emerged almost from the beginning of the process. On the first day of the play-building workshop, we sat in a circle, and each of the 12 teen mothers told their stories. The director asked a series of questions that helped to shape each story: How did you get pregnant? What was going on in your life at this time? How did your parents react? Your friends? What was the pregnancy like? What was your labor like? How much did your baby weigh? What did the baby of the father do? Is he still around? Are you a good mother? What is a good mother? How do you survive now? Where do you live? What is your child's personality like? What are your hopes and dreams for the future? Other participants occasionally asked follow-up questions or commented; the director took notes. I listened without taking notes at this stage; the only question I asked was whether they had been in school at the time they got pregnant.

I was immediately struck by the diversity of the stories. For example, although 10 of the 12 had been out of school at the time they got pregnant, they had left school for different reasons, ranging from a fight with a teacher to family problems to finding the schoolwork too difficult. The major commonality seemed to be that all felt stigmatized in one way or another, although the nature and source of the stigmas varied. A number of young women spoke about the significance of racism in their lives, either as First Nations women or as White women who had given birth to children of mixed race. Several teen mothers spoke of the age barriers to getting on welfare and the indignities they had suffered once they began to receive public assistance.

Based on these 12 accounts of becoming teen mothers, many plays could have been constructed. Ultimately, though, most of the scenes that formed the teen mothers' play seemed fairly conventional, not unlike the narratives of fictive and documentary videos about teen pregnancy and motherhood shown in family life classes. A number of factors help to explain why this happened. First, the time frame for building the play was short; participants had only three days before the pre-scheduled dress rehearsal to build the play, learn their lines, and prepare for performing; the first day was spent listening to individual stories. Therefore, when the students hesitated to suggest scenes, the director described the plot of the previous year's play. Most of its themes, including some of the same scenes, were eventually adapted for re-use.

Second, the director tried to prompt ideas by quoting individual teen mothers, based on notes she had taken of her interviews with them on the first day. Her selection of phrases seemed intended to elicit stories of prevention or warning. (She told me later that an important aim of such a play would be to "deter young women from becoming teen mothers.") For example, the director noted that Ruth had used the phrase "hope-and-pray method of birth control" and wondered aloud about the possibility of building a scene about the use of condoms.

Third, the director stressed the importance of structuring "dramatic tension" into the play, and this seemed to slant the teen mothers' stories toward the negative. At the end of the first day, for example, the director asked the teen mothers what themes had emerged from their discussion. Several identified (a) the prejudices they faced from family, friends, and strangers, and (b) how their lives had become more difficult financially and otherwise.

Two of the more outspoken young women—Tamara and Patricia—emphasized, however, that there were many positive aspects to being a teen mother and that the play should not just dwell on the negative. Ruth responded that she wanted the play to be "realistic" and that becoming a mother at a young age was "not that good." The director followed up on Ruth's comment, telling Tamara and Patricia that "just saying how wonderful it is to be a mother" would be "boring" because the theme lacked dramatic conflict. Thus, the emphasis on conflict toned down an exploration of the positive sense of identity some teen mothers had fashioned from their experiences. It need not have. One might have created dramatic tension while holding onto the theme of positive identity by, for example, having the teen mothers in conflict with a school administrator who refuses to acknowledge their claim to full student rights.

Resistance to the Dominant Discourse

Despite pressures to do so, many of the teen mothers resisted the building of a play that was a simple prevention story. The evolution of a scene that became known as "Friends Visit" illustrates this resistance. A number of teen mothers had described how, once they had given birth, it became more difficult to see their old friends and how, when they did see them, they found they had less in common. The director linked these experiences to a scene developed the previous year in which a teen mother is at home with her baby, unable to attend a party with her friends, abandoned by her boyfriend, and without a baby-sitter; she concludes that her life has changed forever.

When they re-wrote this scene, the teen mothers eliminated mention of the boyfriend and made clear that although the mother has access to a baby-sitter, she decides not to attend a party with her friends because her baby is running a low fever. Her old friends do not understand her concern, nor do they evince interest when she eagerly tells them that her baby has gotten his first tooth. Still feeling the scene was overly negative and incomplete, the teen mothers added a final twist: after her old friends depart, the teen mother phones to invite a new friend—another teen mother she has met at school—and her child over to lunch the next day. The depiction of a teen mother facing tremendous responsibilities alone was thus transformed into one where the responsibilities of parenthood (caring for a sick child) are balanced with the joys of parenthood (witnessing a first tooth) and old networks of support give way to new ones based on changed life circumstances.

The re-writing of "Friends Visit" might not have been possible without a direct confrontation with the director, which occurred in the middle of day two of the workshop. I had observed what I perceived to be growing discontent among the teen mothers with the process of building the play, and I suggested to the director at the lunch break that she might want to call a group meeting. After lunch, she asked people to form a circle and report on their feelings; I took notes. Annie wanted to know what "the point" of the play was, and the director reiterated that it was to increase "understanding" of the lives of teen mothers. Patricia said she did not want to add the condom scene that the director seemed to be advocating. "I don't want to be a teacher, lecturing. I never wanted to hear people lecturing me about birth control." Seizing on the director's own rationale for the play, Tamara added, "We want people to understand what our lives are like, make them more accepting [of us]." Audrey said that unlike Patricia and some others, she had not known about birth control at the time she got pregnant, and she would have liked to have had more information. At least some of the teen mothers seemed to recognize that the explicit rationale of the play (to increase understanding of teen mothers) might be at odds with the implicit rationale (to deter other teenagers from becoming parents).

This recognition may partly explain the resistance to the condom scene. Those like Patricia, who emphasized that teenagers already know about birth control or would reject a heavily didactic play, had known about contraceptives and had been using them at the time of their accidental pregnancy. They may have rejected a scene that positioned them at a time before they got pregnant—that is, with an opportunity to re-write their lives—because this might suggest to potential audiences that they regretted having their child or thought of their child merely as "an accident."

Collective Reinterpretation of Experience

The only scene that eventually focused on contraceptives did re-write the lived experiences of the teen mothers, but through a feminist lens. The kernel of this scene was inspired by Sabrina's account of her pregnancy. She had been dating an immigrant from a strict, religious family. In retrospect, she believed that she deliberately acted "submissive" in the relationship, attempting to emulate the women in his family so that her boyfriend would love her. When they began to have sex, they decided to use condoms, and apparently one failed. When Sabrina told her boyfriend she was pregnant, he denied the child could be his, implied that she was a "slut," and broke up with her. Because she had already had one abortion, she worried that she might not be able to conceive a child in the future if she had a second abortion. Thus, she decided to keep her child. As a result of this experience, Sabrina described herself as "more assertive."

The director asked Samantha to improvise a scene in which she "asserts" herself in an attempt to persuade her boyfriend (played by Annie) to wear a condom. When the boyfriend resists, Samantha, borrowing a line from Ruth's story, says, "I'm sick and tired of using the hope-and-pray method of birth control. If you're not going to wear a condom, then we're through." As originally scripted, the scene ends with the boyfriend calling out Samantha's name after she exits. During rehearsal, however, Annie improvised the final line, "She has PMS." The director objected, and Annie explained that this would be "a guy thing to say." The director replied that ascribing the girlfriend's behavior to PMS would "take away the power" from Samantha's character. Ruth agreed: "If there are guys in the audience, we want them to realize that birth control is their responsibility, too."

The improvisation process combined with guidance from a feminist director show how play-building might provide a framework for fostering a collective reinterpretation of gendered experiences. Yet given that a number of the teen mothers later interpreted this and related scenes as "male-bashing," a more sustained exploration of the complex reasons that many young women find it difficult to negotiate safer sex, the involvement of some young men in the play-building, or both might have clarified the issues and distinguished a feminist from an anti-feminist perspective.

Guidance in developing a feminist (or other) lens need not come from a director. For example, when the group was brainstorming one-liners for the "Prejudice" scene, Audrey said she had not experienced any prejudice. Ruth quickly reminded her of incidents on city buses where they had both been treated with disrespect simply because they were "Native teen moms." Ruth encouraged Audrey to name such experiences as "racism."

The Challenge of Constructing a Counter-Discourse

Beginning to theorize about their experiences and name them was difficult enough. But thinking about how to connect with potential audiences in ways that countered prevailing stereotypes about teen mothers—a key goal of the play-builders—proved even more difficult. Many efforts to resist categorization inadvertently played into other stereotypes. For example, when asked why she decided to carry her pregnancy to term, Patricia explained, "I don't really agree with using abortion as a form of birth control." Although not religious, she appropriated language associated with the pro-life movement; it helped her to counter the stereotype of teen mothers as selfish and irresponsible. Yet in order to explain why she, an "unwed mother," had decided to keep her baby—a decision that pro-life advocates often characterize as selfish—Patricia used a more pro-choice argument: "Adoption wasn't for me. There was no way I could go through the pregnancy and then say, 'Here you go, take my life'."

The difficulty of finding a clear position from which to challenge stereotypes meant that much of the play involved the assumption by teen mothers of the parts of those who had hurt them (family members, boyfriends, school gossips, strangers). The play-builders hoped that by echoing back the many statements of prejudice and unsolicited advice they had heard, their audiences might recognize the cruelty in those words. In

the course of rehearsing these scenes, a number of young women engaged in bawdy humor, which acted as comic relief. In improvising a
scene between two gossips, for example, Ruth said, "I hear Lydia is going
to a school in Pacifica that promotes girls having babies at a young age,"
and Annie quipped, "It's a ho(e)-down." "Ho" was current slang for whore;
using it to form the word "hoe-down"—a square-dancing party—made for
a funny contrast between whores, women outside the bounds of conventional morality, and rigidly conventional "squares." As I will elaborate
below, however, at least some audience members later interpreted the use
of such words as "ho" and the bawdy humor as evidence that the sexual
stereotypes about teen mothers were true.

The Problem of Same-Yet-Different

Compounding the difficulty of dispelling stereotypes, the teen mothers
did not speak with one voice. Some felt that becoming mothers had literally saved their lives, while others wanted to encourage their peers to
practice safe sex. Their lives did not make for neat generalizations. The
director, for example, suggested that many of the young men who fathered the children of the teen mothers were "in denial." Those for whom
this was not true contested the generalization. Even some of those for
whom this was true resisted the statement. Explained Sabrina in a later
interview, "Lots of girls in our class are still with their baby's father, and
lots of them that aren't have boyfriends. And some of them just like being
single."

In short, the group was faced with a problem that has increasingly
concerned feminist theorists: How do we take into account the fact that
women are simultaneously the same and yet different? On the third day of
the workshop, the teen mothers devised a partial solution, a means of
asserting their individuality. As a way of closing the play and leading into
the question-and-answer period, they each would give their name and
age, their baby's name and age, and a statement about being a teen
mother. The statements came from individuals and reflected their own
experience and beliefs, but they were vetted by the collective. Once somebody made a particular statement, subsequent speakers were encouraged
not to repeat the exact sentiment. If the collective felt the statement might
inadvertently reinforce a stereotype, they coached the individual on how
to make her line "sound better."

Sherill, for instance, initially said, "Being a teen mom has kept me
from partying." The director and several teen mothers urged her to re-
phrase her statement because the audience might assume that teen mothers

either do not like to have a good time or that they are former drug or alcohol (ab)users. Sherill finally settled on the line, "I like being a teen mom because it has made my life more stable." Similarly, Audrey initially said she had a daughter who "will always love me and not try to change me—she'll love me just the way I am." Several of her friends advised that this would feed into the stereotype of the teen mother who has a child because she feels unloved and perhaps victimized. Audrey wrote a completely new line, perhaps the only one of twelve that might be categorized as cautionary: "The hard part about being a mom is not having the same freedom as before."

A similar group dynamic emerged as the play-builders prepared for the question-and-answer sessions that would follow each performance. The teen mothers coached each other on how to manage potentially stigmatizing questions. Someone posed the hypothetical question, "How do you support yourselves financially?" Annie responded, "Welfare." Ruth advised her to avoid that word and to say "Social Assistance" instead. Alexis added, "We couldn't stay in school without the [public] support. We're in school because we don't want to be on [welfare] anymore." This provided the response to the frequent complaints that teen mothers are lazy and a drain on taxpayers. Patricia expressed the concern that whoever answered this question "shouldn't say, 'Some of us are on social assistance' because what if they ask, 'Which ones of you are on welfare?'" In order to avoid this, Tamara recommended that the respondent use the phrase, "Most of us."

Another strategy for coping with the "same-yet-different" problem also emerged while practicing how to answer audience questions: the exploration of differences that might constitute a pattern. For example, Patricia was the most insistent that her boyfriend was happy about her pregnancy and supportive throughout; they had plans to marry at the end of the school year. Yet during a question-and-answer session, Patricia cited as an example of her boyfriend's support that he "baby-sat" a lot. Annie called attention to the (unnamed sexist) assumption that a child's father "baby-sits" while a child's mother "parents." From this angle, Patricia's boyfriend (and, indeed, Patricia herself) might be described as "in denial" of the full extent of his parental responsibilities. Patricia accepted Annie's interpretation. This example illustrates Marilyn Frye's observation:

It is precisely the articulation and differentiation of the experiences formulated in consciousness-raising that give rise to meaning. Pattern discovery and invention require encounters with difference, with variety. The generality of pattern is not a generality that defeats or is defeated by variety. (1990, p. 180)

On the eve of their first performance, it was clear how often in their lives the teen mothers had been called upon to justify the choices they had made and to explain who they were in order not to be identified negatively by others (e.g., as "sluts," "stupid," "irresponsible," "welfare bums"). They had been engaged in this exhausting practice from the time they had decided to carry their pregnancies to term, albeit usually in isolation from people who had made similar decisions. Now brought together—first as students in the TAP program, then as play-builders—the teen mothers had begun to develop what one later described in an interview as loyalty to "the image of teen moms."

As this loyalty grew, however, it did not necessarily hold that the loyalty was expressed in the script as a unified voice. What emerged from the play-building process was a highly negotiated script, which reflected compromises among the teen mothers, between the teen mothers and the director, and between the teen mothers and the social attitudes they all knew existed in the wider world.

Performing the Play, Answering Questions

Teen Moms in the Nineties, the title the play-builders gave to their production, took only 10 to 15 minutes to perform. The play consisted of seven parts:

Scene One:	"Prejudice" (one-liners)
Scene Two:	"Asking Boyfriend to Use a Condom"
Scene Three:	"Friends Visit"
Scene Four:	"Bathing the Baby" (one-liners)
Scene Five:	"Conflict with Mom over Boyfriend"
Snapshots:	"Girls at Mall Fantasize about Having Babies"
	"Telling Mom about Being Pregnant"
	"Boyfriend in Denial"
	"Teen Moms Discuss Difficulty of Mothering"
	"Gossips at School"

Closing One-Liners

The scenes were mostly impressionistic, highlighting key topics and relationships. They acted as discussion starters for the main event, the question-and-answer periods, which lasted from 30 to 40 minutes.

For the closing one-liners and thus for the start of the question-and-answer session, the teen mothers stood shoulder to shoulder in front of the classroom audience. No school authority was present as their sponsor. The director, although in the audience, rarely attempted to mediate between the audience and the teen mothers, and she never intervened to interpret for them. In interpreting their own lives, though, the participants found it difficult to find space within the prevailing discourses about teen mothers to present a positive identity or formulate a counter-discourse.

What messages did the teen mothers intend to convey? I looked for the answer to this in three places: the rationales they used in building the play, their closing one-liners, and their responses when asked directly about the play's main message in five of the six question-and-answer sessions. Their intended messages comprise at least three categories: (a) "We're not the stereotype," (b) "Make good decisions," and (c) "It's hard to be a parent, but there are lots of positives, too."

"We're Not the Stereotype"
In the opening scene entitled "Prejudice," the audience hears negative statements about teen mothers based on their age, their marital status, breast-feeding in public, their welfare status, and their knowledge of birth control. These statements suggest that teen mothers are inappropriate, incompetent, promiscuous, ignorant, selfish, lazy, lacking in self-control, and irresponsible. No explicit mention was made of child abuse or neglect, although the line "Do you even know what you're doing?" hints at this.

Ruth chose to draw attention to the multiple ways teen mothers are stigmatized in her closing one-liner: "The hardest part about being a Native teen mother is facing the discrimination and prejudice in society." She elaborated on this during question-and-answer sessions:

> A lot of guys think that if you're young and you have a child, they assume you're a ho [whore]—easy. . . . I've been accused by people and the public of being a sleazy, no-good mom and stuff because I'm Native and because I'm young. And it's nothing like that. I've been going out with my boyfriend since I was twelve; we went to the park together. We grew together. It developed from that into a relationship.

Patricia, among others, underscored the harmful nature of stereotyping when asked about the play's message: "We're not the stereotype. We're not all going out to get laid all the time. [I want you] to understand us better and have respect for all those other mothers out there who are having a hard time."

"Make Good Decisions"

This theme came out mainly when younger students in the audience explicitly asked about the play's message. Tamara stated: "It's your decision. You're responsible for yourself. . . . Make good decisions." Teenage mothers have made a series of important decisions about whether or not to engage in sex, to use birth control, to have an abortion, to give the baby up for adoption. A number of the teen mothers acknowledged that they had made at least some of their decisions by default. They urged their audiences to "think before acting," not to "be in denial," to "think about the consequences," to "take responsibility," and to "do the right thing."

Using "make good decisions" as their central framework, the teen mothers hoped to avoid a simple warning message. Nobody, for example, urged sexual abstinence. Instead they said things like, "If you're going to have sex, be responsible. Use a condom because there's not only pregnancy, there's AIDS and stuff out there" (Ruth). Several, drawing on their own experiences with failed condoms and birth control pills, pointed out that no form of contraception is 100% effective.

In addition to taking into account the consequences of one's decisions, the teen mothers highlighted the importance of communication in relationships, an important part of the context in which decisions are usually made. In the snapshot scene between mother and pregnant daughter, the play-builders underscored the dangers of the mother interpreting events only through her own experience ("I'm too young to be a grandma") and dictating solutions ("You're getting an abortion"). Some teen mothers also stressed the need for communication with dating partners. Annie stated, "There's more to a relationship than just sex." Nancy, who was visibly pregnant with her second child, made this point most vividly in the question-and-answer sessions: "If you think you want to get a baby and you're in some loving relationship, think about this guy and what he may do afterwards. The guy can leave you, and you'll be this big, fat hippo sitting there."

Ultimately, argued the teen mothers, making good decisions depends on particular circumstances and therefore has to rest with each individual. They avoided the dominant discourse that would have portrayed them as negative role models, however, by asserting that they had made good decisions, if not about the use of birth control, certainly about subsequent choices, such as returning to school.

Parenting Is a Difficult Yet Positive Experience

In their closing one-liners, 10 of the 12 performers emphasized why becoming a mother had been a positive experience for them. The experience had resulted in personal growth (maturity, stability, assertiveness, sensitivity, and patience), improved relationships with family members, and joy (of having a new "friend," of experiencing "all the firsts with my baby," of witnessing a unique "character" develop, of being able "to teach someone the things I was never taught"). The teen mothers tended to weigh the positives against the challenges and restrictions of being a new parent. Tamara's comment was typical: "Having [my daughter], my life's a lot better now; I can't see myself without my daughter. But a lot of freedom's taken from me. You mature really fast. Boom, you're an adult—you're a mom."

The teen mothers emphasized that to be a good parent, one must be "emotionally ready." Alexis pointed out: "Having a baby changes your life dramatically." In a snapshot scene of younger girls at the shopping mall fantasizing about babies, the teen mothers exposed what they believed to be the erroneous idea that having a baby is like baby-sitting or playing with a doll. This is countered by a later snapshot scene in which teen mothers talk about the difficulties of being full-time parents. The teen mothers referred back to these scenes in the question-and-answer sessions. Ruth, for example, held up the doll they had been using as a prop in the play and elaborated: "It's not really easy. This is just a doll. [Real babies] don't sit in your lap like this. They cry." Alexis added, "When babies get sick, they don't know what to do. They can't tell you."

What Was Left Unsaid

A subtext of the play—what remained largely unspoken yet was important to the play's meaning—was that teen mothers are stigmatized as likely child abusers. The issue of abuse was not raised in the play itself, perhaps because the play-builders worried about highlighting it as a potential discussion topic. The fear of being seen as neglectful or abusive is a real one; teen mothers are particularly vulnerable to having their children taken from them. This is true despite the fact that careful research suggests that a mother's age is far less important than other factors in determining her parenting behavior, including potential abuse of her children (see Chapter 2).

In six performances, the teen mothers were asked only one question related to abuse and neglect. A Black female student queried, "Do you ever take your frustrations out on your babies?" Tamara responded, "Well, yeah, sometimes. Well, not really. [audience laughter] You get frustrated, for sure. That's why it's good to have someone else around to support you."

Tamara's comment prompted two other teen mothers to describe how they avoided taking their frustrations out on their babies, with Alexis cautioning, "You've got to realize it's not the baby's fault. They don't know any better." Immediately after the performance, the teen mothers let the director know that they felt "offended" by the "frustrations" question; they thought it positioned them as child abusers. Patricia likened the question to "Do you beat your wife?" During a later performance when a student audience member asked, "What is the most absurd question you've been asked," several of the performers mentioned without hesitation the "frustrations" question.

Parenting can be an isolating experience for mothers of any age in the dominant Canadian society as it is presently structured. If there had been a more accepting general climate and adults had been less concerned about simply issuing warnings about teen pregnancy, there might have been more room to discuss the potential negative aspects of the mothering experience and the conditions that might lead to abuse. But because the stigma of being potential child abusers hung over the performers' heads, they did not feel safe enough to raise or explore the issue.

Interpreting the Play

Although the teen mothers—as play-builders and performers—intended to convey certain messages, these were not necessarily the meanings that audience members took away from the play. Their interpretations depended on such things as who they were (e.g., their age, ethnicity, gender, sexual orientation, social class, school status), their values and prior knowledge, and subsequent conversations about the play with peers and teachers.

In this section, I analyze the questions asked in the question-and-answer periods; this analysis is informed by interviews I conducted with, as well as written responses I collected from, audience members after the performances. The questions following each of the six performances were strikingly similar and comprised three categories: questions that were informed by prevailing stereotypes about teen mothers, questions about the effect of pregnancy and parenthood on various relationships, and questions about the experience of pregnancy, labor, or new motherhood. I noted how many of the questions from the audiences possibly implied stigma and the various forms it took. This analysis revealed that concerns of the teachers differed somewhat from those of students.

Interpretations by Teachers and Other Adults

Teachers interviewed after the various performances agreed that the play benefited both the viewers as well as the performers. Explained one, "It made the students in the audience aware of the pressures and problems teenage pregnancy can cause," and the teen mothers "probably gained self-confidence and self-esteem." A concern about some of the play's messages, however, tempered these perceived benefits. Wrote one teacher:

> My concern was that not enough was said about life after the baby was born. It was probably good that abortion was slated as an option, but the real issues and practicalities of bringing up a baby as a teenage mother were not discussed. . . . It was almost like a "rosy" picture was painted. Certainly, we should be trying to discourage teenage pregnancies and teenage motherhood. Adoption was not discussed. Money issues were not discussed. Looking at the future was not discussed.

Here is the prevention discourse that many teachers wanted to see reflected in the play. No doubt such concerns fueled the attempts of teachers to shape student interpretations of the play by issuing warnings. They did this in two ways: through the questions they posed to the performers during the question-and-answer sessions and in the follow-up discussions and activities they conducted in the privacy of their own classrooms. Most of the questions of the teachers sought to prompt the teen mothers to consider their futures as well as those of their babies. Follow-up questions seemed to indicate, and later interviews confirmed, that prevention (of teen pregnancy, child abuse, welfare dependence) was high on the agenda of the teachers. One teacher, for instance, asked, "Are there things that you wished that we as parents or we as teachers had been able to teach you *before* all this happened to you?" This question, designed to elicit warning stories from the teen mothers, instead drew statements affirming the choice they had made; students, to paraphrase bell hooks, were asked to speak from their pain, but some spoke instead in a voice of resistance (1990, p. 152). Ruth answered first: "I'm glad I have a child. I wouldn't change it."

A few of the questions of the teachers were more pointedly judgmental, and the teen mothers highly resented them, as I discuss below. One teacher, for example, asked, "How many of you smoke?" His question led to the following exchange:

Tamara: What, during our pregnancy, or?
Teacher: Now.

Alexis: I smoke.
Teacher: Why?
Alexis: Why does anybody smoke?
Teacher: Aren't you role models for these little kids growing up?
Patricia: It's hard to quit. I've tried. I was down to two cigarettes a day
           when I was pregnant. I used to smoke a pack and a half.

Teachers also attempted to counter the positive stories told by teen mothers by pointing out some of the play's silences to their students and highlighting alternative messages. For example, a family management teacher at one school told me that she planned to discuss the play with students at the next class meeting. She wanted them to realize that "these girls are the cream of the crop of teen mothers because they're still in school." Even at that, she continued, the question-and-answer session revealed some of "the negatives" about teen motherhood—"the girls' worries about money, the fact that their social lives had changed"—and she planned to reiterate these. Another adult present at the same performance found the mixed messages confusing and disturbing. On the whole, she told me, the play made being a teen mother seem like a "groovy thing to do."

These adult interpretations do not necessarily mean that the teen mothers were fully successful in conveying their own messages. But they are evidence that the text that emerged from the play-building process was distant enough from the warning story ideal desired by many teachers to cause concern.

Interpretations by High School Students

Students said they enjoyed the play, especially the question-and-answer format. Many, particularly the younger students and Asian students of various ages, described the play as cautionary. Although student audience members asked relatively few direct questions about contraception, "safe sex" seemed to be a common message that students took from the play. A Grade 12 South Asian girl interviewed one year later described the play's message: "It was to show us the responsibilities teen mothers have, basically, and the obstacles [they face]. And the point of safe sex— that was the other thing that they promoted." Some students liked the emphasis on choices and making good decisions. Most said the play increased their understanding of the lives of teen mothers. Said one female student directly following a performance: "I learned to be supportive of teen mothers. . . . They're just normal human beings who had babies."

This new understanding resulted in three common sentiments: admiration, sympathy, and disapproval. Students' admiration for teen mothers was predicated on the belief that many teens in their community engage in sexual activity and that "mistakes" do happen (e.g., condoms break). Given this, a number of students, girls in particular, said they admired teen mothers for not having had abortions and for coping with hardship.

In addition, I sensed moments when students in the audience identified with the frustration that the teen mothers described in dealing with adults who believed them to be incompetent parents based solely on their age. A White girl in Grade 10, for example, asked, "Do you think your children have an advantage having a younger mom? That you understand them?" Several teen mothers agreed. Ruth's comment, in particular, met with nods and "yeahs" from some students in the audience:

> I think that you try harder because you have so much pressure from society. We get discriminated [against] so often that we strive to be the best that we can, whereas some older parents, they're 25 or 30 or whatever, right? They don't have that pressure. They just naturally think they're such great parents.

A more common sentiment than admiration was sympathy for teen mothers insofar as students perceived them to be victims of various stereotypes, abandoned by the fathers of their children, and destined to live in poverty. During one question-and-answer session, a series of questions forced the teen mothers to defend themselves against the stereotypes of being too young, ignorant about birth control, on welfare, and possibly neglectful. In response, a White boy in Grade 12 said, "I have a question. Everyone has negative things to say about teen moms. What are some of the positives?" Although this question allowed several teen mothers to talk about the joys of parenthood, it also elicited sober reflection in a way that the more pointed questions of the teachers about the future did not. Sherill commented:

> [Our babies] are changing a lot of our lives. A lot of us before were not as responsible and concerned about our educations as we are now. A lot of us were at the dropout point, but now we are back in school because we've got all this responsibility.

A few students expressed disapproval of teen mothers or at least skepticism toward supposed transgressors. Recall that most students offered support to those teen mothers whom they perceived to have made a "mistake." Thus, a fair number of student questions focused on ascertaining who had "planned" to have a baby. As a consequence, students directed the harshest comments and gestures at the one teen mother who was very obviously pregnant a second time. An Asian female in Grade 11 pointed at Nancy, for example, and asked, "You have a baby, right? I see that you are pregnant again. Why would you want to go through this again?" Nancy replied defensively, "I wouldn't. Just before I was going on the birth control pill, I got pregnant [again]. It was too late."

Nancy also acknowledged that she had had multiple sex partners and that two different men had fathered her child and child-to-be. She was later described by some students as "promiscuous," apparently the most damning and common stereotype that teen mothers face from their peers. The most frequent questions asked by students, both boys and girls, had to do with the biological fathers of the children of the teen mothers: what was the nature of their relationship, was marriage a possibility, did the fathers stick around, did they provide support, and so on.

In an attempt to counter the "slut" stigma, some of the teen mothers felt compelled to describe the steady nature of their relationships (e.g., Ruth's description above of playing with her boyfriend in the park since age 12 lent an innocence to the relationship). In an extended exchange about the stereotype that teen mothers are promiscuous, Patricia asserted, "I was on birth control pills. I didn't forget to take it once. I was that one percent. There's always that one percent. Don't forget that." Thus, one of the most staunch opponents of moralizing about birth control during the play-building phase ended up issuing a warning about the Pill in an effort to counter the "slut" label.

Some female students empathized with the teen mothers and said the play made them angry about the sexual double standard still prevalent among many of their peers. Explained one White girl:

> I know, from example, when we asked them, "How many of you are still with the fathers?" . . . maybe about two of them said that they still were, and the rest of them weren't. I mean the attitude is, if you become pregnant, the attitude is that you're a slut, that you sleep with everyone, and that you deserve it, and etcetera. And the attitude is that the father doesn't have to do anything. It's all the woman's fault.

A Chinese-Canadian girl in Grade 11 wrote: "From what I saw, guys are too busy keeping their macho image than thinking about how their mate feels. Because of this, guys usually bail out when their mates are pregnant."

Although some students displayed only one main feeling about teen mothers, more often than not, their comments belied a certain confusion; they simultaneously expressed pity, admiration, and disapproval for teen mothers. Thus, teachers who were concerned about preventing teen pregnancy and teen mothers who were concerned about increasing the understanding by their peers of their lives both had some reason to feel happy about how the high school students interpreted the play. The interpretations of the students provided another indicator that the entire text—the play as scripted and performed *and* the question-and-answer session—was a negotiated potpourri.

Interpretations by Teen Mothers

Among the performers, the immediate response seemed to be a sense of accomplishment and relief that the performances were over. Ruth: "I learned, I guess, that I have the power to change situations that I'm in and to be assertive; being in this workshop helped me learn that."

Eventually, several other teen mothers looked back with puzzled dissatisfaction. Despite their intentions at the outset, the theme of their play, it seemed to them, turned out to be mainly about warning others not to follow their example. They felt they had somehow participated in the reinforcement of their own stigmatization. I began to glean this when conducting the following interviews some months after the last performance.

Sabrina: I didn't think any of that play was really anything that happened in my life other than the fact of getting pregnant and having a baby. We all gave our stories, but it didn't seem like it was anything that happened to any of us, really. Some of us maybe, but me—there was nothing in that play that had to do with what happened in my life, other than having a baby.

Deirdre: If you were going to have it be representative of your life, how would it have been different? What would you have picked to be highlighted?

Sabrina: That's kind of tough, because *in my opinion that play was sort of to warn people* or something [italics added]. But that would be hard for me to do because I didn't find it really awful. I'm glad that all this has happened. So it would be hard for me to give a play of what happened to me by giving warning as well, because I can't really say, "Oh, it was really awful. Watch out."

                              * * *

Deirdre: So I'm just wondering if you can remember back to the play, what message or messages other students took from it.

Samantha: It seemed like it was trying to say, "Don't get pregnant" 'cause it was really negative. But I don't understand how that happened.

Deirdre: So if you had more control over the message that such a play could have, what would it be?

Samantha: That it is hard to be a parent. It's not always negative—there are parts that are negative—but there's a lot of positive things about it. I don't know, it's just as if anybody else that's pregnant, any other aged moms, except that we're going to school.

Thus, although Patricia and Tamara had been the most outspoken at the outset about the play being overly negative about their experiences, I learned that some of the quieter participants like Samantha and Sabrina were equally critical, at least in retrospect. Those still present in the TAP program the following year declined to participate in the play-building workshop again, and ultimately the workshop was canceled for lack of interest among both new and returning students. Although undoubtedly there were multiple reasons for this, I believe that the main explanation was that many of the teen mothers did not feel comfortable having their life experiences reduced by other adults to a mere warning.

What explains their interpretation that the play became a warning? Above all, not all participants understood at the outset that a highly negotiated text results from the play-building process. The teen mothers had been led to believe that their play would give voice to their experiences and help to dispel stereotypes. They did not realize how difficult it would be to convey their own story, let alone forge a collective story about teen mothers that would encompass 12 different lives.

The teen mothers also discovered they could not fully control how their audiences interpreted their intended messages. They did not count on teachers injecting warning messages through the issues they raised in the question-and-answer sessions and afterward. The play-builders may have overestimated the power of art to bring about change in their peers. Commented Sabrina in retrospect, "I think the play got people thinking. I don't think it made anybody change their life." Samantha was less hopeful: "I don't see what kind of impact that play had on anyone; if it did, they would be still talking about it."

Conclusion

In contrast to most curricular material about teen pregnancy and parenthood, the play *Teen Moms in the Nineties* included the self-interpretations of actual teen mothers and was sponsored by adults who wished, in part at least, to combat the negative stereotypes about teen mothers. Even so, the story that could not be fully told—or would not be fully heard—is one that some teen mothers say they would like to convey: (a) they became pregnant for a variety of reasons, just like older women do; (b) they support a young woman's right to choose—including mother-hood—based on individual circumstances; and (c) they believe that being a mother is a challenging yet positive experience. A young woman might either intend to have a child or remorselessly find herself pregnant. And then, with support from state-funded institutions, she might happily com-bine education and motherhood.

These messages were forced to compete, often unfavorably, with the warning message the teen mothers found stigmatizing. The result was complicated enough to prompt one adult observer (not a teacher) to note that while many adults wanted the play to be a morality tale, the produc-tion by the teen mothers presented "the reality":

> I think we [adults] want to say, "It's absolutely terrible, and you're going to be poor and you'll have a terrible time," or "It's going to be fine, and it's going to be wonderful." And it's neither. It's both. And that's true for all of us in our lives.

Ironically, many teen mothers did not see their own play, in the end, as "reality," but as an unsatisfactory construct. To prevent such disillusion-ment, the challenge lies in explaining to play-builders at the outset that they will be in the business of *constructing* a story. There should be no raising of expectations that their individual realities might somehow be combined to form a coherent, singular statement that can be told without clashing into opposing ideologies. The teen mothers should also be told that the play-building process will nonetheless be worthwhile. The script-writing phase, in particular, helped participants articulate their concerns and collectively theorize about their experiences.

Implications for the Use of Play-Building as Curriculum

The analysis of the play-building process with teen mothers suggests some ways in which teachers might rethink classroom practices, taking into account poststructuralist theories of experience and subjectivity. The teen mothers discovered they could not control what sense their audience made of their production. They might not have been so puzzled about how their play became a warning, though, had they (a) fully understood how the play was constituted around multiple, competing discourses; (b) learned to recognize dominant ideologies, (c) gained access to oppositional movements and ideologies, and (d) learned some of the rules of narrative (see Davies, 1993).

By attending to storyline structure, ideological content, and multiple textual interpretations, teachers can help students see "how one discourse can be used to modify or counteract the force of another" (Davies, 1993, p. 159). Although students must learn to recognize the impossibility of overturning stereotypes simply by willing it so, they are not without agency. "[Agency] is the freedom to recognise multiple readings such that no discursive practice, or positioning within it by powerful others, can capture and control one's identity" (Davies, 1991, p. 51).

Educators must also be alert to the limits of play-building as a "liberatory" educational practice for marginalized students such as teenage mothers. Well-intentioned teachers may seek to empower students by encouraging them to create an "authentic" statement that ostensibly grows directly out of their own experiences. Yet students with the same experiential background do not always interpret their experiences in the same way, and their self-interpretations are subject to pressure and even manipulation from outside interests that seek to stigmatize their stories.

Implications for Sexuality Education

With regard to the specific content of the teen mothers' play, I would add my voice to a growing number of calls to reconceptualize sexuality education to include both "discourses of desire and refusal" (Ruddick, 1993, drawing on Fine, 1988). The teen mothers spoke to the pleasures as well as the responsibilities involved in exploring sexuality, giving birth, and becoming parents. When given the space, the teen mothers both gave voice to their desires and urged prevention and the making of informed, responsible decisions. As Ruddick cautions:

> Unless their intimations of pleasure are addressed, they cannot find their experiences within official stories or trust the officials who tell them. They become isolated, less able to name the complexities of their feelings, and thus less capable of becoming choosing people. (1993, p. 134)

Chapter 9

Studying Up, Down, and Across in Schools; Speaking About, For, and With Teen Mothers: Dilemmas of a Critical Feminist Ethnographer

In previous chapters, I discussed how even those adults who identify as feminist or progressive and who intend to help teen mothers sometimes participate in discourses and institutional practices that construct the teen mother as unacceptably different, as the Other. In this chapter, I scrutinize my own practices and explore the dilemmas I encountered in the framing, conduct, analysis, and writing of a critical feminist ethnography.

As a critical feminist ethnographer, I was not just interested in research for its own sake; I sought to challenge and transform unequal relations of power. Researchers can help groups without access to traditional sources of power to articulate their concrete needs, clarify their concerns, and communicate both to broader audiences. They can draw attention to new or marginalized issues and recast old problems. Critical researchers thus attempt to counter or reframe dominant discourses (Kelly & Gaskell, 1996). This partisan approach is at odds with what Rosaldo (1989) calls the "norms of classic ethnography," namely value neutrality and emotional detachment.

I thus began my study of school responses to teen pregnancy and parenthood—in particular, the supported integration of pregnant and mothering teens—committed to the idea that "policy design must be examined for its differential effects based on gender, class, race, age, community, and other dimensions, and these effects need to be evaluated and understood from the lived experiences of those groups or communities affected" (Phillips, 1996, p. 243). An understanding of how teen mothers across various settings interpreted their own experiences and needs was indispensable to what I saw as respectful and rigorous research; I could not simply infer their needs from the policy responses that sought to meet their needs, no matter how progressive these policies may have seemed to me at the outset.

Although teen mothers were not the sole focus of my study, I continue to feel most accountable to them. They constitute a group vulnerable to political scapegoating by virtue of their age, life experiences, social class, and sometimes race or ethnicity (see Chapter 2). I let them know from the beginning that I believed teen mothers had often been misrepresented in the mainstream scholarly literature and popular media (see Chapter 4) and that I hoped my research would present a more complex picture and challenge prevailing stereotypes.

This openness about the values informing the framing of my ethnographic study often strikes people unfamiliar with critical feminist work as a "bias" which threatens the project's credibility. Like many qualitative feminist researchers, I believe the term "bias" is "misplaced" (Olesen, 1994, p. 165). As Nancy Scheper-Hughes argues, "We cannot rid ourselves of the cultural self we bring with us into the field any more than we can disown the eyes, ears and skin through which we take in our intuitive perceptions about the new and strange world we have entered" (quoted in Olesen, 1994, p. 165). All researchers seek knowledge while grounded in a particular *stance,* although that stance is not always acknowledged, let alone explored. Their beliefs, values, and interests shape the topics and interpretive frameworks they select, the questions they ask, and the evidence they gather or co-produce. This does not mean that good researchers (whatever their stance) willfully distort their findings or selectively use evidence to score ideological points or that all truth claims are relative. It does mean that the views of researchers are inescapably partial but that "informed judgments can be made" (Hawkesworth, 1989, p. 555). Although "knowledge is always incomplete . . . some systematic knowledge of the world is possible and . . . such knowledge can be useful" (Alway, 1995, p. 225).

A related misunderstanding about critical feminist ethnographers is that we already know the answer to our research question before we begin the empirical work. As Quantz points out, this is to "misunderstand the question that is being asked":

> The researcher may assume that those to be studied are disempowered, but there is no assumption about how that disempowerment is represented in cultural forms,

how participants respond to their positioning, that they recognize their response as anything other than individual choice, or even that they agree that they are disempowered. The role of empirical study is, therefore, to clarify how material relations become manifested in differing life experiences . . . and how . . . our understanding [can] work toward the restructuring of these relations. (1992, p. 468)

Quantz's characterization of critical ethnography applies to my own project except insofar as it implies only a "studying down" or focus on a disempowered group. I initially conceived of my project as a study of the politics of schools that were interpreting the needs of teen mothers and attempting to lessen stigma by fully integrating them. This focus on the politics of a particular type of curricular detracking seemed to necessitate simultaneously studying up, down, and across, although (as I shall analyze shortly) even this conceptual schema proved inadequate to capture fully the fluidity and complexity of power relations shaping the fieldwork.

I intended to *study up* as I sought to determine how the needs of school-age mothers were being defined and acted upon by government officials, mainstream academics, mass media editors and pundits, politicians, and interested professionals. I intended to *study down* as I sought to understand how teen mothers were positioned within these various, sometimes conflicting discourses about their needs as well as their interpretations and responses to this positioning. I intended to *study across* by selecting two school sites where school and community leaders were committed to reducing the stigma attached to teenage pregnancy and motherhood as evidenced by their support for integration policies, including the provision of on-site child care. What strategies and practices did they use, what barriers did they face, and how could understandings that would emerge from my study of their efforts support them as they endeavored to create more inclusive school environments?

In the rest of this chapter, I will focus on the lessons this critical feminist ethnographer learned about the complex workings of power, how to balance advocacy against self-censorship, and the politics of representing self and others in carrying out the fieldwork (the process of research) and in creating the written account based on my interpretations of the cultural dynamics I documented (the product of research). I sought to minimize the risk of "othering" research participants, particularly the most vulnerable, but because the ethnography was conceived and carried out in contexts of unequal power, I found that the pursuit of this goal necessarily resulted in tensions and dilemmas.

Studying Up, Down, and Across in Schools: Fieldwork Dilemmas

The concepts of studying down, studying up, and studying across are useful when one is thinking through some of the ethical challenges of doing ethnographic research. They rest on some assumptions about power, however, that are open to question. My study of a specific cultural arena for a sustained period and attempts to understand the everyday lives of the people interacting in this arena from both insider and outsider perspectives has confirmed for me, for example, that the oppressed can also be oppressors and that those with privileges in one context may be penalized in another. Power, furthermore, does not always mean hierarchical domination.

Beginning with the Experiences of Teen Mothers: Studying Down?

Studying down implies that a researcher, who is privileged by virtue of her education, social standing, and so forth, makes the object of her inquiry a relatively disempowered group. The inequalities between the researcher and researched create the conditions of possible exploitation, coercion, misrepresentation, and betrayal (Stacey, 1988; for a recent review, see Wolf, 1996).

Although I did not see my only goal as representing the so-called "native's point of view" (Malinowski, 1961, p. 25), I did want to "attend with care to the perceptions and aspirations of subordinate groups" (Rosaldo, 1989, pp. 35–36). By virtue of my age and university position, often my social class, and sometimes my race, ethnicity, and English language proficiency, I was privileged vis-à-vis the teen mothers, and conceiving of my relationship to them in terms of studying down was a useful reminder of the power inequalities and how they shaped interaction (access, rapport, and so on).

But the concept of studying down can mislead as well. It implies that the researched subjects are uniformly and in every context disempowered— a dubious assumption in the case of teen mothers. It directs attention away from power inequalities among those being researched by focusing on the inequalities between researched and researcher. It directs attention away from the commonalities that may exist between researched and researcher—important kindling for the fires of empathy—while focusing on disadvantages that may evoke feelings of disrespect or pity (the phrase studying down here parallels looking down). It assumes exploitation while ignoring potential mutual satisfactions and benefits. It assumes that those being researched are potential victims while ignoring their potential as "active cultural producers in their own right" (Ong, 1995, p. 354) as well as their power to refuse or evade. As Aiwha Ong writes, citing Foucault, "If one considers power as a decentralized, shifting, and productive force, animated in networks of relations rather than possessed by individuals, then ethnographic subjects can exercise power in the production of ethnographic knowledges" (1995, p. 353).

Studying Up and the Difficulties of Knowing Up from Down

Studying up implies that a researcher makes the object of her inquiry a relatively privileged or an elite group; a goal of such studies is a critical analysis of the group's privilege or an exploration of hierarchical power. In perhaps the first use of the term, Laura Nader suggested that studying up as well as down would lead to more adequate theory and increase the democratic relevance of fieldwork. "What if," Nader asked, "in reinventing anthropology, anthropologists were to study the colonizers rather than the colonized, the culture of power rather than the culture of the powerless, the culture of affluence rather than the culture of poverty?" (1972, p. 289). Although he does not use the phrase "studying up," Alvin Gouldner's (1968) description of the work of radical sociologists—"while they take the standpoint of the underdog, they apply it to the study of overdogs" (p. 111)—seems apt.

Ambiguities arise when considering whether the researcher is less privileged than the researched, or equally privileged but within different arenas, and whether deconstruction of privilege(s) is integral to the enterprise. Anthropologist Paul Rabinow described his decision to research elite French male colonial officials as studying up, but given his own positionality based on gender, race, and nationality, Frances Mascia-Lees, Patricia Sharpe, and Colleen Ballerino Cohen contest his claim, because he failed to "deconstruct[] the patriarchy" (1989, p. 19). Feminist ethnographers Judith Newton and Judith Stacey described their research on academic men as studying up: "Although, as white, heterosexual, academic women, we share with the majority of our subjects diverse forms of privilege, most of them are more privileged still" (1995, p. 296).

Thus, as the term "studying up" gets used, the "privilege gap" often seems to be arrived at by comparing the respective locations of the researcher and the researched within multiple, intersecting axes of domination (most commonly, race, gender, social class, ethnicity, age, and sexuality). Less attention gets paid to the specific arenas or institutional settings in which researcher and researched interact and how particular relations of power matter more or less across these varying contexts. It *may* matter little that the researcher is a White heterosexual man who is attempting to study the leadership style of a Latina principal if she decides to use the authority of her office to deny him access to the school she heads and warns her fellow principals against him.

Another attendant ambiguity is how large the privilege gap must be to constitute studying up. In a famous critique of Howard Becker and the study of deviant subcultures (and thus studying down), Gouldner pointed out that Becker's research, with its focus on and implicit sympathy for underdogs as victims, ended up indicting only the rule makers and rule enforcers immediately above the rule-breaking underdogs. Becker's critique, according to Gouldner, was aimed more at the "caretaking institutions who do the mopping-up job, rather than at the master institutions that produce the deviant's suffering" (1968, p. 107). In essence, Gouldner accused Becker of not studying up high enough. A more radical form of studying up, he argued, would focus on the "master institutions" and the "power elite" or "high level officialdom that shapes the character of caretaking establishments" (p. 107), rather than the mid-level bureaucrats who staff and run such caretaking institutions as prisons, courts, hospitals, welfare agencies, and schools.

Despite the various ambiguities inherent in the concept of studying up (which I have summarized as the difficulties of knowing up from down), I still find it evocative of the challenges of researching the relatively powerful. As I sought to connect the development of the integration and school-based day care policies in each site to local, regional, and national politics, bureaucratic funding formulas, and administrative mandates, I attempted the more radical studying up that Gouldner wrote about.

Most of my time, however, was spent studying the implementation of these policies in classrooms, schools, and school districts. In these instances, I had more face-to-face contact with relatively powerful administrators, elected officials, and teachers, who were often marginally privileged over me by virtue of their gender and age but, more importantly, they had power by virtue of their positions of authority within the precise arenas where I wished to do my fieldwork. And although Gouldner's analysis would seem to suggest that mid-level officials are mainly enforcing rules made higher up, I found that they had the power to make rules and shape policies in significant ways and with profound consequences for students (see Kelly, 1998).

When I was observing or interviewing school officials, a significant source of tension for me was the often taken-for-granted set of assumptions they made about teen mothers or, more generally, poor and Native people. I often had to assess whether and when to draw attention to unrecognized White, middle-class privilege and ideology. Like the middle-class mothers studied by Ellen Brantlinger, Massoumeh Majd-Jabbari, and Samuel Guskin, many teachers and administrators "seemed to be unaware of the dichotomy between verbalized liberal ideals and self-/class interest. Generally mystified about class privilege, then, when it was implied, insinuated, or when it became visible in their responses, participants were defensive" (1996, p. 588). In face-to-face studying up, I had to balance deconstructing privilege and provoking defensiveness with maintaining access and rapport.

Studying Across Amid Shifting Configurations of Power: Divided Loyalties and Micropolitical Entanglements

Studying across implies a rough parity between researcher and researched in terms of power and privilege, or at least a willingness to create a dialogue across difference(s), because the researcher shares some political goals with the researched and seeks understanding that would help build alliances in furtherance of shared goals (cf. Newton & Stacey, 1995). In framing my current study, for example, I wanted to forge an alliance with progressive educators and community activists committed to inclusive schooling. I hoped, as one outcome of the research, to identify strategies and practices that educators elsewhere, who were seeking to integrate teen parents fully into regular schools, would find useful.

As I explore in detail in the next section, my efforts to study across met with mixed results and in some ways became derailed. I attribute this partial derailment to two main factors. First, I was attempting *simultaneously* to study across, down, and up. Second, most of the research occurred in the hierarchically structured and contested terrain of schools. The result can be summarized as divided loyalties and entanglements in micropolitics.

My commitment to study across, up, and down meant that I was constantly moving among groups (teen mothers and their peers, teachers and administrators inside and outside the young parent programs, and community members and parents with vested interests in school policy) and trying to attend to the views and interpretations of these various groups. Because schools are arenas of struggle, marked by a diversity of goals and ideological debate, there were inevitably conflicts between groups as well as within groups. Not surprisingly, I felt pressure to choose sides, to display loyalty. By virtue of my commitment to inclusive schooling, I was considered suspect by some. But even among my initial allies, tensions arose because we disagreed, sometimes seriously, about what it meant to be inclusive, to decrease stigma, and to meet the needs of students and teen mothers.

I found it difficult to navigate the micropolitics without entanglement. Such entanglements—exacerbated by a changing cast of characters due to changes in venue, promotions and transfers, student turnover, and in one case, death—put limits around my two main strategies for minimizing othering in the fieldwork, namely collaborating with like-minded educators and community workers and treating teen mothers as co-researchers, potential theorists, and agents of change. The dynamics and dilemmas played out differently at City School and Town School, mainly for reasons related to the differences in the design and history of their respective young parent programs. Because the stories of my involvement at each school differ significantly, I will tell them separately.

City School: Confronting the Grammar of Schooling

I begin with City School, because the main part of the fieldwork there preceded that in Town School and my experiences at City School affected the approach I took at Town School. At any one time, about half of the young women enrolled in City School's Teen-Age Parents Program were fully integrated in regular classes, while the other half spent most or all of their time together doing individualized school work in the TAPP classroom with a full-time teacher, Ms. Connell, and a full-time youth worker, Ms. Dalton. Fully integrated students were expected to check in with the TAPP staff each morning, and TAPP participants regularly ate together in the cafeteria and socialized together at the child care center and at numerous TAPP-sponsored activities scheduled throughout the year. Their sense of belonging to a group, their frequent togetherness in one location, and the self-paced schedule of many allowed me more opportunities to engage them as co-researchers than if they had always been in classrooms dispersed throughout the school of 1,300 students, following completely separate timetables.

From previous research I knew that public schools are not places conducive to participatory action research, particularly when the intended co-researchers are students and minors (Kelly, 1993b). In addition, participatory research requires full collaboration, whereas I approached school sites already knowing what I wanted to study, roughly how I wanted to study it, and that I would carry ultimate responsibility for the analysis, interpretations, and written account. Part of what I wanted to study, however, involved school strategies for lessening the stigmas attached to teen pregnancy and parenthood, and therefore I hoped to use research methods that would avoid treating teen mothers as Other. I wanted to encourage the self-interpretations of students and was open to facilitating small-scale action projects as part of the research, if and when concerns arose and were voiced by teen mothers themselves.

Ms. Connell, the TAPP teacher, was apprised of and initially endorsed my research approach, and based on early conversations with her, I thought we shared a belief in the importance of facilitating the efforts of teen mothers to advocate individually and collectively for themselves. Yet over the course of the first few months, as we—researchers (Sheila and myself), teen mothers, and TAPP staff—participated in a series of shared events and compared views and reactions to those events, I realized that Ms. Connell and I differed ideologically on the meaning of education and how social change occurs.

Our differences were cast into sharp relief as the result of a guest speaker's visit two months into the fieldwork. Ms. Dalton had arranged for an anti-poverty activist to address the teen mothers enrolled in a "life skills" class. Ms. Connell made a point of excusing herself before the speaker arrived; she had heard her speak before and worried that she might provoke an "unproductive anger" among the students and a "we-they situation." According to Ms. Dalton:

> The students already buy into "welfare rights" pretty easily anyway. We worry sometimes that the more they know about the welfare system and how it works, the more they want from it. This can encourage dependence. What we want to encourage is empowerment. We want to help them get jobs and off welfare. (field notes, 10/15/93)

By empowerment, Ms. Dalton and Ms. Connell meant self-assertion, a psychological "inner strength," and individual upward mobility in a system they believed to be largely meritocratic. While I agreed that self-empowerment was important, I offered that social or collective empowerment was equally critical. I was happy that students would be given the opportunity to hear from someone who believed that people working together could challenge an injustice and possibly succeed in changing the conditions of their lives.

These differences need not have translated into mistrust, but a number of my views happened to coincide with those of TAPP's coordinator (an employee of the Community-Based Organization that ran the day care center) and of an outspoken community representative and member of TAPP's Advisory Committee. Both of these women had been at odds with Ms. Connell, often over issues to do with what they perceived as the school's lack of flexibility, its rigid attendance rules and disciplinary routines, its focus on academic needs to the exclusion of the other needs of students—in short, the grammar of schooling.

Historians David Tyack and Larry Cuban suggest that the grammar of schooling can be seen "both as descriptive (the way things are) and prescriptive (the way things ought to be)" (1995, p. 165, n. 2):

> Practices such as age-graded classrooms structure schools in a manner analogous to the way grammar organizes meaning in verbal communication. Neither the grammar of schooling nor the grammar of speech needs to be consciously understood to operate smoothly. Indeed, much of the grammar of schooling has become taken for granted as just the way schools are. It is the *departure* from customary school practice that attracts attention. (p. 85)

When I pursued research methods that might allow for small-scale collective action and self-representation on the part of students, I departed from customary practices at City School and confronted its grammar.

When Researchers Are Sent to the Principal's Office: Is Collective Action "Educational"?

For several months Sheila and I had been hearing many teen mothers complain about the difficulties they were having getting to and from school on the public bus system. At lunch one day, Sheila suggested writing a group letter to the transit authority, because together they would have a stronger voice. Jasmine (age 18) doubted anyone would listen, but others thought it might work. Willow (age 18) then had a suggestion that rallied everyone: Why not ask that the courtesy signs—which directed people to give up a few set-aside seats to "elderly and disabled passengers"—be rewritten to include parents traveling with small children and pregnant women? Sheila offered to write the first draft of a cover letter, and the teen mothers present all agreed to write down their recent bus experiences (positive and negative), which could then be appended to the letter. Later that day, Sheila ran the idea past me, and I endorsed it (field notes, 10/18/93). Afterward, Jasmine wrote in her journal that she felt "accepted" when Sheila offered to help with "the bus ordeal. She makes us feel like we have rights. Usually people just either feel sorry for us or think we deserve it."

A few days later, Sheila showed me an outline of the letter, clearly marked *draft*. She wondered whether to put the letter on university or City School letterhead, and I explained that neither would be appropriate, because this would imply institutional endorsement. I urged her to share with the teen mothers how she had obtained the transit authority's address and contact person's name. Sheila also ran the idea past Ms. Connell, who offered to buy pizza for the teen mothers during a lunch hour set aside to brainstorm and work on the draft (field notes, 10/21/93).

Although seemingly clear on the fact that the letter was a draft, Ms. Connell took a copy to the new principal at City School once Sheila left for the day. After meeting with him, Ms. Connell phoned me to say that he was concerned and saw "no educational value" in the project. Further, he wondered who "this woman" (Sheila) was and said the letter as written was potentially "libelous" and as principal, he could be held accountable if such a letter went out on City School letterhead.

I confessed to Ms. Connell that I was a bit unsettled by the fact that she had taken such an early draft of the letter to the principal. As Sheila's supervisor, I would never have approved a letter even mentioning City School unless both she and the principal had first given their approval. I had gained access to City School through the previous principal, and I did not want the new principal, whom I hardly knew, to think I would try to undermine his authority. I would have to clear this up with him immediately. Although I did not say it, I felt that, in essence, Ms. Connell had sent me to the principal's office!

I suspected she wanted to convey indirectly to Sheila and me that we had infringed on her authority; she wanted to remind us that we were present in the school only with her consent and that of the principal. Sheila's offer of help, although made outside of class time, was discredited as not "educational," not only because she offered to do too much herself but also because she had framed the project as a collective rather than an individual one. By encouraging the teen mothers to write as a group, Sheila was seen as stirring up the kind of divisive "we-they situation" so disliked by Ms. Connell. As Ms. Connell explained to me, "If the students are motivated, they will do this on their own. In communications, we do letters of complaint. I tell them to be polite, to carefully spell out their complaint." And: "They need to learn coping skills" (field notes, 10/23/98).

Teen mothers are often both wards of the state (sometimes literally) and threats to the state, insofar as they are perceived to be a drain on the welfare coffers. Viewed in this light, teachers such as Ms. Connell and others who have some responsibility over teen mothers may come to see the behavior and voiced opinions of the teen mothers as a threat to their professional standing. Furthermore, as multicultural education scholar

Christine Sleeter (1996) argues, "[t]he social locations, vested interests, and ideology of professional educators usually differ in significant ways from that of oppressed communities" (p. 241).

The subsequent meeting Sheila and I had with the principal was cordial. He allowed that Ms. Connell had come to him "with concerns," perhaps prematurely. He mentioned the importance of educational relevance (implicitly distinguishing education from social activism) and following proper channels and suggested we "go slow" and involve teachers from the English department, who could work with the teen mothers on their writing (field notes, 11/1/93). Thus, we were reminded to respect the grammar of schooling, and although the principal said he liked the idea of the project, his suggestion about involving the English teachers seemed to reduce it mainly to a grammar lesson.

Grammar Lesson, Part Two:
How the Journal Writing Project Came to a Halt
From the beginning of the fieldwork, I had hoped to encourage the teen mothers to write journals. Journal writing would allow the young women to reflect on their experiences across many contexts. It would thus complement Sheila's and my observations as we shadowed them through their school day, where we would always be intruding in some way between the teen mothers and teachers, administrators, and other students. In interviews I could ask teen mothers to reflect on instances of acceptance and stigma, but in my experience, interviewees tend to forget or exclude from comment the minutiae of the everyday. Life circumstances change, moods vary; weekly journal entries would perhaps capture this flux by providing numerous snapshots over time.

Equally important, I had hoped that keeping journals would make the students feel more like participants in, rather than objects of, the research. I wanted them to know that their ideas and interpretations of experiences were highly valued resources. In addition, I saw individual journal reflections as the possible basis for eventual group theorizing and perhaps action or some form of self-representation.

I explained my idea to Ms. Connell during the pilot phase of the study and asked for her approval and advice. She liked the idea of journals and told me that the students could get credit for writing either through English or a unit on "self-exploration" in Family Management. She suggested that I provide them with a list of questions to prompt their reflection (field notes, 6/15/93). On the eve of introducing the idea of journals to students and seeking their participation, Ms. Connell suggested that my questions encourage students "to learn to focus on the positive"; she agreed, though, that negative experiences should be reported, too (field notes, 9/8/93).

In response to Ms. Connell's concern, my set of questions led with the following: "Did anybody anywhere say anything to you, or do anything for you, that you felt was a sign that they accepted you? Describe the person. What did he or she say or do? How did you react? Why?" The next set of questions read: "Did anybody anywhere say anything to you, or do anything to you, that you felt was judgmental? Describe the person. What did he or she say or do? How did you react? Why?" These questions, and a set written of guidelines, were approved by Ms. Connell.

On the day I described the journal-writing project to students, all 13 present elected to participate. They seemed to have fun selecting pen names and enjoyed the colorful notebooks I had purchased for the occasion (field notes, 9/13/93). When they were not in use, the journals were kept in a locked filing cabinet in the TAPP classroom. Only Sheila and I knew which teen mothers used which pen names, and I kept track of who had completed their weekly entries in a gradebook provided by Ms. Connell. Most students made regular entries until winter break, and I thought I had found a way for teen mothers who were pressed for time to get credit (the main currency of schooling) for self-reflection.

Even before the break, though, Gina told Sheila that she had got the impression that the journal writing project was over (field notes, 12/1/93); this coincided with a shift in Ms. Connell's attitude toward the study that Sheila and I both thought we detected in the wake of what Jasmine had described as the "bus ordeal." After the break, Ms. Connell told Gina that students would have to write 40 journal entries to get 1 credit—up from 12 entries (field notes, 1/14/94). According to Jasmine, Ms. Connell had discouraged students from writing in their journals, implying that this phase of the research had ended (field notes, 1/17/94). Journal entries slowed to a halt.

Ms. Connell seemed to be sending some indirect signals that she wanted the journal writing project to end. When I talked to her about this, she seemed defensive and commented that she had not looked at the journals but wondered whether they were "educational. I want the work to be aboveboard, not sloppy" (field notes, 1/26/94). I did not want to antagonize Ms. Connell—whose goodwill was critical to the overall study—by questioning her further or taking issue with her explanation.

Yet I was left to wonder: How could Ms. Connell know the quality of the work if she had not read the journals, in violation of the agreement that only Sheila and I would read them? What did she mean by "above-board, not sloppy"? She had read and approved my posted set of guide-lines for journal writing, including: "Don't worry about grammar, spell-ing, crossed-out words. Your journals will not be graded!"

I found the preoccupation with grammar, rather than the content of what the students were trying to communicate, frustrating, and especially so in the case of journal writing, where students were struggling to repre-sent themselves and in relation to others. Learning grammar is important for certain purposes, but overemphasizing it kills the spirit to write and to see writing as a path to self-expression and self-knowledge. I had learned this by watching my brother, Matt, struggle with dyslexia; fortunately, he found an outlet in poetry, which, not coincidentally, tolerates and even celebrates lapses in grammar and spelling.

Although the supposed lapses in grammar and spelling of the teen mothers became the official reason Ms. Connell wanted to halt the jour-nal-writing project, I suspected that her unofficial reason was my violation of the grammar of schooling. The lack of grading, the lack of attention to form, the lack of a minimum word length or amount of time spent writing an entry, the lack of guidelines regarding appropriateness of content—any or all of these may have been grounds for the charge that the work was "sloppy" or not "above board."

Town School: Small Acts of Advocacy, Complicity, Self-Censorship

After my confrontations with the grammar of City School and TAPP, I approached the Town School site (located in the community of Midland) more cautiously. My plan to study a school committed to lessening the stigma attached to teen pregnancy and parenthood went awry when the school district decided to delay the opening of the Young Parents Pro-gram and locate it in a school where administrators were much less sup-portive than the team at the original site. As a result, I could not, as I had anticipated, document the strategies and challenges of progressive ad-ministrators who were intent on creating a fully inclusive environment. Instead, I was confronted with a general silence about the Young Parents Program and issues related to sexuality and I had to grapple with whether and how to interrupt that silence.

Interrupting the Silences

At Town School, where all teen parents were fully integrated into regular classes, the YPP structure allowed fewer opportunities for me to work with program participants as a group. I necessarily spent more time with students who were not parents as well as with a wide variety of teachers. I was struck by the fact that at Town School the silences around sexuality issues of all kinds seemed larger at the same time that the students were more sexually active than at City School (see Chapter 7).

Because of the disjunction between my critical feminist stance and the prevailing discourse on sexuality at Town School, I was inevitably called upon to break the silence: by adding my own voice to the muted chorus of progressive teachers, by advocating on behalf of teen mothers, and by providing information to students in need. Just as inevitably, I was also asked to participate in the silence as a condition of remaining in the school to complete my research. My acts of advocacy were minimal and were done on behalf of individuals; this contrasted with my intentions at City School, where I had hoped advocacy would also take the form of helping teen mothers advocate for themselves. My small acts of advocacy fell into four categories.

A third partner in the school-community collaboration. My initial way into Midland and eventually Town School was through the Youth Society, a progressive, community-based organization that had initiated the Young Parents Program idea and planned to operate the day care. Consequently, I knew a lot more about the project than the administrators and teachers at Town School, who were initially upset that the plan had been "imposed" on them by district administrators. Rumors began to circulate that, if true, might have undermined staff support for the day care (e.g., that 60 "outside" teen mothers were to be accommodated). I found myself dispelling these rumors, at times acting as a go-between or third partner in the fledgling school-community collaboration. But I worried that my intervention might create distance between those most opposed to the day care and me and perhaps reduce my ability to document the multiple, sometimes hidden, agendas that were certain to emerge as the controversial new policy was being implemented.

A resource for progressive staff. As progressive staff members learned more about me, they used me in several ways: (a) as a sounding board, (b) as an "expert" they could cite in support of progressive policies, and (c) as a guest speaker—from outside the community and protected by a university position—who could voice opinions and answer questions they did not always feel safe voicing or answering themselves. I did not volunteer myself as a resource, but I was usually happy to help.

A few examples: Ms. Bosworth, the drama teacher, asked me to review *Dolls,* the play she had selected to be the school's annual feature performance. I reported back that its anti-abortion stance troubled me. In response, she decided to cut the slides and verbal descriptions of fetal development (e.g., "At the end of the first month . . . the baby is . . .") that are intended to be shown throughout the play. As performed at Town School, *Dolls* still did not present abortion as a worthy option, but its pro-life message had been toned down.

In a meeting called to quell the anxieties of staff, the day care coordinator cited me and local statistics to argue against the notion that there was an "epidemic" of teen pregnancy and motherhood. Later a teacher said she sometimes invoked my "expert" findings to conservative colleagues, but just as often she kept quiet, because, she confided, "You don't want to have too many daggers in your back in one day."

This teacher invited me to report back to a Grade 8 class on my interviews with students on issues related to teen pregnancy and to answer their questions. Just prior to the start of class, the teacher encouraged me, if I felt comfortable, to be honest about my views on abortion. As it turned out, the very first question was whether I believed in abortion. I told students that I thought it was a difficult and painful choice, but I was pro-choice because the individual circumstances of people's lives had to be taken into consideration. I was raised in the Catholic church, which condemns abortion, but as I had gotten older, I began to realize that, in certain circumstances, it might be the best choice.

A source for students who needed information. I had to convince school officials to allow me to interview younger high school students; they initially argued that "eighth graders don't know anything about teen pregnancy." Although it was true that many did not seem to be sexually active at this age, others volunteered that they were facing pressure from boyfriends. One such girl (age 14) reported feelings of distress and confusion about her unnamed feelings of sexual desire, yet she had no adult to whom she felt comfortable talking (her assigned counselor was a man). I was able to direct her to two counselors whom I thought she could trust. Another set of eighth grade girls approached me to ask whether they could obtain birth control pills without parental permission, and I told them about the local youth clinic.

An advocate for teen mothers. As I got to know many of the teen mothers at Town School, small moments arose where I could, and sometimes did, serve as their advocate. In one-on-one conversations with school staff, I occasionally cited interim findings to challenge particular stereotypes. For example, the school principal, suspecting that teen mothers were "using their children" as an excuse not to attend school, declared,

"I think that we are getting fiddled and diddled by the young mothers . . . and we have to be tougher." I took the opportunity to remind him about lack of child care support for those with sick children and was able to discuss a number of teen mothers on the honor roll, who probably did not come to his attention as readily as those who were chronically absent. I do not think my comments were decisive, but the principal did eventually support a policy of excusing absences of teen mothers in cases when they were caring for a sick child.

Another example: the day care coordinator asked me to discuss my findings to date with the child care workers. They reported that they were frequently called upon by family members, friends, and acquaintances to respond to negative stereotypes about teen mothers. I shared my judgment that the preponderance of academic research had debunked several myths, including the idea that teens have babies in order to obtain welfare. When it came to light that a TV talk show had fueled fears that children as young as 12 were deliberately planning to get pregnant, I critically analyzed the format of such programs and led a discussion of who might stand to benefit from such sensationalism.

In general, while still conducting fieldwork, I tended to speak out if I felt people were at least open to an alternative interpretation, in a position to make a difference (e.g., perceived to be an opinion leader in the school), or both. At the same time, I listened carefully to opposing views and encouraged staff members to challenge my views.

Participating in the Silences
Although I tried (and continue to try) to interrupt the sexuality-related silences I encountered while doing fieldwork at Town School, I inevitably participated in them as well. I had been warned that Town School's principal was conservative and did not favor the incoming day care. He reluctantly gave me permission to do the research (after I reminded him that I had already received permission from the district superintendent) but told me he wanted "total involvement" regarding who I spoke to and how I obtained their consent. He cautioned me to keep a low profile, which I soon realized was part of his overall strategy to limit the visibility of the Young Parents Program.

Even after the program had been up and running for over two months, the principal forbade me to mention the day care in my cover letter to parents requesting their consent to interview their sons and daughters as part of my study. (The new day care was a cornerstone of Town School's supported integration effort, and I was eager to interview students formally about its impact in the school.) Drawing parental attention to the day care, he said, would "open a can of worms"; we agreed that instead I would couch my study more generally in terms of teen pregnancy (field notes, 11/16/94). In the absence of any official discussion of the day care by school administrators in either daily public address announcements or monthly newsletters, students ironically and erroneously concluded that teen pregnancy was much more prevalent in their school than they realized (they were unaware that the day care served teen mothers from all over town). Some of the students I interviewed read this silence as evidence that school officials were "ashamed" of "not teaching sex ed well enough."

Perhaps more insidiously, I participated in the school's silences through acts of self-censorship. My largely unspoken perspective on the decision of the teen mothers to raise their own children provides the prime example. I respect the right of women of all ages to make this decision, particularly in light of the material and cultural constraints that shape the available choices. Individual women are likely to know better than anybody else what they are capable of handling as well as the specific circumstances informing their decision.

This view clashed with the prevailing ideologies at Town School and in the wider society. To conservatives, the teen mother is Other because she did not "just say no." To liberals, the teen mother is Other because she did not use contraception or have an abortion and then compounded her error by not placing her baby for adoption. Across ideological differences, there is a consensus that "young" women lack the maturity and resources to be good mothers.

Yet I observed many of the young women at Town and City Schools to be fine mothers when they received support from family, community, and the state. Not a few told me that the experience had been difficult but positive and may even have saved their own lives. Yes, most received government money. But most young women who become teen mothers are raised in poverty, and a growing body of research now suggests that postponing childbearing may make little difference in improving their lives (see Chapter 4; Luker, 1996). Even conservatives would probably have a difficult time suggesting that society somehow prevent low-income women in their twenties and older from having children (Jencks & Edin, 1995).

I made the calculation (and would probably make the same one again) that nobody in Town School would take up this more radical discourse as in any way authoritative. To speak in these ways could only alienate me, I felt, from the people whose perspectives I was trying to learn about and eventually portray. Indeed, so hegemonic was the view that becoming a teen mother was a "bad" choice (see Chapter 3), that I was never asked directly to express my views on the matter. In order to maintain access to the research site and prevent a shutdown of dialogue with research participants, I chose to remain silent.

Fieldwork Lessons

As conceptualizations of power have become more complex, so, too, have attempts to give meaning to the idea that critical feminist ethnographers seek, through their research, to understand, challenge, and transform unequal relations of power. Further complications arise when such research is carried out in schools and the ethnographer has an interest not only in understanding the perspectives of variously positioned participants but also in grounding these various perspectives in an understanding of how schools—as contested arenas—work both to reinforce and challenge wider social forces.

An earlier generation of school-based critical ethnographies were often cases of studying down; that is, relatively privileged ethnographers studying marginalized groups of students (see Quantz, 1992 for a review). Immersed in an organization crisscrossed by power relations, I began to see my ethnography as a case of studying up (when, for example, I documented from a critical perspective the perceptions and actions of school and district administrators and school board members with the power to prevent my research from moving forward), studying down (when I, as a relatively privileged middle-class, White woman academic, sought to clarify how teen mothers and other students disadvantaged by age, gender, class, sexuality, and ethnicity understood and responded to their positioning within the school), and studying across (when I sought alliances with progressive teachers, administrators, and community activists).

Because of my more complex understanding of the workings of power and the school as a contested terrain, it strikes me as inevitable that critical feminist ethnographers will collude in unequal relations of power despite our political goals to challenge and transform them. Whether our actions in the field constitute interventions in an oppressive status quo or acts of complicity in that status quo will no doubt depend on nuanced assessments of local contexts.

Therefore, whenever our collusion or collision with power results in self-censorship, we should pay formal, recorded attention by asking some key questions: Is this necessary for me to maintain access to a research site, and if so, at what cost? Can my self-censorship be viewed as an effort to suspend final judgment as I try to listen carefully to a wide range of people, including those in positions of relative power? Is my self-censorship a politically savvy means of retaining credibility with as many participants and outsiders as possible, with an eye toward making the fullest, most persuasive case for my emerging conclusions?

Or, in a more negative light, by remaining silent am I missing an opportunity to submit my provisional findings and conclusions to on-the-spot critiques by those in the research setting? Through my silences and failures to intervene, am I betraying the interests of those participants with the least power to tell their stories and disturb the dominant ways of understanding their lives (Ong, 1995)?

Having grappled with such self-assessments all the way along, the critical feminist ethnographer must be prepared to act on them. She or he must be prepared, under compelling circumstances, to suspend or radically restructure the research process in order to avoid adding another layer of silencing. At a minimum, the ongoing tension between advocacy and self-censorship and the ethnographer's attention to that tension must be explicated in the final written accounts of the research if we are to pay proper heed to the complexities of power.

Speaking About, For, and With Teen Mothers: Writing Dilemmas

In making the transition from fieldwork to writing, similar tensions arise, although they take different form. As a critical feminist ethnographer, I alternately attempt to speak about, for, and with teen mothers as I analyze and write about discourses, including school policies, about and for— but not necessarily or always with—teen mothers. In a different but related context, Elizabeth Ellsworth has cogently summarized the political significance for issues of representation of these "orientations between the teller of the story" (in my case, the ethnographer) and "the subjects of the story":

> Each . . . enacts a particular social and political relationship that profoundly affects the meanings that will be constructed by listeners [and readers]. . . . *Speaking "about"* implies that the speaker/teacher[/researcher] does not share the social and political location of the group being represented, and is in a position to name, describe, analyze, and/or represent a group whose histories and meanings he or she does not live out. *Speaking "with"* implies that the speaker/teacher[/researcher] does not share the social position of the group he or she is representing, but is connected to that group by shared commitments and a history

of shared struggle, and has demonstrated an ability to respond meaningfully in support of that group in ways that have been welcomed and valued by its members. . . . *Speaking "for"* implies that the speaker, policy, curriculum, or teaching [and research] practice in some way represents—stands in for—those who cannot speak for themselves in a particular context and makes present and visible meanings and perspectives that, it is assumed, would otherwise by absent or missed. (1994, pp. 105–106, italics added)

Balancing the Risk of Misrepresentation against Retreat from Analysis

In undertaking to write an ethnography, my speaking about and my speaking for teen mothers raise highly overlapping political issues. As Linda Alcoff notes, "[I]t may be impossible to speak for others without simultaneously conferring information about them. Similarly, when one is speaking about others, or simply trying to describe their situation or some aspect of it, one may also be speaking in place of them, that is, speaking for them" (1991, p. 9). In both speaking about and for teen mothers, I imply that they make up a coherent group with identifiable needs, interests, and goals; whenever I attempt to do so, I run the risk of misrepresentation. The problem of representing others intensifies when those others are not well positioned to correct or reinterpret the ethnographer's written account.

As a critical feminist researcher, I want to avoid "blanket categorization that imposes identities, experiences, and names on individuals that they would not choose for themselves" (Phillips, 1996, p. 243). Indeed, I found that my informants had multiple and shifting identities (see Chapters 6 and 8). Still, they did occasionally highlight their collective identity as young women raising children, albeit using slightly different language depending on their intended audience. Some examples: A group at Town School that was starting an extracurricular club identified themselves as "teen parents" in order to attract fathers as well as mothers to their ranks (field notes, 10/13/93). In their letter to the transit authority, teen mothers at City School elected to represent themselves as "concerned parents," because they felt that (a) their requested policy change would benefit fathers and mothers of all ages and (b) revealing their age or secondary school student status would result in their effort being dismissed as "a Grade 8 school project" (field notes, 10/25/93 and 2/28/94). And finally, an attempt by a dozen students to represent themselves as "teen moms in the nineties," which I explore in Chapter 8, illustrates both the difficulty of constituting themselves as a coherent group as well as the possibility of arriving at a set of agreed-upon messages.

Assuming that a provisional collection of concerns and commitments can be discerned from such efforts—concerns and commitments that I share and have attempted to support—I can claim to speak with teen mothers. I see this task as similar to writing what Laurel Richardson has called a "collective story" (1995) about teen mothers, one that they would recognize and not see as one more attempt to represent them as the Other. If successful, I might help to challenge the negative images of teen mothers, which are used to justify social welfare cuts and restrictions on teen sexuality generally.

Speaking with is a type of advocacy, and one that at least some of the teen mothers applauded. They made clear that they did not see themselves as my book's primary audience. Instead, they wanted me to counter stigmatizing representations of teen mothers, and single mothers generally, that were circulating in the media and their communities. By virtue of their age, they felt they would not be taken seriously by those in power.

Anna (age 17), for example, wanted to see a researcher like me counter the negative portrayals of teen mothers on TV talk shows:

> I think that they need somebody to be there [on TV] as a spokesperson . . . just somebody who can go up there and say, "I've talked to all these girls," and have the actual facts instead of just us going [affecting a repentant tone], "We didn't mean to get pregnant."

In Anna's view, a researcher could speak for teen mothers, or with them, and more effectively challenge prevailing stereotypes.

Gathering and presenting the stories of teen mothers ("the actual facts"), however, is far from straightforward. The individual stories, let alone the collective story, of teen mothers will always be constructions built of multiple, competing discourses. Some teen mothers I spoke to, perhaps as a way to distance themselves from negative images, asserted that other teen mothers *did* fit the stereotypes. Thus, teen mothers, a relatively oppressed group, may nevertheless conceive of themselves and others who are similarly positioned in ways that are contaminated by dominant perspectives. In failing to recognize this, the ethnographer risks the "romanticizing of narratives and the concomitant retreat from analysis" (Fine, 1994, p. 80).

Thus, the ethnographer cannot avoid analyzing the narratives she or he has gathered in context and making judgments about how to generalize across stories and perspectives. Yet, as Michelle Fine (1994) has argued, researchers who "self-consciously translate 'for' Others in order to promote social justice" (p. 79) risk "imperial translation" (p. 80). I ran that risk many times. To give just one example, I analyzed one teen mother's story as a possible case of her boyfriend coercing her into having unprotected sex (see Chapter 7). Although Fran (age 18) did not reject my interpretation outright, neither, understandably, did she want people to see her as a victim.

Writing Lessons

To minimize the risk of imperial translation or "othering," the ethnographer who intends to write a collective story can use several strategies: First, the ethnographer can *put herself more fully into the story* by explicating the location from which she writes, that is, the aspects of her positionality (Alcoff, 1988, esp. p. 433) most relevant to the issue under study. This involves pondering such key questions as: "What are the complexities of the speaker's social identity? What life experiences have shaped it? Does the person speak from a position of relative dominance or relative subordination?" (Rosaldo, 1989, p. 169).

Second, and related to the first strategy, the ethnographer can *aim for relational understanding by providing opportunities for informants to talk back* or put forward alternative interpretations. Renato Rosaldo, for example, emphasizes making

> the researcher's upper-middle-class professional persona culturally visible. The study of differences, formerly defined in opposition to an invisible "self," now becomes the play of similarities and differences relative to socially explicit identities. How do "they" see "us"? Who are "we" looking at "them"? Social analysis thus becomes a relational form of understanding in which both parties actively engage in "the interpretation of cultures." (1989, pp. 206–207)

Allowing informants to talk back, to add to or correct the ethnographer's interpretations and representations, can be a formidable task in certain contexts and among seriously marginalized groups. As I discussed above, the grammar of schooling (as well as the material conditions of their lives) made it difficult for teen mothers to participate more fully in my study. Further, as is common with the most economically disadvantaged people, many of the teen mothers moved frequently and sometimes did not have telephones, and I found it nearly impossible to stay in touch with them over the period of years that elapsed between first meeting them and drafting written accounts to which they could respond.[1]

Third, *recognize diversity within the group.* This strategy goes counter to the widespread practice in the analysis of qualitative data of looking for commonalities and unifying themes. At the time I was doing fieldwork, for example, it was popular among professionals working with teen mothers and progressives in the media and elsewhere to cite "the frequency of sexual abuse in the life histories of girls who become pregnant in their teens" (Musick, 1993, p. 86). This is an important issue to explore, and the supposed causal links between sexual abuse and teen pregnancy get used rhetorically to counter negative images of teen mothers. In the process, however, teen mothers in general often get cast as simply victims.

Mina, age 18 and a City School student, was featured in a news article in which the teen-mother-as-victim-of-sexual-abuse theme was prominent and a pull-quote by a professional working with teen mothers read, "The fastest way from slut to angelhood is becoming a madonna." Citing work by Debra Boyer, the article posits that young women who have been sexually abused may later engage in behavior that others see as "promiscuous"; then, in a subconscious effort to move out of the "bad girl" category, they become pregnant and mothers. Mina objected to how the reporter implied that she was "looking for something other than a boyfriend" (i.e., a "father figure") and that "I was abused and looking for a dad who wasn't abusive, and I mean it wasn't that way."

Fourth, *present people as complex* rather than one-dimensional individuals so they are less susceptible to being read as stock types (Atkinson, 1990, p. 130). As Linda Brodkey notes: "It matters foremost whether representations are simple or complex, if only because complexity provides grounds for resisting the received identities, the stereotypes, that are used to rationalize inequitable social treatment" (1996, p. 197). To continue with the example of sexual abuse, even those teen mothers who told me they were survivors of abuse did not want their lives to be solely interpreted through this lens. The experience of this victimization was one important event among many, and most resisted seeing it as the underlying explanation for their having become teen mothers.

Fifth, *place people's stories* (their interpretations, actions) *into context,* including the unequal material and symbolic relations that shape the wider social order. Context emerges as crucial as the ethnographer seeks to balance the risk of "imperial translation" against a "retreat from analysis" (Fine, 1994). For example, prevailing "notions of good mothering practices" against which teen mothers are judged and often found lacking "take no account of the actual material and social conditions of mothering work" (D. Smith, 1987, p. 168). Attending to the wider order helps the ethnographer avoid depicting people as simply victims or "individual heroes who thrive despite the obstacles" (Fine & Weis, 1996, p. 270).

Sixth, *explore differences within the group that might also form a pattern,* a pattern that group members would recognize and to which they would resonate (see Chapter 8). This strategy shares a particular affinity to Laurel Richardson's idea of the collective story:

> The collective story displays an individual's story by narrativizing the experiences of the social category to which the individual belongs rather than by telling the particular individual's story or by simply retelling the cultural story [which is written from the point of view of the ruling interests and normative order]. . . . Although the narrative is about a category of people, the individual response to the well-told collective story is "That's *my* story. I am not alone." (1995, pp. 212–213)

A seventh and final suggestion, which I call the *same-yet-different* strategy, is intended to foster empathy while guarding against unwarranted claims of full understanding; the results of this self-reflexive process may or may not find their way into writing. Namely, the ethnographer might search for possible commonalities between herself and the group whose story is being told (e.g., experiences of motherhood), commonalities which, in turn, may reveal the larger social, political, and economic relations in which they are embedded. At the same time, however, the ethnographer must constantly bear in mind important differences between herself and the group (e.g., in material wealth and security) in order to avoid misleading and disrespectful generalizations.

As I examined some of the standards of mothering to which the young women in my study were being held and noted their exasperation with much of the unsolicited advice they received, I asked myself how I, a privileged White, middle-class professional, would react were these same standards being applied to me. Teen mothers are frequently criticized for the poor timing of their "choice," yet today's economy does not easily accommodate women of any age who are trying to combine childrearing and paid work or full-time study. So often the "right" time to have a baby never manifests itself clearly. I contemplated pregnancy during my fieldwork at City School, for instance, yet a number of well-intentioned colleagues urged me to wait until I had tenure. The same-yet-different stance kept my gaze focused on restrictive social structures while seeing the teen mothers as active agents, making the best of their circumstances.

Conclusion

The world and our understandings of it have become more complex. Back when Laura Nader wrote about studying up and Howard Becker and other symbolic interactionists began to treat the perspectives of subordinate people seriously, they helped to draw a new vector on the matrix of social inquiry. More than a quarter century later, the graph paper is crisscrossed by vectors, and today's inquiries necessarily are less about choosing a clear direction (studying up or studying down) and more about carefully mapping the complexities of power and locating oneself in them.

Still, our increased understanding of the workings of power and our awareness that no research stance is innocent of ideology need not—and should not—lead either to a retreat from attempts to study and interpret the world or to political paralysis. Faced with a myriad of ethical dilemmas, some critical scholars have foresworn fieldwork altogether.[2] This is not uncommon. Michelle Fine and Lois Weis observe that "as we read and hear our friends (and ourselves) pleading for researchers to be critical and self-reflexive, we note that many of these same friends have long stopped collecting data" (1996, p. 253). Yet Fine and Weis have not retreated from doing critical ethnography; they struggle with "how to best write authentically and critically about the narratives offered [by poor and working-class informants], in ways that serve communities, theory, and public policy" (1996, p. 259).

Why do critical ethnography? Gouldner highlighted the importance of drawing attention to the suffering of those who are ignored or forgotten and of identifying the "forms of suffering that are needless at particular times and places." At the same time, he cautioned sociologists against "voyeurism," about not becoming "zookeepers of deviance" (1968, p. 106). Critical ethnography does not understand those on the margins of society who suffer as mere victims but also as people who, as Gouldner put it, occasionally "fight back" (p. 107) and act as social critics.

Against some trends within poststructuralism, critical feminists want to retain such concepts as political economy, hegemony, and ideology, because oppressive practices continue on a large scale. Explains critical feminist theorist Jodi Dean (1996):

[W]omen face continual violence, degradation, harassment, rape, unwanted pregnancies, and inadequate health care; the United States [Canada] and numerous countries throughout Europe are witnessing a renewed nationalism that expresses itself in racism, anti-Semitism, and organized acts of violence against women. All over the world women's bodies and labor are exploited and abused. (p. 67)

Critiques of these "oppressive ideologies and practices offer insight into existing social conditions, and encourage others to imagine alternative cultural and institutional forms" (Miller, 1993, p. 263).

In short, we cannot allow "investigations into localized configurations of power to replace our awareness of and complicity in larger relationships and interconnections" (Dean, 1996, p. 67). This means grounding ethnographic research in broader social and political forces. As I noted earlier in this chapter, critical social researchers can play an important role in countering or reframing dominant discourses. This is the task I set for myself in researching and writing this book, a text that grows out of one critical feminist ethnographer's work in the field.

Notes

1. It proved easier to remain in touch with school and program staff members, and I communicated key findings to them in a variety of ways: giving a public lecture and a workshop, putting myself on the agenda at a staff meeting, filing an interim report at the school board office, and sending drafts of chapters to key informants. Perhaps due to time constraints, only one person commented on my written analysis. Ms. Long, the coordinator of the fledgling Young Parents Program at Town School, showed an interest in everything I sent her, in several cases using what I had written as the basis of ongoing professional development activities for her staff and Town School teachers.

2. Peter McLaren took this position at an audiotaped symposium, entitled "Plain Talk: Writing Rhetorics and Dialectics Across Ethnographic Genres," at the annual meeting of the American Educational Research Association in San Diego, April 15, 1998.

Chapter 10

Teen Mothers and the Inclusive Ideal: Toward a Critical Feminist Stance

> This ideal cannot be implemented as such. Social change arises from politics, not philosophy. Ideals are a crucial step in emancipatory politics, however, because they dislodge our assumption that what is given is necessary. They offer standpoints from which to criticize the given, and inspiration for imagining alternatives.
> —Iris Marion Young

Only recently have those with critical viewpoints—feminist scholars and practitioners, for example—begun to articulate a position on teen pregnancy and childbearing (e.g., Lawson & Rhode, 1993). This inattention can be partially attributed to the fact that feminists, too, have been caught up in what I have analyzed as the good choices discourse (see chapter 3). In seeking to explain the paucity of feminist analysis in this area, Constance Nathanson (1991) notes that, on the one hand, "empowering women to make their *own* choices" has been a goal of feminism. On the other hand, though, feminists (particularly White, middle-class ones) have found it difficult to view positively young (particularly working-class and ethnic minority) women's choices to have sex and to become mothers: "To 'choose' motherhood is to be suspected by modern feminists either of being victimized or of copping out. In neither circumstance is the choice ideologically acceptable" (p. 222).

To counter the good choices discourse, it is worth trying to articulate a critical feminist stance toward adolescent sexuality, pregnancy, and childbearing in the hopes that it might gain more political force and thus influence policy. In this chapter, I begin to sketch such a stance. In the process, I will critique the dominant discourse—including such ideologically loaded terms as *personal responsibility* and *welfare dependency*—

arguing that it frames the problems facing teen mothers as solely individual rather than also structural. That is, conventional wisdom does not acknowledge that becoming a teen mother might, under certain circumstances, be a "good choice," given the ways in which the current economic and political order restricts other choices for young people.

Reproductive Rights for All Women, Regardless of Age, Class, and Race

Feminists have long supported a woman's right to choose when, where, how, and with whom to give birth. Among mainstream feminists, the struggle for reproductive rights has focused on making contraception and abortion services more widely available, safer, and less stigmatized. Feminists have also stressed the need not only to increase access to sexuality education but to improve it, guided by an invitation to "adolescents to explore what feels good and bad, desirable and undesirable, grounded in experiences, needs, and limits" (Fine, 1988, p. 33).

Feminists who use a multicultural framework have tended to recognize more often than others that reproductive rights must extend beyond prevention issues and abstract talk of rights to the concrete needs of socially disadvantaged women and the ability to bear children and raise them in a healthy, supportive environment. Multicultural feminists, among others, recognize that low-income women, women with disabilities, women of color, and young women have, historically, been more vulnerable to coercive sterilization and birth control policies, supported by people who erroneously believe or imply that social problems are caused by disadvantaged groups of women bearing children (Luker, 1996; McLaren, 1990; Roberts, 1997).

First Nations parents, for example, must cope with the legacy of colonialism (including forced residential schooling), institutional racism, and poverty. As a spokesperson from the Indian Homemakers' Association of British Columbia put it: "The courts are racist towards native women. They don't want to hear the voices of native mothers. We must have a beautiful two-bedroom house with new paint, wall-to-wall carpeting and wonderful curtains. When we don't, they take away our children" (quoted in Bolan, 1993, p. A1).

Mindful of this history, I believe society should respect and support the right of young women to bear and raise their own children. To do otherwise compromises the reproductive rights agenda as a whole. Nearly two thirds of births to teenagers are to women aged 18 or 19 years old; they

are legal adults, entitled to vote as citizens. The available research suggests that were they to postpone childbearing into their twenties, most
would still be poor (see Chapter 4). It would be unfair to deny fellow
citizens the right to have children on the basis of income level. In this
light, restrictive policies, although ostensibly aimed at teen mothers, can
be seen ultimately to threaten the full reproductive rights of all but the
most privileged.

Respect and support for teen mothers means providing a variety of
resources without judgment and surveillance. One model for this is Jessie's
Centre for Teenagers in Toronto, which is run as a feminist collective.
Founder June Callwood describes the Centre's philosophy:

> The feminist approach of respect for teenage women and encouragement to en-
> able them to achieve self-worth and independence happens also to be the most
> effective way of helping their babies to thrive. . . . It provides what young moms,
> what *all* moms, need: friendship, information, relief. (1982, p. 38)

Suggestions by policymakers, both conservative and liberal, to
"restigmatize" teen pregnancy and motherhood are misguided. To start
with, teen mothers, as I have argued elsewhere in this book, still face
considerable stigma, albeit within updated constructs. Were it not so, I
would not in the course of my research be hearing stories from young
women who desperately denied their pregnancies for as long as they
could. To the extent that mores about childbearing outside of marriage
have become less rigid over the last 25 years, calling for "the return of
shame" (to quote a *Newsweek* cover title) is impractical and unlikely to
succeed (Luker, 1996). Although a dubious means of lowering teen pregnancy and birth rates, efforts to increase stigma and shame may produce
more denial. "[A] shame-ridden subject lacks a sense of entitlement, she
settles for less than she deserves; she is more easily dominated" (Bartky,
1996, p. 225).

Nurturing Agency, Promoting Collective
Social Responsibility

Rather than seeking to create more shame-ridden subjects, we should be
nurturing agency in young people, partly by taking collective action to
change the context that currently so limits their sexual and reproductive
choices, and partly by supporting them as they attempt to "do the right
thing" under difficult circumstances. A critical feminist perspective helps
to locate the various choices that culminate in teen motherhood in historical

and social context. It illuminates, among other things: that unequal power relations between men and women complicate the negotiation of contraceptive use; that in the classroom and beyond, pregnancy options are weighted unequally; that material and cultural conditions (e.g., barriers to access to contraception and abortion services; mixed messages about sexuality; and the pervasiveness of poverty and unemployment, child abuse, racism, heterosexism, and sexism) constrict the choices available.

The prevailing policy discourse condemns teen mothers, particularly those on welfare, as lacking in "personal responsibility." A critical feminist discourse would highlight instead how our major institutions have failed young people. In addition to pursuing a reinvigorated campaign for reproductive rights, for example, we need to tackle high youth unemployment. In short, we need to create more and better choices for young people "so that having a baby is not the only or most attractive one on the horizon" (Luker, 1996, p. 183). This strategy could be summarized as the promotion of collective social responsibility.

In addition to trying to broaden and improve the options open to young people, particularly those growing up in poverty, we need to provide second chances. By helping those in need, we model a particular type of responsibility, not one of duty enforced through punishment and reward, but one of empathy, nurtured "through being cared for and respected, and through caring for others" (Lakoff, 1996, p. 108).

Based on interviews and fieldwork with teen mothers enrolled in school full-time, I am convinced that, for the most part, they desired to take responsibility, and with support they found a renewed sense of themselves and joy in demonstrating their competence as parents. Such successes should be built upon and encouraged, not only through the provision of material support but ideologically as well. Critical feminists need to develop their own policy rationales rather than relying on conventional wisdom that stigmatizes teen mothers and considers their needs in isolation from other women facing similar or related difficulties.

Challenging the
Dependence-Independence Dichotomy

Conservatives tend to oppose government-funded support for teen mothers (e.g., day care subsidies) because they believe it encourages "welfare dependency" (construed as a moral failing) and discourages "personal responsibility" on the part of teen parents and their families. Liberals reason that some government support now prevents long-term, intergenerational welfare dependency as well as child abuse and neglect.

Critical feminists, in contrast, avoid and oppose talk about welfare dependency altogether. This discourse blames the poor for poverty and its consequences and perpetuates a false dichotomy between dependence (read: unpaid caregivers) and independence (read: paid workers).

The discourse about dependency also contains at least two major tensions. First, "when the subject under consideration is teenage pregnancy, these mothers are cast as children; when the subject is welfare, they become adults who should be self-supporting" (Fraser & Gordon, 1994, p. 329). Second, when teen mothers gain a measure of personal autonomy through state aid, it is considered "bad" dependency; when these young women are forced to rely on individual men for material support (whether the men are abusive or present by dint of the proverbial shotgun or not), it is considered "good" dependency.

Because of segmented labor markets and unequal pay, benefits, and access to on-the-job training, women—particularly ethnic minorities and those with working-class or poverty backgrounds—do not have the same choices as middle-class, White men regarding how to combine family and paid work lives. Furthermore, a woman with a partner who earns a middle-class salary chooses to be an "at-home parent" with much different consequences than a single mother who receives social assistance.

In contrast to divisive talk about dependence and independence, critical feminists stress *interdependence* and the need to respect and support the diversity of family types. Toni Morrison, for example, has said, "You need a whole community—everybody—to raise a child":

> The notion that the head is the one who brings in the most money is a patriarchal notion, that a woman . . . is somehow lesser than a male head. Or that I am incomplete without the male. That is not true. . . . [The nuclear family] isolates people into little units—people need a larger unit. (in Angelo, 1989, p. 122)

Although the current welfare system provides material support to low-income people and some autonomy to women, feminists argue that it is seriously flawed. It treats recipients in stigmatizing ways, as clients of public charity. Socialist feminists, in particular, have joined with anti-poverty and anti-racism activists to describe the system as "public (capitalist) patriarchy" and "welfare colonialism." The organization called End Legislated Poverty in Vancouver, for example, places an emphasis

> on how the state and its institutions not only keep people poor, but actually make them poor. The state makes people poor when it institutes policies that accept high levels of unemployment as inevitable: if some people are not allowed to work, they certainly cannot provide for themselves. The state makes people poor when it permits employers to pay some workers less than a living wage. The state

makes people poor when it perpetuates an under-valuation of some forms of labour, particularly the labour involved in caring for and raising children. (Cohen, 1993, p. 270)

Feminists disagree in their analysis of the welfare state and what reforms would best serve women. Some argue, for example, that higher welfare payments or more effort to create employment for women would not constitute serious reform. Because women are discriminated against in the home as well as the wage workplace, goes the argument, a wholesale attack on gender inequality, including within family roles, is necessary to deal truly with what makes female poverty unique (L. Gordon, 1990, p. 7).

Diana Pearce argues that in any such reform, "an essential element is the establishment of rights and entitlements for poor women and their families, such as the right to shelter, income support, equal pay, and quality child care" (1990, p. 275). Further, the dichotomy independent-dependent must be challenged as the current premise of the welfare system. Otherwise, "[the single mother] must choose between limiting her paid employment to devote more time to her children or limiting her time with her children in order to take more time for paid employment. Either choice perpetuates her poverty, both of income and of life" (p. 275). Single fathers, who are much less likely to live in poverty, do not usually face these tradeoffs in such harsh form; one out of ten single fathers in Canada lives in poverty compared with almost half of single mothers, a fact that cannot be explained by differences in education (Evans, 1996, p. 162).[1]

Class and race must be factored into the analysis of women's poverty. As socialist feminist scholar Johanna Brenner (1990) argues:

A program that incorporates short-term reforms into the larger goal of expanded social responsibility for caring would counteract both the stereotypical dependence of women as care-givers and the stereotypical independence of men as citizen-workers. This approach would frame the feminization of poverty issue in a way that connects it to the movements of working-class people and people of color. (p. 498)

Challenging the Ideologies of the Good Mother and Good Father

Prevailing ideologies of the good mother and the good father can yield destructive consequences, especially for poor people. The ideology of the providing father hurts poor men (as well as women) because "when fathering is identified with economic support in a way that mothering is not, and when men cannot consider themselves mothers, unemployed, impoverished young men cannot take themselves to be 'parents'" (Ruddick, 1990, p. 230).

The good mother ideology is equally destructive, because our culture is sending young women conflicting and hurtful messages about how to construct their self-esteem. Teenage girls' "futures—their potential for self-fulfillment, much less material security—are cut short because they believe . . . that biological mother love is at any cost the greatest, most meaningful fulfillment for a woman" (Rapping, 1990, p. 543).

What is needed, instead, is a new vision for both women and men, where the norm for both sexes would be to combine paid work with caregiving (i.e., childrearing, care for elders and others unable to work, and homemaking). In general, this would require men to become more like women are now. Such a large ideological shift would require major changes in the organization of the workplace, the welfare state, and the gender order (for an excellent analysis of what she calls the Universal Caregiver model, see Fraser, 1997, ch. 2).

Translating the Critical Feminist Stance into Policy

How might the critical feminist stance that I have just sketched translate into policy? One reform being tried throughout British Columbia and elsewhere in Canada is the provision of government-subsidized, school-based day care centers for the children of teen parents. Critical feminists would support this initiative but would reject as its guiding rationale the prevention of "welfare dependency." Instead, critical feminists might justify the full integration of teen parents and their children by arguing that the school itself is a public place and part of the larger community. They would reject as ideological any sharp distinction between public and private. Issues related to sexuality, procreation, and childrearing are deeply *political*. Categorizing them instead as only *private* or *personal* de-legitimizes struggles to change practices in these areas (Jaggar & Rothenberg, 1993, p. 121).

What might this mean in practice? Official and unofficial rules and structures that operate to exclude student-parents would need to be rethought. For example, critical feminists would support a flexible attendance policy for teen parents, particularly with regard to absences related to caring for sick children. If schools and workplaces introduced more flexible hours, then men and women, students and staff, would be better able to perform school, work, and family duties. Enhancing "flexibility for all [students and] workers offers an alternative that acknowledges pregnancy and child care as a human, not just a woman's, problem" (Minow, 1990, p. 89). Ultimately, as lawyer Patricia Blockson has argued in a different context:

> There needs to be a shift from thinking about parenthood as a personal choice to thinking that society as a whole should bear part of the burden for bringing up children. . . . The current reality is that women bear most child-rearing responsibilities and need accommodation now. (quoted in Cox, 1993, p. A2)

Seen this way, the ideal of an inclusive *school* is impossible to separate from the ideal of an inclusive *society.*

> The very recognition of plurality and of difference makes unprecedented demands on the institutions of this country. In other words, it is not only a matter of admission and inclusion in predefined public spaces; it is, as many of us have begun to see, a matter of transformation of our institutions and our public spaces. (Greene, 1998, p. 19)

Such a critical feminist stance obviously challenges prevailing values and assumptions; its discourse is not easily heard. The prospects for mobilizing around it may seem dim in the current conservative climate. Jill Blackmore (1995) has argued persuasively that when developing gender equity policy, reformers need to be "strategic rather than idealistic . . . depending upon the level of commitment and opposition which exists in specific contexts" (p. 310). Yet it is also worth articulating what is desirable, what might define the good society—a society that would not deny women the right to raise children and maintain their self-worth simply because they are young and live in poverty.

In articulating this definition of the good society, critical feminist policy analysts, scholars, practitioners, and activists would be expanding and challenging the individualistic discourse of "good choices" and "personal responsibility." They would be voicing a rationale for why those *in power* must make "good" choices that respond to the realities of those who, pushed to the margins by present policies, find their personal choices constricted.

Notes

1. Pearce (1990)—citing the U.S. Bureau of the Census publication, *Money Income: 1988*—reports that 44.7% of women-maintained households with children under 18 years old are in poverty, compared to about 7.7% of households maintained by men who have children living with them (p. 267).

References

Acker, J. (1990). Hierarchies, jobs, bodies: A theory of gendered organizations. *Gender & Society, 4* (2), 139–158.

Adler, C. (1982). *Towards a caring community.* Vancouver, BC: Social Planning and Review Council.

Alan Guttmacher Institute. (1994). *Sex and America's teenagers.* New York: Alan Guttmacher Institute.

Alcoff, L. (1988). Cultural feminism versus post-structuralism: The identity crisis in feminist theory. *Signs: Journal of Women in Culture and Society, 13* (3), 405–436.

Alcoff, L. (1991/92). The problem of speaking for others. *Cultural Critique, 23,* 5–32.

Alcoff, L., & Gray, L. (1993). Survivor discourse: Transgression or recuperation? *Signs: Journal of Women in Culture and Society, 18* (2), 260–290.

Allen, P. G. (1986). *The sacred hoop: Recovering the feminine in American Indian traditions.* Boston: Beacon Press.

Alway, J. (1995). The trouble with gender: Tales of the still-missing feminist revolution in sociological theory. *Sociological Theory, 13* (3), 209–228.

American Civil Liberties Union. (1998, August 6). Chipman v. Grant County School District. *American Civil Liberties Union Freedom Network* [On-line]. Available: http://www.aclu.org/news/n080698e.html

Anderson, K. (1989, December 2). Every girl's nightmare: Happy teenage mother backs right to choose. *Calgary Herald*, p. H2. (Reprinted from the *Ottawa Citizen*)

Angelo, B. (1989, May 22). Interview with Toni Morrison: The pain of being black. *Time*, pp. 120–122.

Arney, W., & Bergen, B. (1984). Power and visibility: The invention of teenage pregnancy. *Social Science Medicine, 18* (1), 11–19.

Atkinson, P. (1990). *The ethnographic imagination: Textual constructions of reality.* New York: Routledge.

Austin, R. (1989). Sapphire bound! *Wisconsin Law Review, 3,* 539–578.

Ball, S. J. (1987). *The micro-politics of the school.* London: Methuen.

Barrett, M., King, A., Levy, J., Maticka-Tyndale, E., & McKay, A. (1997). Canada. In R. T. Francoeur (Ed.), *The international encyclopedia of sexuality, Volume 1: Argentina to Greece* (pp. 221–343). New York: Continuum.

Barrett, M. (1985). Ideology and the cultural production of gender. In J. Newton (Ed.), *Feminist criticism and social change* (pp. 65–85). New York: Methuen.

Bartky, S. L. (1996). The pedagogy of shame. In C. Luke (Ed.), *Feminisms and pedagogies of everyday life* (pp. 225–241). Albany: State University of New York Press.

Belyea, S., & Dubinsky, K. (1994). "Don't judge us too quick": Writing about teenage girls and sex. In S. Prentice (Ed.), *Sex in schools: Canadian education and sexual regulation* (pp. 19–43). Toronto: Our School/Our Selves Education Foundation.

Bewley, L. (1984, March 2). This is simply not done. *Vancouver Sun,* p. A11.

Bibby, R. W., & Posterski, D. C. (1992). *Teen trends: A nation in motion.* Toronto: Stoddart.

Billung-Meyer, J. (1982). Forsaken children. *Canadian Woman Studies, 4* (1), 27–30.

Binder, A. (1993). Constructing racial rhetoric: Media depictions of harm in heavy metal and rap music. *American Sociological Review, 58,* 753–767.

Blackmore, J. (1995). Policy as dialogue: Feminist administrators working for educational change. *Gender and Society, 7* (2), 293–313.

Blank, R. M., & Hanratty, M. J. (1993). Responding to need: A comparison of social safety nets in Canada and the United States. In D. Card & R. B. Freeman (Eds.), *Small differences that matter: Labor markets and income maintenance in Canada and the United States* (pp. 191–231). Chicago: University of Chicago Press.

Bolan, K. (1993, August 21). Native leaders label custody ruling racist. *Vancouver Sun,* p. A1.

Boyer, D., & Fine, D. (1992). Sexual abuse as a factor in adolescent pregnancy and child maltreatment. *Family Planning Perspectives, 24* (1), 4–11.

Boyko, J. (1995). *Last steps to freedom: The evolution of Canadian racism.* Winnipeg, MB: Watson & Dwyer Publishing.

Bozinoff, L., & MacIntosh, P. (1992, January 16). Adults offer opinions concerning teenage sexual freedom. *The Gallup Report.* Toronto: Gallup Canada, Inc.

Brantlinger, E. (1997). Using ideology: Cases of nonrecognition of the politics of research and practice in special education. *Review of Educational Research, 67* (3), 425–459.

Brantlinger, E., Majd-Jabbari, M., & Guskin, S. L. (1996). Self-interest and liberal educational discourse: How ideology works for middle-class mothers. *American Educational Research Journal, 33* (3), 571–597.

Brenner, J. (1990). Feminist political discourses: Radical versus liberal approaches to the feminization of poverty and comparable worth. In K. V. Hansen & I. J. Philipson (Eds.), *Women, class, and the feminist imagination* (pp. 491–507). Philadelphia: Temple University Press.

Brewster, K. L., Billy, J. O. G., & Grady, W. R. (1993). Social context and adolescent behavior: The impact of community on the transition to sexual activity. *Social Forces, 71* (3), 713–740.

Bright, S. (1998, June 19). Abstinence blues: Teen sex isn't always traumatic. *Salon Magazine* [On-line]. Available: http://www.salonmagazine.com/col/brig/

British Columbia Ministry of Education and Ministry Responsible for Multiculturalism and Human Rights. (1993, December). BC21: A solution to BC's child care needs. *Ministry News, 10* (3), 2.

British Columbia Task Force on Access to Contraception and Abortion Services. (1994). *Realizing choices.* Victoria, BC: Queen's Printer for British Columbia.

Britzman, D. (1993). Beyond rolling models: Gender and multicultural education. In S. K. Biklen & D. Pollard (Eds.), *Gender and education* (pp. 25–42). Chicago: University of Chicago Press.

Brodie, J. (1996). Canadian women, changing state forms, and public policy. In J. Brodie (Ed.), *Women and Canadian public policy* (pp. 1–28). Toronto: Harcourt Brace and Company, Canada.

Brodie, J., Gavigan, S., & Jenson, J. (1992). *The politics of abortion.* Toronto: Oxford University Press.

Brodkey, L. (1996). *Writing permitted in designated areas only.* Minneapolis: University of Minnesota Press.

Brunet, R. (1992, December 14). Parents fighting planned obsolescence. *British Columbia Report,* p. 23.

Buchholz, E. S., & Korn-Bursztyn, C. (1993). Children of adolescent mothers: Are they at risk for abuse? *Adolescence, 28* (110), 361–382.

Buckingham, D. (1987). *Public secrets: Eastenders and its audience.* London: British Film Institute.

Buie, J. (1987, April 8). Pregnant teen-agers: New view of old solution. *Education Week,* p. 32.

Burdell, P. (1995–1996). Teen mothers in high school: Tracking their curriculum. *Review of Research in Education, 21,* 163–208.

Butler, J. R., & Burton, L. M. (1990). Rethinking teenage childbearing: Is sexual abuse a missing link? *Family Relations, 39* (1), 73–80.

Byfield, T. (1993, May 10). Listen, Abbotsford, as Southams tell you how to raise your kids. *British Columbia Report,* p. 44.

Cable News Network. (1998, April 28). Teenage mother barred from National Honor Society. *Talk back live.* Atlanta, GA: CNN. [Available: On-line]: http://cnn.com/TRANSCRIPTS/9804/28/tl.00.html

Cagampang, H. H., Gerritz, W. H., & Hayward, G. C. (1987). *Pregnant and parenting minors and California schools* (Report No. PC87–4-6-SOR). Berkeley: Policy Analysis for California Education.

Cahill, B. L. (1992). *Butterbox babies.* Toronto: McClelland-Bantam, Inc.

Callwood, J. (1982). Jessie's: Young moms and thriving babies. *Canadian Woman Studies, 4* (1), 37–39.

Canaan, J. (1986). Why a "slut" is a "slut": Cautionary tales of middle-class teenage girls' morality. In H. Varenne (Ed.), *Symbolizing America* (pp. 184–208). Lincoln: University of Nebraska Press.

Canadian Press. (1978, July 15). Pregnant girls off aid: Vander Zalm. *Province,* p. 4.

Canadian Press. (1980a, April 8). Wrong girls keep their babies, professor says. *Vancouver Sun,* p. A17.

Canadian Press. (1980b, October 18). Teen moms "must stay in school." *Vancouver Sun,* p. A19.

Canadian Press. (1990, July 27). Teenage parents emerging problem. *Winnipeg Free Press,* p. 12.

Canadian Press. (1994, December 21). Teen moms better than lesbians, MP claims. *Vancouver Sun,* A6.

Canadian Press. (1995a, March 14). Manning in U.S.: Republican plans to slice welfare labelled too harsh. *Vancouver Sun,* p. A10.

Canadian Press. (1995b, March 22). High schools change as teen pregnancy rates climb. *Canadian Press Newswire* [On-line].

Carlson, D. L. (1994, Fall). Gayness, multicultural education, and community. *Educational Foundations, 8* (4), 5–25.

Chan, C. S. (1994). Asian-American adolescents: Issues in the expression of sexuality. In J. M. Irvine (Ed.), *Sexual cultures and the construction of adolescent identities* (pp. 88–99). Philadelphia: Temple University Press.

Clark, B. L. (1994). On ignoring the hidden laughter in the rose garden; or, how our anxiety of immaturity enables us to belittle students. *Feminist Teacher, 8* (1), 32–37.

Clark, S. (1999). What do we know about unmarried mothers? In J. Wong & D. Checkland (Eds.), *Teenage pregnancy and parenting: Social and ethical issues* (pp. 10–24). Toronto: University of Toronto Press.

Clark, S., Dechman, M., French, F., & MacCallum, B. (1991). *Mothers and children, one decade later.* Halifax, NS: Nova Scotia Department of Community Services.

Cohen, M. G. (1993). Social policy and social services. In R. R. Pierson, M. G. Cohen, P. Bourne, & P. Masters (Eds.), *Canadian women's issues, Volume I: Strong voices* (pp. 264–284). Toronto: James Lorimer.

Collins, P. H. (1990). *Black feminist thought: Knowledge, consciousness and the politics of empowerment.* Boston: Unwin Hyman.

Connell, R. W. (1987). *Gender and power.* Stanford: Stanford University Press.

Coulter, R. P. (1996). Gender equity and schooling: Linking research and policy. *Canadian Journal of Education, 21* (4), 433–452.

Cox, B. (1993, August 26). Stirs controversy at bar meeting. *Vancouver Sun,* p. A2.

Cunningham, D. (1992a, October 12). Is virginity so bad? *British Columbia Report,* p. 28.

Cunningham, D. (1992b, December 14). Rediscovering chastity. *British Columbia Report,* pp. 18–21.

Cunningham, D. (1993, April 26). Institutionalizing infants. *British Columbia Report,* pp. 9–11.

Curtis, B., Livingstone, D. W., & Smaller, H. (1992). *Stacking the deck: The streaming of working-class kids in Ontario schools.* Toronto: Our Schools/Our Selves Education Foundation.

Dale-Johnson, L. (1995). *An analytic inventory of education-based programs with daycare for pregnant and parenting teens in British Columbia.* Unpublished master's thesis, University of Oregon, Eugene.

Daly, K. J., & Sobol, M. P. (1994). Adoption in Canada. *Canadian Social Trends, 32,* 2–5.

Dasgupta, S. D., & Dasgupta, S. (1996). Public face, private space: Asian Indian women and sexuality. In N. B. Maglin & D. Perry (Eds.), *"Bad girls"/"good girls": Women, sex, and power in the nineties* (pp. 226–243). New Brunswick, NJ: Rutgers University Press.

Davies, B. (1991, December). The concept of agency: A feminist poststructuralist analysis. *Social Analysis, 30,* 42–53.

Davies, B. (1993). Beyond dualism and towards multiple subjectivities. In L. K. Christian-Smith (Ed.), *Texts of desire: Essays on fiction, femininity, and schooling* (pp. 145–173). London: Falmer Press.

Dean, J. (1996). *Solidarity of strangers: Feminism after identity politics.* Berkeley: University of California Press.

Delbanco, S., Lundy, J., Hoff, T., Parker, M., & Smith, M. D. (1997). Public knowledge and perceptions about unplanned pregnancy and conception in three countries. *Family Planning Perspectives, 29* (2), 70–75.

Donovan, P. (1997). Can statutory rape laws be effective in preventing adolescent pregnancy? *Family Planning Perspectives, 29* (1), 30–34, 40.

Donovan, P. (1998a). While nationwide birthrate is stable, Black women achieve a record low, and teenagers' rates decline. *Family Planning Perspectives, 30* (3), 151–152.

Donovan, P. (1998b). School-based sexuality education: The issues and challenges. *Family Planning Perspectives, 30* (4), 188–193.

Drenth, J. J., & Slob, A. K. (1997). Netherlands and the Autonomous Dutch Antilles. In R. T. Francoeur (Ed.), *The international encyclopedia of sexuality, Volume 2: India to South Africa* (pp. 895–961). New York: Continuum.

Dube, F. (1993, April 22). Today's teens: It's payback time for rebellious children of the '60s. *Vancouver Sun,* p. A4. (Reprinted from the *Ottawa Citizen*)

Dunkle, M. C. (1990). Schools today aren't making the grade: A survey identifies some shortcomings. *Public Welfare, 48* (3), 9–15.

Durning, A. T. (1997, August 3). Stemming the tide: Region isn't powerless to deal humanely with population pressures. *Seattle Post-Intelligencer,* pp. E1, E3.

Earle, J. (1990). *Counselor/advocates: Keeping pregnant and parenting teens in school.* Alexandria, VA: National Association of State Boards of Education.

Ebert, T. L. (1996). *Ludic feminism and after: Postmodernism, desire, and labor in late capitalism.* Ann Arbor: University of Michigan Press.

Edelman, M. (1988). *Constructing the political spectacle.* Chicago: University of Chicago Press.

Ellsworth, E. (1994). Representation, self-representation, and the meanings of difference. In R. A. Martusewicz & W. M. Reynolds (Eds.), *Inside/out: Contemporary critical perspectives in education* (pp. 99–108). New York: St. Martin's Press.

Epstein, S. (1987). Gay politics, ethnic identity: The limits of social constructionism. *Socialist Review, 17* (93–94), 9–54.

Ericson, R. V., Baranek, P. M., & Chan, J. B. L. (1991). *Representing order: Crime, law, and justice in the news media.* Toronto: University of Toronto Press.

Esping-Andersen, G. (1990). *The three worlds of welfare capitalism.* Princeton: Princeton University Press.

Evans, P. (1996). Single mothers and Ontario's welfare policy: Restructuring the debate. In J. Brodie (Ed.), *Women and Canadian public policy* (pp. 151–171). Toronto: Harcourt Brace and Company, Canada.

Fallon, C. (1979). *The rise in adolescent pregnancy and parenthood: Proposed intervention strategies for this population.* Unpublished paper, School of Social Work, University of British Columbia, Canada.

Fine, M. (1988, February). Sexuality, schooling, and adolescent females: The missing discourse of desire. *Harvard Educational Review, 58* (1), 29–53.

Fine, M. (1991). *Framing dropouts: Notes on the politics of an urban public high school.* Albany: State University of New York Press.

Fine, M. (1994). Working the hyphens: Reinventing self and other in qualitative research. In N. K. Denzin & Y. S. Lincoln (Eds.), *Handbook of qualitative research* (pp. 70–82). Thousand Oaks, CA: Sage Publications.

Fine, M., & Weis, L. (1996). Writing the "wrongs" of fieldwork: Confronting our own research/writing dilemmas in urban ethnographies. *Qualitative Inquiry, 2* (3), 251–274.

Fournier, S., & Crey, E. (1997). *Stolen from our embrace: The abduction of First Nations children and the restoration of aboriginal communities.* Vancouver, BC: Douglas & McIntyre.

Fraser, N. (1989). *Unruly practices: Power, discourse, and gender in contemporary social theory.* Minneapolis: University of Minnesota Press.

Fraser, N. (1992). The uses and abuses of French discourse theories for feminist politics. In N. Fraser & S. L. Bartky (Eds.), *Revaluing French feminisms* (pp. 177–194). Bloomington: Indiana University Press.

Fraser, N. (1997). *Justice interruptus: Critical reflections on the "postsocialist" condition.* New York: Routledge.

Fraser, N., & Gordon, L. (1992). Contract versus charity: Why is there no social citizenship in the United States? *Socialist Review, 22* (3), 45–68.

Fraser, N., & Gordon, L. (1994). A genealogy of *dependency:* Tracing a keyword in the U.S. welfare state. *Signs: Journal of Women in Culture and Society, 19* (2), 309–336.

Frye, M. (1990). The possibility of feminist theory. In D. L. Rhode (Ed.), *Theoretical perspectives on sex difference* (pp. 174–184). New Haven: Yale University Press.

Furstenberg, F. F., Jr. (1991). As the pendulum swings: Teenage childbearing and social concern. *Family Relations, 40,* 127–138.

Furstenberg, F. F., Jr. (1997). Foreword. In K. M. Harris, *Teen mothers and the revolving welfare door* (pp. i–xi). Philadelphia: Temple University Press.

Furstenberg, F. F., Jr., Brooks-Gunn, J., & Chase-Lansdale, P. L. (1989). Teenage pregnancy and childbearing. *American Psychologist, 44* (2), 313–320.

Furstenberg, F. F., Jr., Brooks-Gunn, J., & Morgan, S. P. (1987). *Adolescent mothers in later life.* Cambridge: Cambridge University Press.

Fuss, D. (1989). *Essentially speaking.* New York: Routledge.

Gallman, V. (1995, March 6). War on teen pregnancy: Policy-makers consider moralizing about sex. *San Jose Mercury News,* pp. 1A, 8A.

Gaskell, J. (1995). *Secondary schools in Canada: The national report of the Exemplary Schools Project.* Toronto: Canadian Education Association.

Geronimus, A. T. (1997). Teenage childbearing and personal responsibility: An alternative view. *Political Science Quarterly, 112,* 1–15.

Geronimus, A. T., & Korenman, S. (1992). The socioeconomic consequences of teen childbearing reconsidered. *Quarterly Journal of Economics, 107,* 1187–1214.

Geronimus, A. T., Korenman, S., & Hillemeier, M. (1994). Does young maternal age adversely affect child development? Evidence from cousin comparisons in the United States. *Population and Development Review, 20,* 585–609.

Glenn, E. N. (1994). Social constructions of mothering: A thematic overview. In E. N. Glenn, G. Chang, & L. R. Forcey (Eds.), *Mothering: Ideology, experience and agency* (pp. 1–29). New York: Routledge.

Goffman, E. (1963). *Stigma: Notes on the management of spoiled identity.* Englewood Cliffs, NJ: Prentice-Hall.

Golding, P., & Middleton, S. (1983). *Images of welfare: Press and public attitudes to poverty.* Oxford: Martin Robertson.

Goodman, E. (1993, December 23). Marital misery: Humbug; Dan Quayle missed the point. *Vancouver Sun,* p. A3.

Gordon, D. E. (1990). Formal operational thinking: The role of cognitive-developmental processes in adolescent decision-making about pregnancy and contraception. *American Journal of Orthopsychiatry, 60* (3), 346–356.

Gordon, L. (1990). Introduction. In L. Gordon (Ed.), *Women, the state, and welfare* (pp. 3–8). Madison: University of Wisconsin Press.

Gouldner, A. (1968). The sociologist as partisan: Sociology and the welfare state. *American Sociologist, 3,* 106–116.

Grant, J. (1993). *Fundamental feminism: Contesting the core concepts of feminist theory.* New York: Routledge.

Green, T., & Steel, B. (1993, February 1). An isolated objection [Letter to the editor]. *British Columbia Report,* p. 3.

Greene, M. (1998). Moral and political perspectives: The tensions of choice. *Educational Researcher, 27* (9), 18–20.

Griffin, K. (1991, April 22). Play rings true with new Canadians' pain. *Vancouver Sun.*

Griffith, A. I., & Smith, D. E. (1991). Constructing cultural knowledge: Mothering as discourse. In J. Gaskell & A. McLaren (Eds.), *Women and education* (2nd ed., pp. 81–97). Calgary, AB: Detselig Enterprises, Ltd.

Griffiths, V. (1990). Using drama to get at gender. In L. Stanley (Ed.), *Feminist praxis* (pp. 221–235). London: Routledge.

Grindlay, L. (1993, September 5). Proud of their novel conception. *Province,* p. A23.

Grindstaff, C. F. (1988). Adolescent marriage and childbearing: The long-term economic outcome, Canada in the 1980s. *Adolescence, 23* (89), 45–58.

Harari, S. E., & Vinovskis, M. A. (1993). Adolescent sexuality, pregnancy, and childbearing in the past. In A. Lawson & D. L. Rhode (Eds.), *The politics of pregnancy: Adolescent sexuality and public policy* (pp. 23–45). New Haven: Yale University Press.

Harris, K. M. (1997). *Teen mothers and the revolving welfare door.* Philadelphia: Temple University Press.

Hawkesworth, M. E. (1989). Knowers, knowing, known: Feminist theory and claims of truth. *Signs: Journal of Women in Culture and Society, 14* (3), 533–557.

Hays, S. (1996). *The cultural contradictions of motherhood.* New Haven: Yale University Press.

Henshaw, S. K. (1997). Teenage abortion and pregnancy statistics by state, 1992. *Family Planning Perspectives, 29* (3), 115–122.

Herr, K. (1991, April). *The context of schooling for pregnant and parenting teens.* Paper presented at the annual meeting of the American Educational Research Association, Chicago, IL.

Hoffman, S. D. (1998). Comment: Teenage childbearing is not so bad after all . . . or is it? A review of the new literature. *Family Planning Perspectives, 30* (5), 236–239, 243.

Holm, G. (1995). Handled but not heard: The managed lives of teenage mothers in school. *Qualitative Studies in Education, 8* (3), 253–264.

hooks, b. (1990). *Yearning: Race, gender, and cultural politics.* Boston: South End Press.

Horowitz, R. (1995). *Teen mothers: Citizens or dependents?* Chicago: University of Chicago Press.

Hudson, F., & Ineichen, B. (1991). *Taking it lying down: Sexuality and teenage motherhood.* New York: New York University Press.

Hume, S. (1996, September 14). What is education for, anyway? *Vancouver Sun,* pp. D1, D4–5.

Ingrassia, M. (1993, August 2). Daughters of Murphy Brown. *Newsweek,* pp. 58–59.

Irvine, J. M. (1994). Cultural differences and adolescent sexualities. In J. M. Irvine (Ed.), *Sexual cultures and the construction of adolescent identities* (pp. 3–28). Philadelphia: Temple University Press.

Jacobs, J. L. (1994). Gender, race, class, and the trend toward early motherhood: A feminist analysis of teen mothers in contemporary society. *Journal of Contemporary Ethnography, 22* (4), 442–462.

Jaggar, A. M., & Rothenberg, P. S. (Eds.). (1993). *Feminist frameworks: Alternative theoretical accounts of the relations between women and men* (3rd ed.). New York: McGraw-Hill.

Jencks, C., & Edin, K. (1995). Do poor women have a right to bear children? *The American Prospect 20,* 43–52.

Jones, E. F., Forrest, J. D., Goldman, N., Henshaw, S., Lincoln, R., Rosoff, J.I., Westoff, C. F., & Wulf, D. (1986). *Teenage pregnancy in industrialized countries.* New Haven: Yale University Press.

Jones, K. B. (1993). *Compassionate authority: Democracy and the representation of women.* New York: Routledge.

Keetley, K. (1981). *Native teen pregnancy and parenting: A problem in perspective.* Vancouver, BC: Social Planning and Review Council.

Kelly, D. M. (1993a). *Last chance high: How girls and boys drop in and out of alternative schools.* New Haven: Yale University Press.

Kelly, D. M. (1993b). Secondary power source: High school students as participatory researchers. *American Sociologist, 24* (1), 8–26.

Kelly, D. M. (1996). Dilemmas of difference: Van Tech's schools-within-a-school model. *Alberta Journal of Educational Research, 42* (3), 293–305.

Kelly, D. M. (1998). Teacher discourses about a young parents program: The many meanings of "good choices." *Education and Urban Society, 30* (2), 224–241.

Kelly, D., & Gaskell, J. (Eds.). (1996). *Debating dropouts: Critical policy and research perspectives on school leaving.* New York: Teachers College Press.

Kerby, W. (1993, May 3). Anti-choice and pro-abortion [Letter to the editor]. *British Columbia Report,* p. 3.

Ketting, E., & Visser, A. P. (1994). Contraception in the Netherlands: The low abortion rate explained. *Patient Education and Counseling, 23* (3), 161–171.

Kline, M. (1993). Complicating the ideology of motherhood: Child welfare law and First Nations women. *Queen's Law Journal, 18* (2), 306–342.

Krangle, K. (1980, March 1). Lure of teen motherhood is having someone to love. *Vancouver Sun,* pp. A1–2.

Lakoff, G. (1996). *Moral politics.* Chicago: University of Chicago Press.

Lambert, B. (1997, October 10). N.Y. woman finds 17-day-old baby in daughter's closet. *Vancouver Sun,* A17.

Lamont, M., & Fournier, M. (1992). Introduction. In M. Lamont & M. Fournier (Eds.), *Cultivating differences: Symbolic boundaries and the making of inequality* (pp. 1–17). Chicago: University of Chicago Press.

Laucius, J. (1999, February 19). Professors want prospective parents to meet strict criteria: Require licence, education. *National Post,* pp. A1–A2.

Laumann, E. O., Gagnon, J. H., Michael, R. T., & Michaels, S. (1994). *The social organization of sexuality: Sexual practices in the United States*. Chicago: University of Chicago Press.

Lawson, A., & Rhode, D. L. (Eds.). (1993). *The Politics of pregnancy: Adolescent sexuality and public policy*. New Haven: Yale University Press.

Lees, S. (1994). Talking about sex in sex education. *Gender and Education, 6* (3), 281–292.

Lenskyj, H. (1990). Beyond plumbing and prevention: Feminist approaches to sex education. *Gender and Education, 2* (2), 217–230.

Lesko, N. (1990). Curriculum differentiation as social redemption: The case of school-aged mothers. In R. Page & L. Valli (Eds.), *Curriculum differentiation: Interpretive studies in U.S. secondary schools* (pp. 113–136). Albany: State University of New York Press.

Lesko, N. (1995). The 'leaky needs' of school-aged mothers: An examination of U.S. programs and policies. *Curriculum Inquiry, 25* (2), 177–205.

Lesko, N. (1996). The dependency of independence: At risk youth, economic self-sufficiency, and curricular change. In D. Kelly & J. Gaskell (Eds.), *Debating dropouts: Critical policy and research perspectives on school leaving* (pp. 44–59). New York: Teachers College Press.

Lever, J. (1995). Bringing the fundamentals of gender studies into safer-sex education. *Family Planning Perspectives, 27* (4), 172–174.

Lindberg, L. D., Sonenstein, F. L., Ku, L., & Martinez, G. (1997). Age differences between minors who give birth and their adult partners. *Family Planning Perspectives, 29* (2), 61–66.

Lipsky, D. K., & Gartner, A. (1996). Inclusion, school restructuring, and the remaking of American society. *Harvard Educational Review, 66* (4), 762–796.

Little, D. (1990). Preservice teacher education in Canada: Is it meeting the challenge of mainstreaming? *B.C. Journal of Special Education, 14* (2), 184–193.

Lu, J. (1997). *Teen pregnancy, Thompson Health Region: A report of the medical health officer to the Thompson Regional Health Board.* Kamloops, BC: South Central Health Unit.

Luker, K. (1991, Spring). Dubious conceptions: The controversy over teen pregnancy. *The American Prospect 5,* 73–83.

Luker, K. (1996). *Dubious conceptions: The politics of teenage pregnancy.* Cambridge: Harvard University Press.

Lustig, D. F. (1997). Of Kwanzaa, Cinco de Mayo, and whispering: The need for intercultural education. *Anthropology and Education Quarterly, 28* (4), 574–592.

Lykken, D. T. (1996, February 9). Giving children a chance in life. *Chronicle of Higher Education,* pp. B1–2.

Males, M. (1994, January). Poverty, rape, adult/teen sex: Why "pregnancy prevention" programs don't work. *Phi Delta Kappan,* pp. 407–410.

Malinowski, B. (1961). *Argonauts of the Western Pacific.* New York: E. P. Dutton.

Martineau, S. (1992). *Corporal punishment in the family: A review of psychology, sociology, and women's studies abstracts, 1983–1992.* Toronto: Institute for the Prevention of Child Abuse.

Martineau, S. (1993). *Mainstream madness: Child abuse as gender socialization in the middle class.* Unpublished senior undergraduate thesis, University of Toronto, Ontario.

Marx, F., Bailey, S. M., & Francis, J. (1988). *Child care for the children of adolescent parents: Findings from a national survey and case studies.* Wellesley, MA: Center for Research on Women, Wellesley College. (ERIC Document Reproduction Service No. ED 302 937)

Mascia-Lees, F. E., Sharpe, P., & Cohen, C. B. (1989). The postmodernist turn in anthropology: Cautions from a feminist perspective. *Signs: Journal of Women in Culture and Society, 15* (1), 7–33.

Massat, C. R. (1995). Is older better? Adolescent parenthood and maltreatment. *Child Welfare, 74* (2), 325–336.

Maternal Health Society (Vancouver, BC). (1982). *Maternal Health News.*

Maynard, F. (1982, October). Teen-age mothers: A nationwide dilemma. *Chatelaine*, pp. 91, 126–132.

McCrate, E. (1990). Labor market segmentation and relative black/white teenage birth rates. *Review of Black Political Economy, 18* (4), 37–53.

McCrate, E. (1992). Expectation of adult wages and teenage childbearing. *International Review of Applied Economics, 6* (3), 309–328.

McCreary Centre Society. (1993). *Adolescent health survey: Report for the greater Vancouver region of British Columbia.* Vancouver, BC: McCreary Centre Society.

McDade, L. (1987). Sex, pregnancy, and schooling: Obstacles to a critical teaching of the body. *Journal of Education, 169* (3), 58–79.

McDonough, J. (1988). *Dolls.* Schulenburg, TX: I. E. Clark, Inc.

McGowan, W. N. (1959). What's happening in California secondary schools. *California Journal of Secondary Education, 34* (8), 485–489.

McLaren, A. (1990). *Our own master race: Eugenics in Canada, 1885–1945.* Toronto: McClelland & Stewart.

McNeil, L. (1986). *Contradictions of control: School structure and school knowledge.* New York: Routledge & Kegan Paul.

Meadmore, D., & Symes, C. (1996). Forces of habit: The school uniform as a body of knowledge. In E. McWilliam & P. Taylor (Eds.), *Pedagogy, technology and the body* (pp. 171–191). New York: Peter Lang.

Miller, B. C., & Moore, K. A. (1990). Adolescent sexual behavior, pregnancy, and parenting: Research through the 1980s. *Journal of Marriage and the Family, 52,* 1025–1044.

Miller, G. (1993). New challenges to social constructionism: Alternative perspectives on social problems theory. In J. A. Holstein & G. Miller (Eds.), *Reconsidering social constructionism: Debates in social problems theory* (pp. 253–278). New York: Aldine de Gruyter.

Minow, M. (1984). Learning to live with the dilemma of difference: Bilingual and special education. *Law and Contemporary Problems, 48* (2), 157–211.

Minow, M. (1990). *Making all the difference: Inclusion, exclusion, and American law.* Ithaca: Cornell University Press.

Minow, M. (1997). *Not only for myself: Identity, politics and the law.* New York: New Press.

Mitchell, A. (1993, November 9). Family thriving, study finds. *Globe and Mail,* pp. A1, A7.

Mitchell, A. (1998, January 17). Teen-age pregnancy on the rise again. *Globe and Mail,* pp. A1, A6.

Mohanty, C. T. (1991). Cartographies of struggle: Third world women and the politics of feminism. In C. T. Mohanty, A. Russo, & L. Torres (Eds.), *Third world women and the politics of feminism* (pp. 1–47). Bloomington: Indiana University Press.

Moore, K. A. (1995). Executive summary: Nonmarital childbearing in the United States. In *Report to Congress on out-of-wedlock childbearing* (pp. v–xxii). Washington, D.C.: U.S. Dept. of Health and Human Services.

Morgan, R. (1973, January 8). Pregnancy no barrier to completing school. *Victoria Times,* p. 21.

Musick, J. S. (1993). *Young, poor, and pregnant: The psychology of teenage motherhood.* New Haven: Yale University Press.

Nader, L. (1972). Up the anthropologist—Perspectives gained from studying up. In D. Hymes (Ed.), *Reinventing anthropology* (pp. 284–311). New York: Pantheon Books.

Naples, N. A. (1997). The "new consensus" on the gendered "social contract": The 1987–1988 U.S. congressional hearings on welfare reform. *Signs: Journal of Women in Culture and Society, 22* (4), 907–945.

Nathanson, C. A. (1991). *Dangerous passage: The social control of sexuality in women's adolescence.* Philadelphia: Temple University Press.

National Center for Health Statistics, Division of Vital Statistics. (1997). Births and deaths: United States, 1996. *Monthly Vital Statistics Report, 46* (1), Suppl. 2.

National Education Association. (1970, October). Pregnant teen-agers. *Today's Education* [NEA Journal], pp. 27–29, 89.

Newt's axis: Preston Manning gets a warm welcome from conservatives in the American capital. (1995, March 27). *Maclean's,* pp. 30–31.

Newton, J., & Stacey, J. (1995). Ms.representations: Reflections on studying academic men. In R. Behar & D. A. Gordon (Eds.), *Women writing culture* (pp. 287–305). Berkeley: University of California Press.

Noonan, P. (1992, September 14). You'd cry too if it happened to you. *Forbes,* pp. 58–69.

Oakes, J. (1992). Can tracking research inform practice? Technical, normative, and political considerations. *Educational Researcher, 21* (4), 12–21.

Oakes, J., Gamoran, A., & Page, R. N. (1991). Curriculum differentiation: Opportunities, outcomes, and meanings. In P. Jackson (Ed.), *Handbook of research on curriculum* (pp. 570–608). New York: Macmillan.

Olesen, V. (1994). Feminisms and models of qualitative research. In N. K. Denzin & Y. S. Lincoln (Eds.), *Handbook of qualitative research* (pp. 158–174). Thousand Oaks, CA: Sage Publications.

O'Neill, K. (1998). No adults are pulling the strings and we like it that way. *Signs: Journal of Women in Culture and Society, 23* (3), 611–618.

O'Neill, T. (1993, January 11). Message to trustees: Be careful with your new teen-parent programs [Editorial]. *British Columbia Report,* p. 2.

Ong, A. (1995). Women out of China: Traveling tales and traveling theories in postcolonial feminism. In R. Behar & D. A. Gordon (Eds.), *Women writing culture* (pp. 350–372). Berkeley: University of California Press.

Ormiston, S. (1993, October 28). Teen moms. *W5.* Toronto: CTV Television Network Ltd. Transcript available: Media Tapes and Transcripts Ltd., Ottawa, Ontario, Canada.

Orton, M. J. (1999). Research report on adolescent pregnancy: Change the high-risk policies and programs to change high-risk sexual behaviours. In J. Wong & D. Checkland (Eds.), *Teenage pregnancy and parenting: Social and ethical issues* (pp. 121–150). Toronto: University of Toronto Press.

Orton, M. J., & Rosenblatt, E. (1991). *Adolescent pregnancy in Ontario, 1976–1986: Extending access to prevention reduces abortions and births to the unmarried.* Report No. 3. Ontario Study of Adolescent Pregnancy and Sexually Transmitted Diseases. Hamilton, ON: McMaster University.

Ouston, R. (1997, July 9). Native Indians seek resolution over issue of adopted children. *Vancouver Sun,* pp. A1, A6.

Page, R., & Valli, L. (Eds.). (1990). *Curriculum differentiation: Interpretive studies in U.S. secondary schools.* Albany: State University of New York Press.

Page, R. (1984). *Stigma.* London: Routledge & Kegan Paul.

Parker, B. & McFarlane, J. (1991, May–June). Identifying and helping battered pregnant women. *American Journal of Nursing, 16,* 161–164.

Parsons, C. (1993, 14 September). Guilt over abortion is rare, study finds: Adoption trauma seen as more severe. *Globe and Mail,* pp. A1–A2.

Pearce, D. (1990). Welfare is not *for* women: Why the war on poverty cannot conquer the feminization of poverty. In L. Gordon (Ed.), *Women, the state, and welfare* (pp. 265–279). Madison: University of Wisconsin Press.

Petchesky, R. P. (1984). *Abortion and woman's choice: The state, sexuality, and reproductive freedom.* Boston: Northeastern University Press.

Petrie, A. (1998). *Gone to an aunt's: Remembering Canada's homes for unwed mothers.* Toronto: McClelland & Stewart.

Phillips, L., & Fine, M. (1992). What's "left" in sexuality education? In J. T. Sears (Ed.), *Sexuality and the curriculum: The politics and practices of sexuality education* (pp. 242–249). New York: Teachers College Press.

Phillips, S. D. (1996). Discourse, identity, and voice: Feminist contributions to policy studies. In L. Dobuzinskis, M. Howlett, & D. Laycock

(Eds.), *Policy studies in Canada: The state of the art* (pp. 242–263). Toronto: University of Toronto Press.

Phoenix, A. (1991a). Mothers under 20: Outsider and insider views. In A. Phoenix, A. Woollett, & E. Lloyd (Eds.), *Motherhood: Meanings, practices and ideologies* (pp. 86–102). London: Sage Publications.

Phoenix, A. (1991b). *Young mothers?* Cambridge: Polity Press.

Pillow, W. S. (1997, July–September). Exposed methodology: The body as a deconstructive practice. *International Journal of Qualitative Studies in Education, 10* (3), 349–363.

Pollitt, K. (1992, July 20–27). Why I hate "family values" (Let me count the ways). *The Nation,* pp. 88–94.

Pozsonyi, J. (1973). *A longitudinal study of unmarried mothers who kept their first born children.* London, Ontario: Family and Children's Services of London and Middlesex.

Pregnancies in 14-year-old girls show alarming increase. (1980, October 15). *Province,* p. A5.

Prendergast, S., & Prout, A. (1980). What will I do . . . ? Teenage girls and the construction of motherhood. *Sociological Review, 28* (3), 517–535.

Quantz, R. A. (1992). On critical ethnography. In M. LeCompte, W. Millroy, & J. Preissle (Eds.), *The handbook of qualitative research in education* (pp. 447–505). San Diego: Academic Press, Inc.

Rains, P. M. (1971). *Becoming an unwed mother: A sociological account.* Chicago: Aldine-Atherton.

Rappaport, J. (1986). In praise of paradox: A social policy of empowerment over prevention. In E. Seidman & J. Rappaport (Eds.), *Redefining social problems* (pp. 141–164). New York: Plenum Press.

Rapping, E. (1990). The future of motherhood: Some unfashionably visionary thoughts. In K. V. Hansen, & I. J. Philipson (Eds.), *Women, class, and the feminist imagination* (pp. 437–548). Philadelphia: Temple University Press.

Rathie, E. (1989, November). Teen moms. *BC Woman to Woman,* pp. 8–13.

Rhode, D. L. (1993). Adolescent pregnancy and public policy. In A. Lawson & D. L. Rhode (Eds.), *The politics of pregnancy: Adolescent sexuality and public policy* (pp. 301–336). New Haven: Yale University Press.

Rhode, D. L., & Lawson, A. (1993). Introduction. In A. Lawson & D. L. Rhode (Eds.), *The politics of pregnancy: Adolescent sexuality and public policy* (pp. 1–21). New Haven: Yale University Press.

Richardson, L. (1995). Narrative and sociology. In J. Van Maanen (Ed.), *Representation in ethnography* (pp. 198–221). Thousand Oaks, CA: Sage Publications.

Rincover, A. (1991, December 10). Teenage mothers lacking resources needed to help raise their children. *Vancouver Sun*, p. C3.

Rivers and Associates. (1995, December). *School based young parent child care: An evaluation.* Prepared for the Ministry of Women's Equality. Victoria, BC: Rivers and Associates.

Roberts, D. (1997). *Killing the Black body: Race, reproduction, and the meaning of liberty.* New York: Pantheon Books.

Roosa, M. W., Tein, J., Reinholtz, C., & Angelini, P. J. (1997). The relationship of childhood sexual abuse to teenage pregnancy. *Journal of Marriage and the Family, 59,* 119–130.

Rosaldo, R. (1989). *Culture and truth: The remaking of social analysis.* Boston: Beacon Press.

Rosaldo, R. (1993). Introduction to the 1993 edition. *Culture and truth: The remaking of social analysis* (2nd ed., pp. ix–xix). Boston: Beacon Press.

Ruddick, S. (1990). Thinking about fathers. In M. Hirsch, & E. Fox Keller (Eds.), *Conflicts in feminism* (pp. 222–233). New York: Routledge.

Ruddick, S. (1993). Procreative choice for adolescent women. In A. Lawson & D. L. Rhode (Eds.), *The politics of pregnancy: Adolescent sexuality and public policy* (pp. 126–143). New Haven: Yale University Press.

Saenger, E. (1991, December 9). Learning to accommodate teen moms. *British Columbia Report*, p. 23.

Sandell, J. (1996). Adjusting to oppression: The rise of therapeutic feminism in the United States. In N. B. Maglin & D. Perry (Eds.), *"Bad* girls"/"good girls": Women, sex, and power in the nineties (pp. 21–35). New Brunswick, NJ: Rutgers University Press.

Sayo, C. (1996, July 17). Young women face double standard. *Vancouver Sun*, p. A2.

Schlesinger, B. (1979). The unmarried mother who keeps her child. In B. Schlesinger (Ed.), *One in ten: The single parent in Canada* (pp. 77–86). Toronto: University of Toronto.

Schlesinger, B. (1982). Changing sexual mores: The student in the 80s. *School Guidance Worker, 37* (5), 43–47.

Schmidt, P. (1996, November 29). A student's plan to escape poverty runs afoul of new rules on welfare. *Chronicle of Higher Education,* pp. A29–A30.

Schmidt, P. (1998, January 23). States discourage welfare recipients from pursuing a higher education. *Chronicle of Higher Education,* p. A34.

Schur, E. M. (1980). *The politics of deviance: Stigma contests and the uses of power.* Englewood Cliffs, NJ: Prentice-Hall.

Schwartz, S. (1991, March 18). Teens live with joy, stigma of motherhood. *Montreal Gazette,* p. B4.

Scott, J. W. (1991). The evidence of experience. *Critical Inquiry, 17,* 773–797.

Sears, J. T. (1992). Dilemmas and possibilities of sexuality education: Reproducing the body politic. In J. T. Sears (Ed.), *Sexuality and the curriculum* (pp. 7–33). New York: Teachers College Press.

Sedlak, M. W. (1983). Young women and the city: Adolescent deviance and the transformation of educational policy 1870–1960. *History of Education Quarterly, 23* (1), 1–28.

Seguin, R., & Unland, K. (1996, October 25). Quebec plans education reforms. *Globe and Mail,* p. A4.

Skrtic, T. M. (Ed.). (1995). *Disability and democracy: Reconstructing (special) education for postmodernity.* New York: Teachers College Press.

Sleeter, C. E. (1996). *Multicultural education as social activism.* Albany: State University of New York Press.

Smith, C. P. (1982). A needs-based curriculum for teenage mothers. *Education, 102* (3), 254–257.

Smith, D. E. (1987). *The everyday world as problematic: A feminist sociology.* Boston: Northeastern University Press.

Snider, W. (1989, May 17). Study: Schools violating rights of pregnant girls. *Education Week,* p. 5.

Solinger, R. (1992). *Wake up little Susie: Single pregnancy and race before Roe v. Wade.* New York: Routledge.

Solinger, R. (1998). Introduction: Abortion politics and history. In R. Solinger (Ed.), *Abortion wars: A half century of struggle, 1950–2000* (pp. 1–9). Berkeley: University of California Press.

Southam Newspapers. (1999, March 6). Teen mothers forced back to class. *Vancouver Sun,* p. A14.

Stacey, J. (1988). Can there be a feminist ethnography? *Women's Studies International Forum, 11* (1), 21–27.

Stacey, J. (1996). *In the name of the family: Rethinking family values in the postmodern age.* Boston: Beacon Press.

Stainback, S., Stainback, W., & Ayres, B. (1996). Schools as inclusive communities. In W. Stainback & S. Stainback (Eds.), *Controversial issues confronting special education: Divergent perspectives* (2nd ed., pp. 31–43). Needham Heights, MA: Allyn and Bacon.

Stanley, J. C. (with Parrish, M.). (1998). "The vision thing": Educational research and AERA in the 21st century—part 5. *Educational Researcher, 27* (9), 34–35.

Statistics Canada. (1997). *Births and deaths, 1995.* Ottawa: Minister of Industry. (Catalogue No. 84–210)

Stern, G. (1993, May 27). Learning curve: School day care helps teen moms, but risks condoning pregnancies. *Wall Street Journal,* pp. A1, A7.

Stevens, W. (1979, December). Teenage pregnancy: When they say chic I hear chick. *off our backs,* pp. 10–11.

Strom, M. (1993, August 26). Adoption: Mom's the word. *Vancouver Sun,* p. A11.

Study contradicts Osterman comments. (1989, March 18). *Calgary Herald*, p. B2.

Sussel, T. A. (1989, December 8). Pregnant student files human rights complaint. *Education Leader*, p. 2.

Taylor, S. E., & Langer, E. J. (1977). Pregnancy: A social stigma? *Sex Roles, 3* (1), 27–35.

Thompson, S. (1995). *Going all the way: Teenage girls' tales of sex, romance, and pregnancy.* New York: Hill and Wang.

Thorne, B. (1987). Re-visioning women and social change: Where are the children? *Gender & Society, 1* (1), 85–109.

Trubisky, P. (1995, January). Congressional briefing highlights sexual behavior survey. *Footnote* [newsletter of the American Sociological Association], *23* (1), p. 1.

Trudell, B. N. (1993). *Doing sex education: Gender politics and schooling.* New York: Routledge.

Tyack, D., & Cuban, L. (1995). *Tinkering toward utopia: A century of public school reform.* Cambridge: Harvard University Press.

U.S. Department of Education. Office of Educational Research and Improvement. (1987). *Dealing with dropouts: The urban superintendents' call to action.* Washington, D.C.: GPO.

U.S. General Accounting Office. (1995, September). *Welfare to work: Approaches that help teenage mothers complete high school.* (GAO/HEHS/PEMD-95-202). Washington, D.C.: GPO.

U.S. General Accounting Office. (1998, June). *Teen mothers: Selected socio-demographic characteristics and risk factors.* (GAO/HEHS-98-141). Washington, D.C.: GPO.

Upchurch, D. M., & McCarthy, J. (1989). Adolescent childbearing and high school completion in the 1980s: Have things changed? *Family Planning Perspectives, 21* (5), 199–202.

Vancouver: Would like high school daycare. (1981, Autumn). *News Bulletin of the Task Force on Teenage Pregnancy and Parenthood* (Social Planning and Review Council of British Columbia), p. 4. (Reprinted from the *Vancouver Sun*)

Vanier Institute of the Family. (1994). *Profiling Canada's families.* Ottawa: Vanier Institute of the Family.

Victor, S. (1995). Becoming the good mother: The emergent curriculum of adolescent mothers. In J. Jipson, P. Munro, S. Victor, K. F. Jones, & G. Freed-Rowland (Eds.), *Repositioning feminism and education: Perspectives on educating for social change* (pp. 37–60). Westport, CT: Bergin and Garvey.

Wadhera, S., & Millar, W. J. (1997, Winter). Teenage pregnancies, 1974 to 1994. *Health Reports, 9* (3), 9–17.

Ward, W. P. (1981). Unwed motherhood in nineteenth-century English Canada. *Canadian Historical Association, Historical Papers, 34–56.*

Warland, P. (1993, 2 December). Welfare system breeds poverty [Letter to the editor]. *Vancouver Sun,* p. A14.

Weatherley, R. A., Perlman, S. B., Levine, M., & Klerman, L. V. (1985). *Patchwork programs: Comprehensive services for pregnant and parenting adolescents.* Seattle: Center for Social Welfare Research [School of Social Work, University of Washington].

Weedon, C. (1988). *Feminist practice and poststructuralist theory.* New York: Basil Blackwell, Inc.

Weiner, R. (Ed.). (1987). *Teen pregnancy: Impact on the schools.* Alexandria, VA: Education Research Group.

Whitehead, B. D. (1994, October). The failure of sex education. *Atlantic Monthly,* pp. 55–81.

Willis, E. (1996). Villains and victims: "Sexual correctness" and the repression of feminism. In N. B. Maglin & D. Perry (Eds.), *"Bad girls"/ "good girls": Women, sex, and power in the nineties* (pp. 44–53). New Brunswick, NJ: Rutgers University Press.

Wolf, D. L. (Ed.). (1996). *Feminist dilemmas in fieldwork.* Boulder, CO: Westview Press.

Wolpe, A. (1988). *Within school walls: The role of discipline, sexuality and the curriculum.* London: Routledge & Kegan Paul.

Woollett, A., & Phoenix, A. (1996). Motherhood as pedagogy: Developmental psychology and the accounts of mothers of young children.

In C. Luke (Ed.), *Feminisms and pedagogies of everyday life* (pp. 80–102). Albany: State University of New York Press.

Wrigley, J. (1992). Gender and education in the welfare state. In J. Wrigley (Ed.), *Education and gender equality* (pp. 1–23). London: Falmer Press.

Young, I. M. (1990). *Justice and the politics of difference.* Princeton, NJ: Princeton University Press.

Young, I. M. (1997). *Intersecting voices: Dilemmas of gender, political philosophy, and policy.* Princeton, NJ: Princeton University Press.

Zabin, L. S., & Hayward, S. C. (1993). *Adolescent sexual behavior and childbearing.* Newbury Park, CA: Sage Publications.

Zellman, G. L., & Feifer, C. N. (1992). Education for teen mothers. In M. C. Alkin (Ed.), *Encyclopedia of educational research: Volume 4* (6th ed., pp. 1391–1397). New York: Macmillan Publishing.

Index

('n' indicates a note; 't' indicates a table)

AC / SS — Adolescent Cultures, School & Society

General Editors: Joseph & Linda DeVitis

As schools struggle to redefine and restructure thems⟨
be cognizant of the new realities of adolescents. Thu⟨
monographs and textbooks is committed to depicting ⟨
adolescent cultures that exist in today's post-industrial so⟨
intended to be a primarily qualitative research, practice, and poli⟨
devoted to contextual interpretation and analysis that encompas⟨
broad range of interdisciplinary critique. In addition, this series will see⟨
provide a pragmatic, pro-active response to the current backlash of con⟨
servatism that continues to dominate political discourse, practice, and
policy. This series seeks to address issues of curriculum theory and
practice; multicultural education; aggression and violence; the media and
arts; school dropouts; homeless and runaway youth; alienated youth; at-
risk adolescent populations; family structures and parental involvement;
and race, ethnicity, class, and gender studies.

Send proposals and manuscripts to the General Editors at:

Joseph & Linda DeVitis
Binghamton University
Dept. of Education & Human Development
Binghamton, NY 13902

To order other books in this series, please contact our Customer Service
Department at:

(800) 770-LANG (within the U.S.)
(212) 647-7706 (outside the U.S.)
(212) 647-7707 FAX

or browse online by series at:

WWW.PETERLANG.COM